Teaching Creative W

Teaching Creative Writing

Edited by Graeme Harper

 continuum
LONDON • NEW YORK

Continuum

The Tower Building   80 Maiden Lane
11 York Road   Suite 704
London SE1 7NX   New York NY 10038

British Library Cataloguing-in-Publication Data

A catalogue record for this book is available from the British Library.

  ISBN: 978-0-8264-7726-2 (hardback)
        978-0-8264-7727-9 (paperback)

Library of Congress Cataloging-in-Publication Data

A catalog record for this book is available from the Library of Congress

Typeset by YHT Ltd, London
Printed and bound in Great Britain by Biddles Ltd., King's Lynn, Norfolk

Contents

Acknowledgements

To all the writers here in *Teaching Creative Writing* – this book is a fine 'gathering' and I am pleased to say that work on it has been undertaken with considerable enthusiasm, delight and commitment from all the writers – my sincerest thanks to you all.

Thanks also to Pip Lamberti, my PA, who has assisted greatly with co-ordination and formatting, chasing things from us all when necessary, and following up a myriad of queries, from the mundane to the wild and woolly. Thanks to her!

A great many thanks go to Jenny Lovel, Commissioning Editor at Continuum, who has maintained keen interest in, and commitment to, this book from start to finish in a manner that warrants celebration. Thanks so much, Jenny. Fantastic!

Thanks also to Sophie Cox, a fine copy-editor.

And, finally, to Louise, Myles and Tyler Harper who, in order that I can complete such books, have maintained the cave, hunted the mammoth, fed the sabre tooth, and chased away the Tyrannosaurus, since before the dawn of time. Much love, always.

Graeme Harper

Notes on Contributors

Katharine Coles's books include the novels *Fire Season* and *The Measurable World* and three collections of poems, *The Golden Years of the Fourth Dimension, A History of the Garden* and *The One Right Touch*. Her stories, poems and essays have appeared or are forthcoming in *The Paris Review, The New Republic, The Kenyon Review* and *Poetry*, among other journals. Her poems have been included in numerous public arts projects, including *Passages Park*, for which she served on the design team; her ongoing collaboration with visual artist Maureen O'Hara Ure has resulted in two major installations and an artist's book, *Swoon*. She has received awards from the National Endowment for the Arts and PEN, among many other organizations. She is on the faculty of the English Department at the University of Utah, where she teaches creative writing and literature and directs the Utah Symposium in Science and Literature.

Chad Davidson is the author of *Consolation Miracle*, winner of the Crab Orchard Prize in Poetry. His work has appeared in *AGNI, The Paris Review, Prairie Schooner, Shenandoah, Virginia Quarterly Review, The Writer's Chronicle* and others. He teaches literature and creative writing at the University of West Georgia.

Jack Epps, Jr wrote and directed several award-winning short films while an undergraduate at Michigan State University. After moving to California, Mr Epps co-authored over 25 screenplays while working for every major studio in Hollywood. He has seven produced motion pictures including *Top Gun, Legal Eagles, The Secret of My Success* and *Dick Tracy*. Mr Epps also wrote several television shows including *Hawaii Five-O* and *Kojak*. He has written for Tom Hanks, Tom Cruise, Robert Redford, John Voight, Al Pacino, Debra Winger and Michael J. Fox. In addition, Mr Epps has worked with directors Ivan Reitman, Tony Scott, Herb Ross and Warren Beatty. He is an active member of the Writers Guild of America, west, and the Academy of Motion Picture Arts and Sciences. Mr Epps is an Associate Professor at the University of Southern California (USC) and teaches at the School of Cinema-Television in the Writing Division. Currently Chair of the BFA Curriculum Committee, he has been instrumental in creating several new classes for the writing programme at USC.

Gregory Fraser is the recipient of a grant from the National Endowment for the Arts. His poetry has appeared in journals including *The Southern Review, The Paris Review* and *The Chicago Review*. Fraser's first book of poems, *Strange Pietà*, was published in 2003 by Texas Tech University Press. He teaches literature and creative writing at the University of West Georgia.

Graeme Harper (aka Brooke Biaz) is Professor and Head of the School of Creative Arts, Film and Media at the University of Portsmouth. Holding such awards as the National Book Council Award for New Fiction (Aust), the Premier's Award for New Fiction, the Literature Board Travelling Fellowship and the CCVP Commonwealth Doctoral Scholarship in Creative Writing, he is also recipient of awards, grants and fellowships from NESTA, the AHRC, British Academy, Australia Council, ACE, ACW, Eastern Frontier Foundation, BBC World Service, UEA, European Commission and others. He has been three times short-listed for the rich Vogel Award for fiction writers under thirty-five, and has been a visiting writer in the UK, USA and Europe. His previous creative works include *Black Cat, Green Field, Swallowing Film* and *Dancing on the Moon*, while his most recent works of fiction are *Small Maps of the World* and *Filming Carol*. He was recently a BBC Talent featured fiction writer. He is Director of the UK Centre for Creative Writing Research-Through-Practice and Editor-in-Chief of *New Writing: The International Journal for the Practice and Theory of Creative Writing*.

Jeri Kroll was born in New York City. She completed her PhD at Columbia University and taught in the US and England before moving to Australia in 1978, where she has received state and federal writing grants. She is Associate Professor of English and Program Co-ordinator of Creative Writing at Flinders University in Adelaide as well as past President of the Australian Association of Writing Programs. Her publications cover children's literature, Samuel Beckett, contemporary poetry and the pedagogy and theory of creative writing. She has published over 20 books for adults and young people, including poetry, picture books (two Children's Book Council Notable Awards), novels and anthologies. In addition to Australia, some have been released in Canada, Korea, New Zealand, the UK and the US. Her most recent books are *Mickey's Little Book of Letters* (novel) and *The Mother Workshops* (poems).

Martin Lammon's poetry and essays have appeared in *Black Warrior Review, Chelsea, The Gettysburg Review, Mid-American Review, Ploughshares, Poets & Writers, Puerto del Sol* and many other journals. A recent creative non-fiction essay won the Lamar York Prize and appeared in *The Chattahoochee Review*, and another essay was runner-up for the Iowa Award and published in *The Iowa Review*. Those essays are part of a Costa Rica memoir, 'Nine Degrees North' (in progress), which recounts how in 1995 he sold his house and most of his possessions to live for a season in the Caribbean village of Cahuita. Lammon has won several awards for his poetry, including a Pablo Neruda Prize, for poems selected by W. S. Merwin and published in *Nimrod*, and the Arkansas Poetry Award, for the collection of poems *News from Where I Live*. Lammon is also the editor of *Written in Water, Written in Stone: Twenty Years of Poets on Poetry*. A past president of the Association of Writers and Writing Programs, Lammon currently directs the Master of Fine Arts Program in Creative Writing at Georgia College & State University, where he holds the Fuller E. Callaway/Flannery O'Connor chair and also edits the journal *Arts & Letters*.

Cynthia Lewis is Professor of English Education at the University of Minnesota. Her research focuses on young people's responses to literature as well as their digital literacy practices, and she is interested in the implications of this research for the teaching of literature and writing. She is author of *Literary Practices as Social Acts: Power, Status, and Cultural Norms in the Classroom* and co-editor of *Identity, Agency, and Power: Reframing Sociocultural Research on Literacy*. Her study on social identities and Instant Messaging is forthcoming in *Reading Research Quarterly* and chapters on adolescents' digital literacy practices will appear in the *Handbook on Teaching Literacy through the*

Communicative, Visual and Performing Arts and in the *Encyclopedia of Children, Adolescents, and The Media*.

Steve May has written more than 40 plays for BBC radio, including *No Exceptions* (1983), which won a Giles Cooper award, and *Fair Hearing* (1995), which was runner-up for the Writers' Guild Best Original Script award (and for which he also wrote the music). His latest radio credits include *Facing the Mirror, Chess Wars* and *Arthur* (episodes 4–6), all broadcast in 2004. His latest novel for young people, *One Chance*, was also published in 2004. He has won prizes for fiction and poetry, written for publications as diverse as *Penthouse, Medieval English Theatre* and the *Daily Telegraph*, and leads the undergraduate creative writing programme at Bath Spa University.

Rob Pope is Professor of English Studies at Oxford Brookes University, a UK National Teaching Fellow and a Fellow of the English Association. He has taught at universities in Wales, Russia and New Zealand, and has led curriculum and staff development programmes in North and South America, Australia, South East Asia, the Middle East and Central Europe. He is a regular speaker and workshop and conference organizer for the British Council and an adviser for the Open University (UK) and the European Society for the Study of English. In 2002 he was Visiting Professor at Yokohama City University, Japan. His publications include *Textual Intervention: Critical and Creative Strategies for Literary Studies; The English Studies Book: Language, Literature, Culture* and *Creativity: Theory, History, Practice*. He is currently co-writing a further book on critical-creative rewriting (including adaptation, imitation, parody, critique and intervention) and is collaborating on the redesign of these materials for interactive use electronically.

Thomas Swiss's collaborative poems appear on-line in such journals as *Postmodern Culture* and *electronic book review*, as well as in museum exhibits and art shows. He is Professor of English and Rhetoric of Inquiry at the University of Iowa and the editor of *The Iowa Review Web* – a journal of new media writing and art. The author of two collections of poems, *Rough Cut* and *Measure*, his latest books include *Unspun* and *New Media Poetics: Texts, Technotexts, Theories*, an edited anthology on poetry in a digital age.

Stephanie Vanderslice has an MFA from George Mason University and a PhD in English with a creative dissertation from the University of Louisiana-Lafayette. She has published stories and essays both personal and academic in *The American Literary Review, New Writing, Writing-On-the-Edge, Other Mothering, Profession* and many others. She is currently editing, with Dr Kelly Ritter, *This is (Not) Just to Say: Lore and Creative Writing Pedagogy*, a book that examines the lore and myth that surrounds the teaching of creative writing. She is also Associate Editor of *New Writing: The International Journal for the Practice and Theory of Creative Writing*. Dr Vanderslice is Associate Professor in the Department of Writing and Speech at the University of Central Arkansas, in Conway, Arkansas, where she lives with her husband and two sons.

Michelene Wandor is a playwright, poet, fiction writer and musician. Her dramatization of 'The Wandering Jew' was produced at the National Theatre in 1987, the same year her adaptation of 'The Belle of Amherst' won an International Emmy for Thames TV. Her prolific radio work includes original plays and dramatizations (novels by Fyodor Dostoyevsky, Jane Austen, George Eliot, Rudyard Kipling, Sara Paretsky and Margaret

Drabble), many nominated for awards. Her books on contemporary theatre include *Postwar British Drama: Looking Back in Gender*. Her poetry, *Gardens of Eden Revisited*, and her short stories, *False Relations*, are published by Five Leaves. She is completing a book about Creative Writing and holds a Royal Literary Fund Fellowship at Birkbeck College, 2005–06. Her poetry collection *Musica Transalpina* was a Poetry Book Society Recommendation for 2006.

Introduction

In universities and colleges in North America, the United Kingdom and Australasia – and elsewhere, beyond the 'Western' world as well – the subject of 'Creative Writing' has seen steady to phenomenal growth, periods of relative stasis and periods of considerable change. Today, it is not only a subject found among English speakers, nor is it only to be found in undergraduate and postgraduate courses, nor is its story really one that can be told in a single narrative, starting from a single entry point and ending at a single exit, with little real sense of comparison and contrast.

Creative writing, as an art, as an action and an activity, as a mode of engagement with the world, as the producer of artefacts in the form of books and plays and poems and television and films and websites and much more, and as a site of knowledge where there is teaching and learning undertaken, both in informal and formal ways, has a complex and distinctive character.

This book, *Teaching Creative Writing*, is written largely by those concerned with higher learning in contemporary universities and colleges. Yet its relevance to those involved in creative writing elsewhere will quickly become evident.

One of the most important facts about the learning of creative writing is that it gains nothing at all from being considered the remit of only one type of learner or one type of teacher. It doesn't gain much either from being considered one of the 'new' university subjects to be 'traded' as Western higher education – there is a great deal more to creative writing than any such commodification can suggest. Two thoughts immediately come to mind, both brought about by the words of Ivan Illich.

Illich, described variously as 'educationalist', 'radical', 'sociologist', 'former priest', 'polymath' and 'polemicist', was perhaps best described in his obituary in the *Guardian* newspaper in December 2002 where he was called, simply, a 'thinker'. In an essay entitled 'The Alternative to Schooling', first published in the *Saturday Review* some 35 years ago, Illich wrote:

> We must now recognise the estrangement of man from his learning when it becomes the product of a service profession and he becomes the consumer. (Illich, 1974: 400)

This prompts my first thought – that the spread of formal courses in Creative Writing in universities and colleges has raised questions about the nature of the modern university, not least about the relationship between formal, scheduled, 'institutionalized' teaching and learning and the many other kinds of teaching and learning that universities are capable of providing.

Although Illich was a critic of both institutions and of claims to expertise, he was also interested in changing practices of reading, thus very far from being against scholasticism. His *In the Vineyard of the Text* (1993) explores these changing practices from the medieval, through the period following the invention of the early printing press, to the age of computers, doing this through an examination of the *Didascalicon* of Hugh of St Victor. Hugh of St Victor's *Didascalicon* is a key medieval text relating the growth of knowledge to the whole person, each element integrated, and is a significant text in the history of schools and pedagogy.

The year before his death, in a talk entitled 'Text and University: on the idea and history of a unique institution', Illich said this:

> I needed to stress that what defines the university is not some post- Enlightenment science, but the new medieval writing technique that appeared in the twelfth century. It is this that makes university culture unique. (Illich, 1991: 1)

> In a special way, this university was conceived as an adventure. Today, many of those here assembled remember the origins. ... (Illich, 1991: 2)

These words prompt my second thought about the growth and spread of Creative Writing courses in higher education – that it has raised questions about the nature of creative writing itself.

As you are about to read a book composed largely by writers working in higher education institutions, but not necessarily writers who have been 'institutionalized' by this, the mention of Illich seems at very least a useful 'point-to-counterpoint' to the discussion that follows.

What is at stake here?

If creative writing can be seen as something that can be taught and learnt through higher education – and I'm placing the 'if' here only to be conciliatory, I personally have no doubt about this – if this is the case in higher education then, in essence, what is to be taught and what is to be learnt?

This question produces some now very familiar responses. For example, the response that runs along the lines of 'creative writing cannot be taught, only encouraged and supported'. And the response that runs along the lines of 'so many students of creative writing do not go on to be creative writers, therefore the whole enterprise of claiming to teach creative writing is, at very least, a little questionable'.

What neither of these responses considers is, on the one hand, the historical picture of the university, the changing nature of higher education in relation to the economy and to society and, on the other hand, the historical picture of the writing arts in relation to technology, culture, the individual and society. To judge the success or failure of the teaching of creative writing in universities and colleges on a fixed sense of what it means to teach and learn creative writing is as false as such a judgement would be with any other field, or site, of knowledge.

Likewise, emphasizing commercial criteria – including the infamous 'publishability' definition that still now and then finds its way into discussions of Creative Writing, most often in graduate prospectuses – will confirm that much of what is undertaken in creative writing teaching and learning in universities is a failure. Equally, emphasizing criteria noting 'improvement of life skills' or 'increasing the ability to communicate effectively in words', or the wonders that studying creative writing provides in relation to 'under-standing literature' or 'developing creativity', will rightly confirm that the term 'Creative Writing' fails as an accurate definition of the subject.

Placing emphasis on either of these criteria is plainly wrong.

Creative writing teaching and learning is about creative writing, a particular set of activities and understandings forming a large component of the writing arts. It is not *primarily* about whether creative writing maps onto the needs and functions of the contemporary publishing industry, or contemporary film-making, web-design or performance industries for that matter. Neither is it *primarily* about whether the things learnt in learning creative writing are of use in other areas of our lives, relate to other sites of knowledge, or can be 'transferred' (to use a still relatively contemporary university buzzword) and thus put to good use in other ways.

The activity, and consideration of the activity, of creative writing informs a *site of knowledge* that can be accessed and understood both formally and informally, that has a relationship with other sites of knowledge, and that gains substantially from keeping its borders open to movement outward and inward. *Nevertheless*, it is still distinct, and it has long been found in and around environments devoted to higher education, from the ancient to the contemporary, and in a variety of manifestations.

SITE OF KNOWLEDGE

Knowledge can be gained through experience or learning (*a posteriori*), or through deductive reasoning (*a priori*). In essence it is the awareness and understanding of facts, truths or information and, as a term, it is connected with other terms such as 'meaning' and 'representation'. Knowledge is studied, of course, as the subject of epistemology, and it is generally defined in that field as something along the lines of 'justified true belief'.

From there, discussions about knowledge become increasingly more difficult and, to many, increasingly more interesting. Is knowledge, for example, a biological phenomenon, as Q. V. Quine suggests? Is it largely connected with the senses, as Wilfred Sellars might argue? Or is it about evident belief, as Roderick Chisholm once touted?

It is not the perceived place of a book about creative writing to spend a significant number of pages debating epistemological questions. And yet, creative writing has been poorly served by many in their failure to consider it a specific site of knowledge, and therefore to ground a discussion of creative writing in a way that approaches 'justified true belief', thus improving our understanding of it – which seems a genuinely valuable aim that no one could question.

One of the most obvious problems has been that concerning the application of the tenets of literary criticism to the practice and understanding of creative writing. This has come about largely through the relationship between creative writing and the subject of English Literature in higher education and has been most often defended on the grounds that the formal study of Literature provides key critical viewpoints, important historical information, and related aesthetic understanding that makes its relationship with creative writing both logical and positive. The same is said, though less often, about the relationship between the subjects of Media Studies and Film Studies and scriptwriting and about the relationship between Theatre Studies and playwriting.

Much about these relationships has indeed been positive – extremely positive. However, creative writing is not, to take the key example, the 'post-event' study of Literature, even when it involves the creation, and consideration of the creation, of prose fiction and poetry – the primary fodder for the critical work of university Literature departments. Therefore, to find the subject approached as if it is not a site of knowledge in its own right creates a situation in which the chances of achieving a 'justified true belief' are considerably diminished.

It would be wrong to say that this situation has arisen because all those involved in critical literary study simply want to colonize creative writing. Certainly the belief that creative writing is part of the study of Literature is often suggested for genuinely conversant epistemological reasons, linked to the commonplace notion that textual materials that appear to have connections might benefit from similar analytical grounding and that cultural artefacts that elicit similar responses might best be discussed by those who have experience in deconstructing those responses.

However, it would be naïve to believe that this is where the relationship or, indeed, the tension between creative writing and the post-event discussion of Literature (or film, drama, poetry or multimedia, for that matter) ends. Throughout their history, universities and colleges have frequently seen 'turf wars'. The emergence of the subject of English itself followed a history in which the subject of Classics had a key, antecedent role, alongside other subjects such as Philology. As Colin Evans (1993) points out, tracing that subject history:

> Classics was the means by which one group sought to hold on to power and privilege, and English was the means by which other social groups attempted to wrest that power from them. (p. 9)

> Palmer shows how the main objection to English at Oxford and Cambridge and in public schools was that English was, in the modern parlance, a soft option. That is why, even when it had some legitimacy, it was despised – known as the 'courier Tripos' in Cambridge, and relegated to an inferior place in public schools. (p. 10)

> So the rise of English is part of a modern phenomenon of professionalization and institutionalization. . . . The role of the university is to legitimise . . . . The rise of the university feeds on and is fed by the rise of professionalization, in a long symbiotic process. (p. 12)

The growth of formal study of Creative Writing in academe has seen analogous debates, tensions and developments to these Evans notes in relation to the birth of English as a university subject, except that we are located here around a century and a half later. In fact, in the case of Creative Writing, these debates, tensions and developments continue, and there is little doubt that stating this here does little to resolve the situation, perhaps even exacerbates it.

That said, regardless of this seeming political naïvety, more important than whether Creative Writing needs to be 'shown to be "hard" and this means not only hard for students . . . but also hard for researchers, hard in the modern sense' (Evans, 1993: 11), as English once needed to do, is whether Creative Writing is given full opportunity to seek out 'justified true belief', or whether the subject is currently in some way pressed upon within academe by inaccurate assumption regarding its nature as a site of knowledge.

Is it inaccurate to say that Creative Writing is a branch of post-event literature analysis; or, additionally, a branch of film analysis, drama, media or 'new' media? Is it in some way about aesthetics, or aesthetics of a particular kind? Is it more than solely a craft pursuit in which the skills and mechanics of application are the primary concern? Is the fact that it is pursued most often by individuals of significance? Has it particular approaches to culture, society, individual or group? Is it concerned with psychology? Is its relationship with the physical environment distinctive (e.g. does it have practices and ideals that reflect particular notions of time and space, or that investigate them)? In dealing with human nature does it relate a condition of human physiology? As creative writers are often pursuing the depiction and discussion of human intentions, feelings and reasons do they have a set of approaches to this and, if so, in what ways are these articulated? Is the condition of human agency that produces and explores creative writing distinct to it, or could it be said to share characteristics with human agency in the pursuit of other arts, for example – if so, what kind? Are there structures, social rules and cultural meanings that impact upon the pursuit of creative writing, are reflected in it, and perhaps enable or disable certain ideals or intentions? Are their certain dispositions, individual and behaviour patterns reflective of the nature of creative writing? Has creative writing something specific to pursue in terms of modes of meaning, ways of seeking information, styles of instruction, methods of communication and types of representation?

Even if any one of these questions produces an affirmative answer, then is creative writing not a site of knowledge distinctive enough to be considered a subject in its own right in academe and, as a subject – however much it might have a relationship with other subjects – is it not essential that we acknowledge the pursuit of justified true belief in relation to it, first and foremost?

Naturally, the conclusion here is going to be that affirmative answers can be given to a great many of the questions posed above; in fact, to all of them. Likewise, that the reason that creative writing is not *solely* about whether creative writing maps onto vocational strategies in academe, or whether its site of knowledge can provide opportunity for 'transfer' to other fields is because these should not be seen as primary concerns. Rather, they reflect a starting point for understanding creative writing which is at odds with its true nature, its *actual* site of knowledge.

The nature of knowledge is undoubtedly a complex subject, but one simple thing is largely agreed and that is that knowledge is certainly more than information. Rather, it is information with purpose or use, information connected with intention. The intention of defining and pursuing work in the site of knowledge that is creative writing is not only to seek out the truth of how creative writing, and creative writers, approach their field, but also to determine what truths creative writing is capable of pursuing, what information about ourselves it is actively considering, and what aspects of the world it is able to cast light upon. As a subject found in a variety of educational settings, including universities and colleges, *and* as a specific site of knowledge, this is essential.

THE WRITERS' APPROACH

The writers contributing to *Teaching Creative Writing* were asked to creatively interpret the book's template. Many books on the learning of creative writing fix creative writing dead with chapters/subdivisions created not in the action or in the process of creative writing, but in responses to completed versions of it. Many 'how-to' creative writing books seem bound in approaches that emphasize compartmentalization not interaction, separation not synthesis, discontinuity not continuity.

In essence, these 'how-to' creative writing books are working from the point of view of the *intellect* not from the point of view of the *intelligence*, to borrow an approach from philosopher and Nobel Prize Laureate, Henri Bergson. The intellect, to quote Bergson:

> ... always starts from immobility, as if this were the ultimate reality: when it tries to form an idea of movement, it does so by constructing movement out of immobilities put together. (1998: 155)

Creative writing certainly cannot be understood as 'immobile', even if its end-products might often be fixed in books, magazines or journals or in the final productions of the screen arts. Thus, in Bergsonian terms, creative writing cannot be thought of as an *intellectual* enterprise; but, rather, as an *intelligent* one. Creative writing is an action, affected by the dispositions, intentions, feelings, reasons and behaviour patterns of writers, most often individually, and by the cultural, social and economic factors of society, most often as a whole with limited address to the individual.

So the instructions to the writers in *Teaching Creative Writing* were to use my editor's template as a guideline, to endeavour to work to an overall chapter length that would make their chapters of a similar length to others in the book, if only to ensure a degree of parity, and to otherwise feel empowered to say what they felt was most important to say in the way they felt was most appropriate to say it.

The chapters thus draw on the writers' personal understanding of creative writing in the genre or area with which the writers are dealing. Each writer had key expertise in the areas covered and each writer, or pair of writers, approached the task independently of the others.

In order to assist the reader, I've set out below the template I presented to the writers. In each chapter I've added numbers corresponding to those below, to show the reader where the writers begin and finish each of their guideline sections. The writers largely followed the numbering, in order; however, a few preferred to swap the order of sections 3 and 4. I have indicated this, using brackets in the text. My guidelines offered to the writers were as follows:

1: a section concerned with the writers' personal/creative/critical thoughts on, and about, teaching/learning the genre or area with which they were dealing;

2: the writers to highlight their key points in teaching/learning the genre or area with which they were dealing;

3: the writers to offer their choice of notable readings in/of/about the genre or area with which they were dealing;

4: the writers to outline, as they thought best, the favourite exercises/strategies for teaching/learning/understanding the genre or area with which they were dealing.

What emerges in this book is the result of the creative and critical understanding of the writers. Despite its title, this is most certainly a book both about the teaching of creative writing *and* about the learning of it. It is, in this sense, more like what that notable philosopher of education, R. S. Peters, once called 'initiation':

> Terms like 'training' and 'instruction' – perhaps even 'teaching' – are too specific. Education can occur without these specific transactions taking place in ways which fail to satisfy all the criteria implied by 'education'. The term 'initiation', on the other hand, is general enough to cover these different types of transaction if it is also stipulated that initiation must be into worthwhile activities and modes of conduct. (Peters, 1974: 370)

While not entirely sure what Peters might consider *not* 'worthwhile activities and modes of conduct' his notion of initiation into a field of knowledge is a useful pointer towards the fluidity both of consciousness and of teaching and learning. *Teaching Creative Writing* is, in that sense, most importantly a mnemonic, recalling teaching and learning choices, encouraging the reader to think on the ideas, approaches and texts, both those mentioned, and their own, personal alternatives. It is not a specific road map. Nor is it a marble tablet chiselled with the words 'How To'. Such things simply do not recall the nature of creative writing or its modes and methods of enquiry.

Teaching Creative Writing is a series of movements, in the Bergsonian sense, a synthesis, in historiographical terms; a gathering, in social terms; and a collaborative work, in artistic terms.

Graeme Harper

WORKS CITED

Bergson, H., *Creative Evolution* [1911] (New York: Dover), 1998.

Evans, C., *English People: The Experience of Teaching and Learning English in British Universities* (Buckingham: Open University Press), 1993.

Illich, I., 'The Alternative to Schooling' [1965], in J. Bowen and P. R. Hobson, *Theories of Education: Studies of Significant Innovation in Western Educational Thought* (Brisbane: Wiley), 1974.

Illich I., 'Text and University: on the idea and history of a unique institution', trans. L. Hoinacki (www.pudel.uni-bremen.de/pdf/TEXTANTL.pdf), 1991.

Illich, I., *In the Vineyard of the Text: A Commentary to Hugh's Didascalicon* (Chicago, IL: University of Chicago Press), 1993.

Peters, R. S., 'Education as Initiation', in J. Bowen and P. R. Hobson, *Theories of Education: Studies of Significant Innovation in Western Educational Thought* (Brisbane: Wiley), 1974.

Chapter 1

Short Fiction

Katharine Coles
University of Utah

THE ELEPHANT IN THE ROOM

1. THE TROUBLED WORKSHOP AND A NEST OF BOXES

Box 1: Say the box is a glass, and fill it

Cocktail conversation at the annual conference of the Association of Writers and Writing Programs (AWP, a US organization), as I've unsystematically tracked it over 25 years, reveals two things. First, writers adapt readily to trends in drinks – apple martinis, vintage red wines – while refusing to surrender the reliable, tweedy habits of whisky and cigars. Second, though most pay little attention to trends in pedagogy, many if not most writers teaching creative writing in higher education in the United States feel deeply uneasy with the old-fashioned workshop, even as they cling to its conventions.

Box 2: The workshop story and the death of literature

Indeed, critics from outside and inside the creative writing community insist that the workshop, even as it has increased the number of writers, has led to the decline, even the end, of literature in the United States. The now ubiquitous 'workshop story', competent but uncompelling, arises, our critics tell us, not in spite of but because of our labours: our workshops create and enforce conformity, channelling students into predictable avenues and preventing them from achieving the heights they might, without our meddling, achieve. 'Workshop stories' infest literary journals and first books, choking out otherwise promising roses and marigolds – or perhaps the workshop pansies and bluebells, domestic and expected, prevent wind-born exotics from taking root?

Box 3: The workshop, whatever it is

So, precisely what 'conventional workshop' practices produce the 'workshop story'? A student turns in a story and the class convenes, prepared to pick the story apart. The students frame their comments in the language of 'likes' or 'dislikes': 'I really like this sentence, but I don't like the one that follows'; or 'I just love the dialogue in this story, but I can't sympathize with the main character'; or, perhaps, 'I have always hated that word'. Advanced students adopt another common elocution – 'This is/isn't working' – which appears objective on the surface, though it represses 'for me' barely if at all. The professor directs the discussion with questions or looks benignly on, weighing in only at the end, when she dispenses her wisdom and thereby neatly divides the class up into 'right' and 'wrong', letting everyone know whether the writer (and, by extension, her supporters) is 'good' today or not, chosen or bereft. This model has become the workshop standard, its box containing us as invisibly as and strictly as narrative; all writers who have spent any time to speak of in the US academy are familiar with its terms.

No wonder we're uneasy.

Box 4: The heart of the matter/the writer in the academy

What form of self-hatred could have led academic writers to internalize so fully the voices of their critics? Many US writers feel a certain malaise about the academy generally, even though (or perhaps because) the US academy was first to formalize the writer's presence *as creative writer* within it.[1] Our creative writing programmes – which offer by far the most popular courses in English departments – have required departments to hire working writers whose primary research focus is their own work and whose most important teaching credentials, at least until the programmes themselves were well established, could not be the graduate degrees that were only just coming into being (though of course these degrees would eventually be required), but rather the publication and ongoing production of literary works.

While Britain has a longer tradition of sheltering writers within the academy, Britain's academic writers have until recently been different animals than ours. An incomplete, semi-arbitrary survey of British academic writers over the last 150 years gives us Lewis Carroll, a lecturer in Mathematics; C. S. Lewis, who taught Philosophy and English Language and Literature; Philip Larkin, a university librarian; and Kingsley Amis, A. S. Byatt and David Lodge, who taught Literature. Renowned writers all, none of these came into the academy to teach creative writing. If they found shelter in universities, they found it as academics. Amis, Byatt and Lodge left academia after their writing began to support them, and even sufficiently distanced themselves from the academy to train their gimlet writers' eyes on its eccentricities.

If the US academy enables ordinary journeymen writers without scholarly aspirations to pursue their art without starving, the institutionalization of the writer *as artist* has had some odd results. Even as it has placed the writer at the heart of departmental efforts to attract and retain students, it has also positioned her as department outsider and opposed her discipline – creative, wayward, *undisciplined* – to the department's primary mission, the production of scholarship, criticism and now theory. For the advent of theory did not, as academic writers commonly believe, create the writer's alienation. This arose much earlier, directly from the uncomfortable proximity of living writer to textual scholar, whose work even before Derrida required the writer's absence, preferably her death, to flourish.

But tenure allows writers to complain about the ivory tower even from within its whited walls – not cats in the chicken house so much as, well, chickens in the cat house. The claws of an academic cat are purely theoretical, but they give the chickens something to cluck about – writers love nothing so much as a good story – and illustrative, possibly apocryphal tales abound: about amorous writers pursuing innocent students; drunk writers sleeping it off on seminar tables while workshop continues, literally, over their prone carcasses; writers parrying clumsy and delivering exquisite cruelties, raging through mailrooms, shouting death threats down the hallowed halls. Never mind that these tales reveal the writers as predators themselves, or that most of these storied events took place in earlier, purer days, before the lamented 'professionalization' of the writer. Like all origin tales, they remind us who we want to be; and everyone knows where the remaining bad (mostly) boys and (some) girls are, ageing and toothless as they now must be.

Nonetheless, present-day unease creates real problems for our students, not least the disagreements between scholars and writers about what creative writing students should study, and how much of it. (During the spring 2005 meeting, the AWP Board revised its hallmarks to state unambiguously that the proper study for writers in non-workshop classes is literature, not theory.) In PhD programmes, where scholarly classes and exams often carry weight equal to workshops and creative dissertations, this difference is often intensified. At Utah, students take more than half their coursework in literature and critical theory. Because the scholarly component of our PhD is strenuous, we recruit students who demonstrate serious commitments to literary study in addition to creative work, as well as literature and theory faculty who commit themselves to literary study. Still, our students struggle to divide themselves between two competing, apparently disparate pursuits. Though they believe intuitively that their scholarly work and their creative work are related, they aren't sure how, and their educations don't help them to clarify matters.

Box 3: The workshop, whatever it is, reprise

How could this be? Somehow, we are failing to reinforce our students' sense of the project: to make literature. In this, we might take a lesson from our best scholarly colleagues, whose classes rivet the attention of teacher and student on the text itself. In the olden days, writers learned their craft from the perfected dead and the imperfect living, through reading. But though conventional workshop discussion focuses largely on formal and technical concerns, the way it formulates its concerns – 'I like'; 'I don't like' – draws attention *away* from the work and *towards* the reader, onto her preconceived set of personal preferences about, well, you name it: words, line breaks, how sentences are assembled, political and sexual matters, tastes in food and dress, *whatever*, as my undergraduates say. The student/critic may address a formal or technical issue, but the subject of each sentence is 'I', and the verb expresses taste in a way that often becomes strangely personal, directed not only at the writing, but through it at the writer's own character.

Isn't the workshop's job to teach students what they're doing right or wrong? Of course. But publicly subjecting students to personal critiques teaches them primarily to seek praise (from each other and especially from the teacher) and avoid blame, and so to steer clear of the kinds of risks that might result in catastrophe. Shouldn't we rather be teaching them aspiration, courage and grace?

Box 2: The workshop story and the death of literature (do I contradict myself?)

So, yes, I too am uncomfortable with the workshop. And it must now appear that I believe the conventional wisdom. But the workshop poses no threat to literature. Even badly taught, it cannot doom a voracious student to produce mediocre work; it cannot so blunt her instincts or ravage her talent. Our most interesting, interested students are still *readers*, and they will keep learning by reading even as they take what they can from us (a hint on dialogue here; something about tone over there) and run with it; they will use our classes, often through muscular resistance, to learn what they might have learned without us, though more laboriously and slowly. The rest they will eventually shrug off. A bad class may slow a good writer down; it may simply fail to speed her up. But if she has the drive, as Michael Ventura (1993) puts it, to cultivate the 'talent of the room', the painful ability to 'sit alone in a room for years', it will hardly put her off altogether. It may even help her to focus, to harden her resolve.

So how do I account for all the 'workshop stories', good enough perhaps even to get published but not to last? First, even great writers create apprentice stories, which in retrospect we read as signs of progress rather than catastrophe. But further, consider the valiant others, who, left to their own devices, would never have written even competent stories, but who through work and good teaching may become competent, at least. The large numbers of such writers emerging from graduate programmes represent not failure but success – and if the idea of all those merely plausible stories exhausts us, well, we've made our bed. Even a bed of oysters will contain its surprising, rare pearl: the student a teacher may have misjudged as *merely* competent, who suddenly, through sheer determination and hard work, somehow *gets it* and astonishes everyone. This student repays all the hours and tears invested in a hundred unrewarding others, and she disproves one of our most dearly held myths.

Box 1: Another round, on me

For our pervasive unease about workshops reflects more than our writerly discomfort, closely guarded and nurtured, with the academy. It also reflects our cherished idea that creative writing can't be taught, which means we can't really help that poor mollusc of a student, at least not directly. Of course, people who believe creative writing can't be taught have no business taking money to teach it, however hard they might find selling insurance or cleaning toilets instead. But, paradoxically, teaching writers themselves cling to this myth, perhaps because it reinforces our sense of special-ness, which we perpetuate through the sorting we do in workshop, at the same time that it allows us to be lazy, to respond to student stories haphazardly, out of our own unexamined preferences (however better educated than those of our students) rather than with real engagement. In other words, all this cocktail chatter reveals our right sense that there's more we could and should be doing for our students – the rare one who will write her name across the literary firmament, the one who will publish a few modest stories here and there then settle into a suitable career in accounting or law, and the one who chafes herself until she finally realizes she's sitting on a pearl.

I don't know. But, ready or not, my box runneth over. I must go on to build, and fill, the next.

2. ATHENA AND THE ELEPHANT: FORM AND CONTENT

It matters to meaning, whether this essay is a garden or a set of nesting boxes or Athena or an elephant. So form and content rub up against each other. My esteemed editor, Professor Harper, has provided a strict form (hence the abrupt close of the last section, which ran a word over): four boxes, already labelled. I had only to uncollapse them, tape them open, send them back full.

Of course Professor Harper hoped to control not only my form but through it my content: so many words to philosophy and whatnot (just enough rope, there, to hang), so many to exercises, recommended reading. But my essay will be different from the others, the others from mine. And I – will I obey the charming Professor's outline? Will I let content or form run away with me, shape my remarks precisely as asked, or look at ways to shape the boxes themselves just a little differently?

Athena and the claims of form

Our minds divide to conquer. In the classroom, we focus our attention mostly on form. This is hard on beginners. They value content, or at least intention, over form; in the US they've been taught they have *something to say*, and they want us to tell them in ten easy lessons how to get their content, themselves, out onto the page, where they will know it when they see it. True, almost any life might provide compelling raw materials for fiction. But when accountants and marketing managers say to the teachers of their evening classes 'Everyone has a story', they imagine their stories already exist, intact in Platonic space, waiting to blow straight from the head of Jove. One might as well say *I am* and expect the two words to go off and reproduce in private, then assemble their brood into typescript. As the writer says to his barfly friend in the old *New Yorker* cartoon, what we really hate about writing is that 'it's just work', and, while it's not exactly ditch digging, teasing a full-grown goddess from left hemisphere to page can give a person a headache.

A decade and a half after Eve Shelnutt published her essay 'Notes from a Cell' in the *AWP Chronicle* (Shelnutt, 1990), the idea that we can teach form – or, more precisely, craft – through structured readings and exercises is no longer controversial. Only building the box (now Athena-shaped) can make fiction present, can give a story an inside and an outside. Ideally, the student will become adept at box building, enter into skilled play, and distract herself from her original intentions, her desire to make her case to the world, long enough to make something interesting. To do their stories, as opposed to themselves, justice, students must stop thinking of writing as self-expression and learn to create shapes that might be possessed by, and possess, someone else. If we want a story to spend more time in readers' hands than our own, it must be as much about reader as writer.

So, we ignore what they want, these beginners who don't know what's good for them, and put them through their paces on description, dialogue, scene, the lathe-turned sentence. I remind my students of the joke about the blind men trying to describe an elephant: make a foot, a tail, a bizarre tooth and a peculiar breathing apparatus; imagine from these a beast that walks and trumpets and feeds itself, however improbably, with its nose – a beast someone might recognize. Our box takes the form, now, of a creature with mind, language, an enormous, beating heart – an interior made of flesh and blood and grief. But our exercises may or may not enable a given student to create a box that could hold anything, much less become a beast with agency and charming, wrinkly knees. We tell them to make the pieces then assemble them, not to wrestle the creature whole from their heads. *Do as we say, not as we do.* We can't hope to teach them how to bring everything together. We were never taught ourselves. Content, we secretly believe, just *happens*, as if by magic. We don't tell our students the whole Rube Goldberg machine is held together by spit, duct tape, and bungee cords, and also by faith – the faith of the writer, and the cultivated faith of the reader.

The elephant in the room: faith and content

In workshop, standing in for readers, we don't grant this faith, and withholding it works admirably up to a point. But our advanced workshops too remain focused on mechanics. Because our discussions become more nuanced and sophisticated as students master elements of form, we expect our methods to continue to serve, even as our students, and we too tire of the same old nitpicking and positioning. We look forward to reading the stories of our one or two 'stars', but, having little new to tell them, we earn our salaries by quibbling with their placements of commas and scenes. We bring the same kind of advice but a different tone to bear on 'workshop stories'; we faint with damned and damn with faint praise.

We understand, though we don't say, that there is an elephant in the room. Our focus on form ignores what art critic Dave Hickey calls 'the slippage ... between how it looks and what it means' (1993: 54) – not how form creates and embodies content, but how the two cannot quite account for each other in the experience of the viewer. According to Hickey, modern painting flattens its surface to deny the viewer entry, to exclude the viewer as active participant, and so eradicates the wonderful tension of the painter-subject-viewer triangle, in which viewer and painter take on the subject together. Now, the viewer merely watches, from outside the frame, as the painter wrestles with his subject.[2]

Our workshops too, in their focus on 'fixing' stories, encourage the flat, smooth surface. But this tidy surface, its impenetrability, is what makes the workshop story not merely adequate but actually inadequate, if by adequacy in fiction we mean something a reader might finish reading if she's not being paid to do so or sitting in a dentist's waiting room. As in painting, that surface denies the reader entry, denies her necessary role as an active agent who might inhabit and interpret the delicious 'slippage' between form and content. To succeed beyond mere adequacy, then, a story must finally escape, not adhere to, our prescriptions and proscriptions.

How do we continue to sharpen our students' awareness of form while teaching them when to ignore its requirements? I believe we may do so not by eradicating but by offering ourselves up to a story's slippage, the loose skin at the elephant's knees, prepared not only to inhabit and be charmed by it but, more importantly, to perform this elusive charm before the writer. So I have been experimenting for the last dozen years or so with a workshop in which, instead of addressing content obliquely and implicitly through discussions of form, we face it head on, also through form. To do this, we reframe the question, asking of each story up for discussion not *Does it work?* but *How does it work?*

The second question assumes a positive answer to the first. This presents a difficulty, since by asking the first question endlessly we've trained ourselves to assume a negative answer. But now I ask my students to approach their colleagues' work with the same curious, analytic mind with which they might pick up a story by Byatt or Munro. (Imagine the advice our students would give in response to a Byatt or Munro draft – the frenzy of tidying and trimming.) Then, I ask them to articulate their reading practice, to perform it, for their colleagues and me. They must deploy the language of description and analysis and, most difficult, abandon the language of evaluation, positive or negative, within the workshop. I encourage them to swap prescriptive advice in the bar after class, and if they require praise or blame from me, I invite them to seek it privately, in my office.

This has had many happy results. First, all writers know from the misunderstandings that sometimes emerge in traditional workshops that there might be vast differences among the interpretations students bring to class with them – but until we routinely elicit these various interpretations and place them entire on the table, we cannot understand just how varied they are. The new workshop often reveals these differences as great enough to disable questions like 'is it working?' until we know what 'it' is. Now, when we reach the point of discussing whether a story works – *if* we reach that point – everyone including the writer knows which, among a number of different stories inhabiting any particular story before us, we might be talking about.

Second, the new workshop makes visible to the writer her collaboration with her reader in all its variability and richness. As students begin to see different good minds at work on their stories, they see how many possibilities for interpretation they have built into their works, possibilities that may create unanticipated confusion or surprising moments of clarity. A writer can watch one reader follow a path she intended and another a path she never herself saw, perhaps into interesting underbrush. She sees how she controls (or fails to control) the direction we take, the pieces of landscape we cross, and how we make from those pieces a whole geography. Rather than coming to class to watch us disassemble, perhaps snarkily, what she has made, she watches us work good-heartedly to put it all together. The writer begins to see *how* the story works – or does not. She may at first have trouble interpreting what she sees, but that's what individual consultation is for.

Students can no longer see, to my astonished pleasure, whose work I most wanted, on first encounter, to devour whole, and whose I could have left alone. No longer working to tailor their responses to what they believe mine will be, they set aside aesthetic judgements and alliances by which they might dismiss some stories out of hand and engage the work as it is, treating all of it with respect. Instead of jostling for position, they compete fiercely to give the smartest, most generous readings of each other's stories. In composing these readings, they also begin to heal the rift they experience between their scholarly and their creative work – they begin to see how to use the critical eye in relation to their own work.

I also work harder in these classes, preparing a detailed written reading for each story that comes in. This is more difficult than hovering over the pages with a pencil, looking for things to adjust. Now, my graduate workshops exhaust me, but they are well worth the effort. The students rise to the occasion, learning to take their own work more seriously. Even the less ambitious among them begin to take risks, hazard new and dazzling complexities.

We have not, in the process, abandoned our attention to form; we have simply reconfigured it. The poet Cynthia Macdonald taught me the most important thing I learned as a student: to look for the heart of a piece in the place where form is failing me, or rather where I am failing form: that place where the surface of the work simply refuses to adhere to my intentions. There, I should look not for something to excise ('This isn't working – you should cut it') nor for something to smooth over ('I like it, but it would sound better if you changed the word "mutant" to "defective"') but rather for what refuses to be subdued however we may try to tame it or eradicate it. Thus form, or its failure, remains the mechanism for entering the conversation, not to close it down but to blow it open.

(3) 4. MAKING THE ELEPHANT (VISIBLE): TEACHING STRATEGIES

Undergraduate workshops: making the elephant

Some creative writing teachers believe there should be no workshops at the early post-secondary levels – only reading, craft exercises and teacher response, all focused on form. But the workshop serves important functions at this level, not the least of which is to teach students workshop vocabulary and methodologies they can take with them into advanced classes. With this in mind, my workshop sessions even at the beginning level open with descriptions of the pieces at hand before moving on to craft questions; as the semester proceeds, after we've extensively modelled critical analysis in talking about the reading, we introduce analysis into workshop.

Beyond this, my undergraduate creative writing classes are structured to keep the students reading and writing and especially to focus their attention towards developing formal strategies and away from pleading their own cases.

Sudden fiction exercise 1 – Imitation: same old
Sudden fictions – stories under 500 words – allow students to practise making beginnings, middles and ends on stories whose boundaries are visible from everywhere. Sudden fictions also help students learn how much can be accomplished within small spaces, that small stories might become very large on the inside with the application of certain techniques – multilayered dialogue, white space, voice, image. Sudden fictions are also wonderful tools for helping students learn how to workshop as well as how to revise. Most of these sudden fictions should be complete as they are, but some may lend themselves to extension when the students begin to write longer stories later in the semester. There are a number of excellent contemporary anthologies of sudden fictions. I also present students with brief stories by writers like Chekhov and Kafka as well as with prose poems and self-contained chunks of lyric prose from larger works.

For the first sudden fiction exercise, students choose an object of imitation from a range of short fictions and prose poems. Sometimes, I ask them to work from sentence structure – every sentence in their sudden fictions must follow, in order, the syntax of the sentences in the pieces they imitate. Sometimes, I ask them to imitate some less tangible element of a story, such as its use of image. Imitations allow me to focus my written and workshop comments about their work very closely on writing and technique.

Sudden fiction exercise 2 – Dramatic monologue: the awful other
This in-class exercise uses cues. It helps displace students' attention away from themselves

while locating possible content within their own lives. The resulting stories provide good vehicles for discussing authorial complicity, round characters and tone, as well as how to use action, description and image to convey meaning.

Some cues:

- Think of and write down the name of a person you deeply dislike.
- You will now begin to write. Beginning with the words 'the truth is', speaking in the first person, in that person's voice, tell a lie.
- Modify the lie – correct it in some way, either towards or further away from the truth.
- You are performing a repetitive task. Talk about the task, explaining how you do it, how it feels to be doing it – what kind of skill it might take, what you might have to wear to perform it, the extent to which it absorbs or bores you.
- As you work, focus in on a particular, visual aspect of the task, something about it you can see. Create a visual image from/around the repetitive task. Develop the image – extend it. Keep extending the image, even as it becomes improbable.
- Make a confession – tell a deep secret.
- Return to the repetitive act or the image.
- Correct or alter the confession.
- Return to the task and finish it.

Foster characters

One of our PhD graduates, Lynn Kilpatrick, noting that her students persist in writing stories in which nobody does much besides drink beer and/or coffee and try to have sex, has taken to assigning her students characters. Sometimes Kilpatrick develops these characters – name, sex, age, background, work history – herself; sometimes she has students develop characters to give to each other; sometimes she assigns students to write stories around characters from Studs Terkel's *Working*.

The Zoning Committee

You can use similar exercises to encourage students to think in a larger way about place. Sometimes, I get the whole class to collaborate in developing a town, which will become the setting for all their stories. Every student takes a hand in the town's making, but the town will also contain neighbourhoods, businesses and other elements that may be alienating or unfamiliar to individual students. As students write from this town, they continue to develop it, and they continue, as they read each other's stories, to borrow from and cross reference each other. When this works well, the students create a wonderful intertextual conversation, even asking permission to bring other students' characters into their own stories in cameo roles.

Envisioning the elephant: the content-based workshop

But my primary teaching focus is now on the postgraduate, content-based workshop, the philosophy of which I have already described. In this class, each workshop story becomes the primary responsibility of one student, who creates a formal reading of it. I ensure that every student is responsible for an equal number of stories by using a daisy-chain approach, in which the student whose story was last discussed performs the reading on the next story.

Making and managing the groups

1. During the orientation class, ask for a student volunteer to perform the first work-shop reading.
2. Divide the class up into groups.
    a. I make four groups of three or four students for a fourteen-week semester of weekly, three-hour classes. This gives us time to do three stories by each student, devoting 45–60 minutes per story.
    b. The student who has volunteered to give the first critical reading automatically becomes a member of the last group, since her own final story of the term will be the last story we discuss. Beyond this, you can divide the students any way you wish. They will stay in the same groups for the whole term.
3. Once group 1 has been formed, have your volunteer choose whose story from the group she will read in the first workshop.
4. Then have the student whose story was selected decide from the remaining group members whose story she will read, and so on until all the stories in the group have been discussed. The student from group 1 whose story is chosen last will have no story to read during the group 1 workshop.
5. At the end of the group 1 workshop, when group 2 distributes its stories, have this leftover student decide which story she will read to lead off the following week's workshop. Group 2 will then follow the same procedure outlined above, again with a student left over to start off the readings on group 3.

How the workshop operates

1. Assign each student doing a reading to prepare and present a brief (ten-minute) analysis, a pressured close reading. This reading might look at how a specific image builds in the story; it might address the story's use of metonymy, something inter-esting about dialogue in the story, or how the language in a scene shapes the reader's response to the events it narrates. Later in the semester, students may chafe against the analytic structure with interesting results, finding ways to make their responses innovative and playful. One student of mine, in response to a highly-wrought, ima-gistic three-part story, created her own altarpiece-style triptych. Others have responded with collages, musical compositions, dramatic monologues, poems, even treasure maps.
2. Open the student's analysis to conversation by engaging her with questions about her reading. You may ask about inconsistencies or things that contradict or remain unaccounted for by the student's reading; you may encourage the student to take her account one step further.
3. Begin to invite the other students to break in with their own questions, quibbles and alternate readings. Keep the focus on the story and the various developing readings of it, and on the questions: *What does the story do*, and *How?*
4. At the end of the discussion, invite the writer to ask questions – not, again, to discover whether or not something is 'working', but to clarify the readings and interpretations

or to ask for an interpretation of some piece of the story on which nobody has yet touched.

Tips and cautions

1. Hold yourself to the same standards to which you hold your students. Prepare your own typed analysis of each story that comes up for workshop, perhaps three or four double-spaced pages. You will not present these to the class – the focus will be on the student analyses – but you may summarize or even read brief sections when they will add to the discussion, not only but especially when you realize in class, as you sometimes will, that you have misread the story in some way. This information is *extremely* useful to the student, who can use it to gain insight into how she might have led you in the wrong direction or merely to understand how far astray even good readers can go. In addition, owning up publicly about your own misreadings makes you vulnerable in a workshop situation in which you've asked the students to make themselves in some ways more, or at least differently, vulnerable than usual.

2. Prohibit evaluative language absolutely – both to your students and to yourself – at least until the term's last full round of stories. Use only the descriptive (*What?*) and the analytic (*How?*). You will be tempted to transgress, and your students will test you, but you must enforce this rule, even as students push against it. It takes time to get used to the format and also to begin to see its benefits, and once you open the discussion to evaluation the students will revert to it aggressively.

3. Expect the first efforts to be stiff and a little hesitant. Most students are used to responding to literature this way – but they are not used to thinking of their own work, or that of their fellows, as literature. It makes them feel uncomfortable to be taken so seriously, to have their work read as if to have it read was what they had intended all along.

4. Condition any recommendations you do make in private or during the last round of stories. Remember that a decision about what to do with a story will depend on which story or stories within the work the writer decides to pursue and develop.

5. As the term proceeds, ask students to read stories by students in their group whose work they haven't read before. This creates variety and collegiality. If you forget to ask, chances are the students will arrange this themselves.

Also important

1. Leave class time to talk about assigned reading. I assign recent books by the guest writers who are visiting our campus during the academic year. In these discussions I invite students to be not only analytic but also evaluative, and especially to reveal and defend aesthetic biases – an exercise useful not only to them but also to the fellow students who rely on their readings.

2. Help the students move beyond content that comes easily. Send or take them on field trips – to galleries, factories, morgues. Assign them to embark on individualized, miniature reading programmes: three books in a non-literary discipline – the circus, alchemy, cosmology, jazz, ship building. Have them report in their final portfolios on how their excursions and readings have influenced their work.

A final word

Yes, this is a difficult kind of workshop to run, and students will resist it at first. But by all reports they come in the end to value the experience, and they will carry its lessons and many of its practices back into their conventional workshops in ways that are productive and useful to them and to your fellow teachers.

(4) 3. NOTABLE READINGS FOR YOUR STUDENTS AND FOR YOU

Lower division: resources for exercises and workshop strategies

With *Sudden Fiction*, editor Robert Shapard (1987) coined the term now freely applied to the short-short story. This anthology and its follow-up, *Sudden Fiction International* (edited by Shapard with James Thomas, 1989), provide wonderful examples of the sudden fiction form.

The Story Behind the Story, edited by Andrea Barrett and Peter Turchi (2004), contains stories of varying lengths by such writers as Robert Boswell, Chuck Wachtel, Antonya Nelson, and Karen Brennan. Each story is followed by a brief essay in which the author talks about the story's creation – its genesis, the writer's struggles with craft, etc. Because it shows how messy the writing process can be, it's a wonderful book for undergraduate students, especially at the intermediate level.

The strength of *The Passionate, Accurate Story: Making Your Heart's Truth into Literature* by Carol Bly (1990) is that it actually asks undergraduate students to consider content as primary, providing advice and exercises to this end. She is right to try to move students towards engagement and emotional depth in their work. Unfortunately, the book is marred by Bly's conviction that real content always works from and towards a particular political point of view – her own – and that no other 'heart's truth' does either. Even when they agree with Bly's politics, students are smart enough to recognize – and reject – this aspect of the book.

History of pedagogy and resources for upper division teaching

D. G. Myers's *The Elephants Teach* (1995) provides an interesting overview of the history of creative writing in the US. It also presents the argument, somewhat provocative in 1995, that writers teaching creative writing in academia represent one of three distinct positions in relation to the teaching not of creative writing but of literature, 'demand[ing] that literature be taught (in the sensible phrase of Allen Tate) as if people intended to write more of it' (p. 6). I agree with this argument, which provides additional insight into why writers often feel themselves opposed to their departments' literary scholars.

For an overview of the pedagogy discussion currently going on in the US, I would direct interested readers to the essay by Kassia Fleisher and Joe Amato, 'Reforming Creative Writing Pedagogy: History as Knowledge, Knowledge as Activism', at www.altx.com/ ebr/riposte/rip2/rip2ped/amato.htm#classroom, and also to the excellent review by Kirsten Young in the *electronic book review*, which can be traced from www. electronicbookreview.com/v3/servlet/ebr?command=view_essay&essay_id=youngend, and which includes a lively follow-up discussion with responses by Marjorie Perloff and others. The account of creative writing history in the US academy given here by Fleisher and Amato is less detailed and more irreverent than that of Myers in *The Elephants*

Teach, but it is still quite thorough enough for most purposes (its information differs slightly from that on the University of Iowa website, www.uiowa.edu/~iww/about.htm, which is the one I used). The essay, review and follow-up discussion also provide an interesting account of arguments about 'craft' versus 'process' being made in the US academy today. Among other salient points in the follow-up discussion, Perloff makes the case – accurate if somewhat hyperbolic – that Creative Writing Programmes are the last places in the 'Englit' department in which the close reading of literature is still practised and taught.

In *Metro: Journeys in Writing Creatively*, Katharine Haake, Hans Ostrom and the late Wendy Bishop (2001) present exercises designed to move writers into what they call 'active writing'.

Bishop, a pioneer in creative writing pedagogy in the US, has authored and edited numerous other books, including most notably *Colors of a Different Horse*, also with Hans Ostrom (1994); *Released into Language: Options for Teaching Creative Writing* (1998); *On Writing: A Process Reader* (2003a); *The Subject Is Writing: Essays By Teachers and Students* (2003b), and *In Praise of Pedagogy*, with David Starkey (2000).

Though less well known than Bishop, Haake is one of America's most interesting fiction writers and thinkers about fiction and teaching. The stories in *No Reason on Earth* (1986) and *The Height and Depth of Everything* (2001) enact some of this thinking, dramatizing and examining the position of the writer – and therefore of the reader – in relation to her fiction.

The Writer's Chronicle, AWP's bimonthly magazine, began as a membership news pamphlet, the *AWP Newsletter*, and was also for many years known as the *AWP Chronicle*. It has for almost four decades provided an invaluable resource to US writers looking for the practitioner's take on craft and teaching as well as for information about prizes and publishing opportunities. Though I have found very little that specifically addresses the kind of workshop I'm trying to teach, an interview with Jane Smiley in the March/April 1994 issue (p. 1) includes an interesting early discussion of the value of a more neutral, analytic workshop.

According to AWP Director David Fenza, Joseph Moxley's *Creative Writing in America* (1989), which gathers essays by 27 teaching writers, is one of the few books on pedagogy that has caused 'a small ripple' rather than the usual 'minute impact' of such works on the field. This book includes Shelnutt's 'Notes from a Cell', which originally appeared in the *AWP Chronicle*.

From outside the discipline of creative writing comes dancer Liz Lerman's essay 'Toward a Process for Critical Response' (available at www.communityarts.net/readingroom/archivefiles/2003/10/toward_a_process.php). Though Lerman is still focused on 'fixing' what is 'wrong' in a piece, she has useful ideas for bringing the artist into the critical discussion as an active, even a controlling member.

Last but certainly not least, Dave Hickey's *The Invisible Dragon: Four Essays on Beauty* (1993) mounts an urgent defence of the value of beauty and through this an equally urgent plea on behalf of the beleaguered viewer of art. I recommend these essays as wholeheartedly to writers as to artists.

Chapter 2

Poetry

Chad Davidson and Gregory Fraser
University of West Georgia

1. DISPELLING MYTHS AND GETTING STARTED

Who are poets? Conduits for 'the muses'? Especially gifted people with an ear or an eye or a hand for the stuff of poetry? How do they invent the language of poetry? What students entering the classroom think of poetry will inevitably be their only reference point until the class offers alternatives. Student preconceptions regarding what poetry is then (i.e. merely self-expression, catharsis, a place for the soul, and so forth) easily inhibit what poetry could be, what its potential for each practitioner will ultimately be. In a similar manner, we might also challenge facile definitions of 'the poet' or 'the artist'. In *The Creative Mind: Myths and Mechanisms*, Margaret Boden (2004) argues that there are a few predominant myths about artists and that these myths are perpetuated at the expense of both artists and non-artists. Viewing artists as somehow gifted, imbued with special talents, or just plain 'creative', cheapens the act of creation while excluding those who feel they are not especially gifted. Romantic and inspirational myths surrounding the creative process do not accurately portray the difficulty that artistic creation poses, the long hours spent with seemingly little or no progress, the endless drafts of the same poem. Believing these myths about artistic creation means accepting the premise that some of us are merely 'hardwired' for creativity and that it cannot be learned. Guidebooks, however, continually stress the 'showing up for work' mentality of writing, that writing is a practice as much as it is an art, that the two are inseparable.

If the romantic myth of the writer is bankrupt, so too is the notion that poets are merely scribes for what comes to them from the ether. Gone is the idea that there needs to be little drafting after the original inspiration. The practice of writing is just that: practice. In this sense, students might find it useful to think of poetry writing in terms of sports or dance analogies: all the endless free kicks pay off during the game. All the formal dance moves, once internalized, come freely to the dancer performing on stage. One learns in order to unlearn. One internalizes in order to call forth one's knowledge without having to think about it. One naturalizes, embodies, enacts. Thus, what we are teaching may not be so much 'poetry writing' as it is the avoidance of 'non-poetry writing'. And we aren't teaching as much as we are helping untrained writers to unlearn their preconceptions and biases regarding this very different use of language.

Another useful distinction to make at this point is that between writing poetry and practising poetry. Writing seems to have finality attached to it. Writing seems immutable ('Put it in writing,' we say, and, 'I want that in writing'), whereas what poets do is probably closer to practising. Immersion in the practice of poetry writing is what instructors of poetry writing should encourage their students to do. Not 'writing finished poems' but 'practising the art of writing'. Not 'writing as a means to some final goal or product' but 'writing as an autotelic activity'. In other words, writing for the sheer enjoyment of writing. The writer-in-training privileges the immutable finished product. We want to privilege the act that gave rise to that product.

An excellent starting point in any poetry-writing class is to define what we mean by poetry. Here it might be useful to draw distinctions, with the students' help, between the terms *poesy, prosy* and *poetry*. Common definitions of poetry, such as 'self-expression in words', 'cathartic release' and 'overwhelming emotion recorded in writing', may then be situated tentatively in one of the three categories. By sharpening the students' awareness of the differences between the language they use every day and the language found in poetry, the instructor will already have stimulated the students' sensitivity to language. Finally, the terms *poesy, prosy* and *poetry* are fairly arbitrary. We encourage instructors to find their own distinctions and delineations between the common usages of language, the preconceived notions of poetry, and the poetry that we come back to continually.

Under *poesy* falls the 'overly poetic', the expected poetic clichés, the saccharine and the 'Hallmark'. Words and concepts such as *soul, spirit, embrace, rose, kiss, broken heart, love* and *rapture*, for example, come easily to mind when an untrained writer thinks of what is 'poetic'. In addition to trite poetic vocabulary, we may also add anachronisms such as *thou* and *methinks*, along with abstractions such as *hope, desire* and *eternity*. The idea of poetry as mere self-expression, too, might belong here, as it fails to acknowledge any difficulty or deliberate craft. After all, we express ourselves whether we choose to or not. Even the clothing we wear 'expresses' something about us, and we do nothing more than buy the clothes we like and put them on. One way of enlarging the scope of this argument, though, is to talk about the 'art' of dressing well. Artful dressers are capable of taking seemingly incongruous or haphazard items of clothing and blending them in such a way that their look is entirely surprising and challenging. This is a closer analogy to what poets do with language. Again, poets use the same words that everyone else uses every day to buy bread, to communicate with the postal worker, to order a pizza over the phone, to talk with a friend. But the use to which poets put language, the tests to which they subject the words, is much different.

In his essay 'The Poet in an Age of Distraction', Sven Birkerts notes that 'it has always been the task of the poet to make sure there is bullion to back the currency that we pass so casually from hand to hand' (1989a: 40). If his assumption is correct, then part of what poets and instructors of poetry writing do entails the reinvigorating of the common currency of language. Just as we trade words symbolically (for words, at least in much daily communication, stand for something else), so do we sometimes forget the histories and precariousness of the meanings behind those words. We also forget the more visceral ways in which words 'mean' – the shapes, the contours, the colours of language. Combining words in unexpected ways, pushing language to perform difficult acts, then, becomes part of the poetic practice. In this way, writing that does not somehow test language's elasticity or challenge language to take surprising leaps might be deemed 'prosy'. By that word is intended no derogation towards prose but rather an easy and unself-conscious falling back into the 'symbolic currency' of ordinary usage and a denial of the myriad ways in which language may be significant in poetic contexts. Because of the sheer amounts of 'prose' students digest daily (street signs, news broadcasts, news-papers, Internet chat rooms, biology texts), training their minds to be responsive to the 'poetic' – that is, the surprising, the fresh, the vibrant – uses of language will take some time. To begin, students should aim at recognizing when language is performing difficult acts and not merely lying down orderly in the everyday prose of commerce.

Still, though, we have yet to define what poetry *is*. Even Dickinson's gorgeously visceral definition – that poetry makes her feel as if the back of her head has been blown off – or Coleridge's terseness – the best possible words in the best possible order – assert little in terms of concrete definitions. Other art forms may provide meaningful analogies. Just as musicians may talk of cadence, rhythm and volume, poetry students too may talk of a poem's musical aspects. Just as visual artists, painters and photographers may talk of composition – the spatial placement of the shapes in a work – so too may poetry students begin by discussing the poem's composition on the page. Students might also talk, as sculptors and architects might, of a poem's 'architecture'. That is, can we look past the façade of language and witness any of the structure that is holding the entire poem up?

To help students re-imagine their notions of what poetry is, instructors might have them generate a list of these preconceptions in class. Again, these should be words that they easily associate with poetry (*embrace, kiss, soul, flowers*), bald and facile poetic concepts (desire, love) and anachronistic language (outdated or tired expressions). As a way of challenging the students, instructors may then make this list taboo. That is, the students must avoid using the words and concepts on the list. We have found that not only do students find the act of navigating around these words interesting and enter-taining, they also begin to develop their own taboo words and begin to challenge what they feel is tired or overused in poetry. This works just as well in upper-division work-shops with more nuanced notions of what is cliché. For example, one might discuss the preponderance of 'the way' or 'how' constructions in contemporary poetry (for example, 'the dark coffee, how it stains the parquet'). Similarly, John Poch in his essay on poetic clichés appearing in *The Writer's Chronicle* (2005) talks of overused contemporary poetic material such as cicadas, the homeless and the attention to the 'failure of language'. The variations are limitless here. For untrained writers, such an exercise propels them into the province of surprising language and unexpected connections. For more advanced (or 'trained') writers, inventing their own lists of taboos is a way of heightening their sensitivity to contemporary poetry.

Developing such keen sensitivity to language also helps students with a particularly troublesome roadblock: approaching the process of making poems from a 'readerly' point of view. In our workshops and one-on-one conferences with students, we call attention to this phenomenon and try to address its potential pitfalls. By 'readerly approach', we mean that tendency in maturing poets to confuse the movement and shape of the reading process with the movement and shape of the writing process.

Yet poems aren't written the way they're read.

While reading is predominantly a linear act, the process of making poems tends to be non- or extra-linear – letting in the random and embracing the recursive as the poet haphazardly quests for something – anything – potentially poetic. Non- or extra-linear processes are especially necessary in the early stages of making. In reading, one starts at the beginning of a text and follows its logic to conclusion. Poems, however, are not typically written from start to finish, with clear-cut beginnings, middles, or ends. Some are, of course, but these tend to be exceptions. More frequently, strong poems are pieced together from disparate parts, not unlike Victor Frankenstein's creation. (Henry James, by the way, said essentially the same thing about the making of novels.)

We do not intend to undermine the value of copious reading. We constantly insist that students become voracious readers of poetry – especially but not exclusively contemporary poetry. Such practice is absolutely necessary for the internalization of the complex tones, structures and movements of poems. Indeed, we have required students to memorize at least a hundred lines of poetry over the course of the term, for 10 per cent of their final grade. There's no substitute for deep and eclectic reading, but as instructors we find it necessary to draw meaningful distinctions between the finished products that are master poems and the kinds of extra-linear uses of language involved in the making of those poems.

That many students adopt a readerly approach early in their writing lives should come as no surprise, of course. The largely linear act of following a text from start to finish has been ingrained by years of critical coursework devoted to the complex architectures of poetry. It makes sense for many students to assume that the process of writing poems should be similar. Their thinking might run this way: 'I've read and studied this masterful Shakespeare sonnet. It moves from this point to that point in a richly structured way. First, it builds one argument, then tests out another, then comes to a volta and reverses fields, then reaches its conclusion. I'm going to sit down and write a poem that moves in similar ways.' Such a readerly perspective, when applied to the act of writing, typically forces the process to occur too quickly, in an overly sequential and predictable manner. It dangerously suggests that the student should 'write the poem as she goes', or produce the poem in linear time. Readerly points of view tend to be product-oriented, forcing the premature completion of an artefact. As instructors of poetry writing, part of our job may be to help students learn not to be duped by the readable finished products of published poems. Polished poems are con artists of sorts, magicians that keep their processes secret. Remember Horace's understanding that a good writer is boxing your ears as he strokes your cheek. Polished poems announce: 'Look at how pristine and complete I am. Just imagine what kind of genius could sit down and produce such a work of art.' But such bravado is ironic. One look at any poet's notebook reveals the unruly histories of individual poems. The births of poems tend to be messy affairs, and we do well to remind our students to dwell in messiness much longer than they might like to.

2. KEY POINTS IN TEACHING/LEARNING POETRY

Such high-minded talk of poetry's risk-taking with language, however, holds little import for writers at the beginning of their apprenticeship. And, really, over-analysis of one's language at the beginning may inhibit the free association and imaginative leaps necessary for poetry to live. What first needs to happen – as in the case of a painter, say – is that the writer needs a palette of colours from which to work. Most student-centred guides to writing poetry offer advice along these lines. In *The Triggering Town*, Richard Hugo (1992), for example, stresses the importance of having truth conform to music rather than music conform to truth, which is another way of suggesting that the beginning writer focus more on the sounds and textures of language than on denotative meanings. *Cranium* and *skull*, for example, carry very similar denotations. Their connotations, however – what they 'conjure' in our heads, the images they summon forth – are very different. Thus, a doctor is more likely to say that a patient suffers from a fractured cranium than from a cracked skull. Literal definitions may therefore be similar, but their literary significances are quite different. In *Writing the Australian Crawl*, William Stafford (1978) argues for an intuitive approach much like Hugo's, whereby a writer 'trusts' his or her imagination and that the first steps in writing will require the writer to write poorly, to take risks, to allow room for mistakes. The first lesson, then, should be to write often and voluminously, if only to provide a palette of colours, of textures, of language.

Contemporary critical theory – with its emphases on ideological, psycho-social and historical contexts – has questioned New Critical notions about the self-defining, or 'autotelic', text. Since the mid-1970s or so, Anglo-American literature classrooms have tended to preserve the New Critical emphasis on close reading while at the same time interrogating the belief that poems can exist unto themselves, that stable meanings can be derived through rigorous examinations of texts alone, with little reference to wider contexts. Yet while the concept of the 'autotelic' text may be considered dubious from the perspectives of present-day literary and cultural analysis, the encouragement of an autotelic attitude among developing poets may help them expand and deepen their writing processes.

Mihaly Csikszentmihalyi, the founder of 'flow theory', essentially regards the creative act as autotelic, where writing (along with painting, sculpture, dance, music, and other art forms) needs to be practised and understood as an end in itself. For Csikszentmihalyi, great artists master the art of 'flow' by enjoying an activity for its own sake and leaving 'the boundaries of the ego' (1997: 112). We have found that numerous benefits accrue when students read and apply some of the basic tenets of flow theory. When they begin the process by writing lines and passages not for the sake of any specific message to be conveyed, but for the sheer thrill of the process itself, they tend to tap more fully into their linguistic, visual, oral and auditory imaginations.

Robert Frost said that unless one surprises oneself as a poet, one will never surprise a reader. And the notion of autotelic flow – of giving over to the free play of language and imagery and sound – can be a powerful way to stimulate surprise, especially early on in the writing process, even though strategies of flow can prove productive during later revisions, as well. We advise students to let the poem dictate where it goes, rather than having any pre-formed idea of where the text should go. We suggest that instead of waiting for an idea to form, or beginning the writing process with a preconceived notion or destination, it is often more productive to let words and images help one 'stumble into' an idea. If a writer has too many answers before the process begins, then flow can be impeded.

One helpful exercise involves giving students a list of five passages from one or more published works. Each student's task is simply to 'riff' on the published passages. There are many ways to riff – reversals of imagery, plays on sound (as we will see in the 'recursivity' sub-section below), translations of concepts to other contexts, and so on. Many students use such passages as prompts or springboards: they pretend that the published writing is theirs, and they try to extend the piece, developing logics and moving in directions that are their own. The main idea here is to remain detached from any pre-set notion and to build a 'junkyard' of unexpected images, sounds and phrases that can be mined later in the writing process. As in jazz, where an underlying melody may form a musical foundation on top of which all improvisation is laid, the published passage roots the apprentice poet in strong language, and then asks her to embellish, elaborate, enlarge, retract, and play with, and off of, the original.

Below is a student improv from a recent workshop. The foundation passage, from Edward Hirsch's 'I Need Help', runs like this: 'I admit I'm desperate, I know / that the legs in my legs are trembling / and the skeleton wants out of my body'. These are the notes that the student jotted down in a ten-minute, in-class improv session:

Light in a cage of glass

we warm our hands by fires caged in glass

radiance trapped by the bulb

radiance trapped inside the tulip bulb I bury

I warm my hands by light
trapped inside the tulip
bulb I bury.

The fires folding their arms at dusk

I hear the crackle of distant fires.

I fear the gaping cracks between night's distant fires.

I ride black rivers running over stars.

It is possible to speculate about the thought processes underlying these riffs. The first line appears to play on Hirsch's concept of imprisonment, where bones caged inside the body long to escape. The student has transferred Hirsch's notion into the sphere of light, imagining radiance trapped inside a light bulb. From there, the student plays on the word *bulb* and takes a leap from a light bulb to a flower bulb. After this, the flow of imagination seems to return the poet to the concept of fire, and gradually the imagery moves from the terrestrial to the celestial realm, and also to images of fire and water.

There are innumerable ways to riff, and students rapidly become quite proficient in letting language and imagination lead during improv sessions, especially after they have become more sensitive to the types of language that are most evocative and powerful. Some of the lines cited above are certainly worthy of entering into a notebook or 'junkyard', and, interestingly, the last one appears to have fallen naturally into iambic pentameter. In fact, as the semester progresses, adding some formal constraints to previously written improv lines, asking students, for example, to modify a former improvised passage so that it follows a traditional metre, can prove worth while. Overall, though, the main goal of this exercise is to liberate maturing poets from their culturally inherited product orientation and to cultivate autotelic flow.

Flow and improv can indeed help to overthrow the product-centred approach that hinders many poetic apprenticeships, but these concepts and activities also set the stage for discussions about attachment. Students tend not to become overly attached to their improvisational or flow-generated pieces of writing, which teaches them to keep some necessary distance from their words. Committing too early to an idea or to a particular piece of writing can be dangerous, for until surprise is felt – until an Einsteinian 'aha!' experience comes about – it is often best to remain in an inductive, experimental mode, refusing to force premature conclusions and avoiding attachment until it is fully warranted. Time and again, we have seen students begin with pre-set ideas, work through poems in a linear fashion, and submit their pieces to workshop for review. Typically, the writing is predictable. There's little if any surprise in the lines. The poem's messages are told to, rather than experienced by, the reader. But these kinds of submissions reveal next to nothing about individual students' poetic gifts. They are more a sign of a process that allows students to think in terms of product and completion, to become attached to ideas too early, and to forgo the free play of flow and improv.

In *Aspects of the Novel*, E. M. Forster offers a particularly compressed piece of modernist *ars poetica* when he asks, 'How can I tell what I think till I see what I say?'

(1956: 101). This kind of attitude is one that we invite our students to embrace. Indeed, a good deal of the pedagogical process in the writing classroom can be devoted to questions of attachment and detachment. By not getting wedded to ideas at the outset of the process, students can 'ride their drafts', and this leaves open many more opportunities for the writing to move in unusual directions. The developing text is less stable and fixed, and so it can veer towards history (as Adam Zagajewski or Geoffrey Hill might do); it can swerve into the animal kingdom for a controlling idea (in the manner of Ted Hughes or Marianne Moore); the draft can adopt a mask and take on another's voice (à la Robert Browning or Ai); it might venture into classical myth. But these forays are possible only if the poet is relatively detached from the idea that the poem needs to be finished or that it needs to express a pre-established idea or emotion.

When we talk to students about 'committed detachment', we ask them to commit to the process of unfolding language, following sound, and discovering rather than imparting meaning. In short, we strive to break the attachment students often have to their first efforts on the page. It may be more fruitful, we say, to dwell, to improv, to let the poem surprise you into being. This helps them think in broader, more flexible terms, where a sudden reordering can change the whole face of the poem. The student who says, 'But that's not what I meant' still hasn't given over to flow, and still hasn't grasped what Keats meant when he described 'negative capability' and the 'chameleon poet', or what Eliot was driving at in his notion of the 'extinction of personality'. Ultimately our goal is to illustrate to students that what they 'meant' to say is seldom as surprising and evocative as what they 'come' to say once language is allowed some freedom.

3. NOTABLE READINGS IN/OF/ABOUT POETRY

We have found Richard Hugo's collection of poetry-writing essays, *The Triggering Town* (1992), especially helpful in empowering young writers at the beginning of their apprenticeships. Hugo's continual self-effacement and homespun analogies lend to his arguments a pleasing informality. After urging students not to worry initially about transparent 'communication', for example, Hugo offers this bit of advice: 'If you want to communicate, pick up the telephone.' All joking aside, with his guiding metaphor of the triggering town Hugo manages to couch the poet's complex act of faith in the imagination in terms students easily understand. Additionally, his reminiscences of being in Theodore Roethke's classes and his painful retelling of life-altering experiences as a bomber in the Second World War also encourage young writers to trace poetry's trajectory through the turbulent mid-century, and to consider the importance of constantly historicizing poetry. That some of the thin volume also addresses more generally the poet's place in the academy will be of specific interest to teachers of creative writing.

University of Michigan Press 'Poets on Poetry' series contains more than 90 volumes devoted to the art of poetry. Notables on this diverse list include *Blue Notes: Essays, Interviews, and Commentaries* by Yusef Komunyakaa (2000); *Made with Words* by May Swenson (1998); *Writing Like a Woman* by Alicia Ostriker (1983); *Poets Teaching Poets: Self and the World*, edited by Gregory Orr and Ellen Bryant Voigt (1996); and *Writing the Australian Crawl* by William Stafford (1978). Stafford's essays are particularly illuminating as regards the building of confidence in young writers. Many of Stafford's ideas have informed our discussions of the craft, and his book is filled with such timeless wisdom as 'any time we adopt a stance that induces an analytical feeling, we may be subverting what art depends on' (p. 47).

Additionally, we recommend *The Poet's Work*, edited by Reginald Gibbons (1989). This volume reprints essays by the likes of Lorca, Stevens, Montale, Moore, Bogan, and many more. Sven Birkerts's eminently readable *The Electric Life: Essays on Modern Poetry* (1989b) still imbues the study of poetry with enormous worth from a cultural standpoint, and effectively bolsters student perceptions of what poetry can do. For more practical, hands-on guides, see *The Poet's Companion: A Guide to the Pleasures of Writing Poetry* by Kim Addonizio and Dorianne Laux (1997); *Writing Poems* by Michelle Boisseau and Robert Wallace (2004); *The Portable Poetry Workshop* by Jack Myers (2005); and *The Practice of Poetry: Writing Exercises from Poets Who Teach*, edited by Robin Behn and Chase Twichell (1992).

John Frederick Nims and David Mason's *Western Wind* (1999) has arguably been one of the most important pedagogical tools in the teaching of poetry since the mid-1970s. While the authors devote most of the book's energy to aiding students in the under-standing and explication of poetry, they also suggest enough 'writing-centred' exercises to suggest a somewhat hybridized methodology. At the end of the chapter on images, for example, they ask students to generate a catalogue of 'concrete terms' in lieu of the 'abstract concepts' provided. What's more, the wonderfully rich anthology portion of the book – with which their myriad exercises are in constant dialogue – enables the book to be literally an 'all in one' poetry text. Meticulously updated, *Western Wind* is still a must for any instructor of poetry writing.

We have also consulted the following entries – a blend of critically and creatively minded texts – and continue to use excerpts from them in classrooms: *The Dyer's Hand* by W. H. Auden (1990); *Place of Writing* by Seamus Heaney (1989); *Poetic Meter and Poetic Form* by Paul Fussell (1979); *The Verse Book of Interviews: 27 Poets on Language, Craft & Culture*, edited by Brian Henry and Andrew Zawacki (2005); *Writing Through: Translations and Variations* by Jerome Rothenberg (2004); *Making Your Own Days: Rhyme's Reason: A Guide to English Verse* by John Hollander (2001); *The Poetry Home Repair Manual: Practical Advice for Beginning Poets* by Ted Kooser (2005); *Forces of Imagination: Writing on Writing* by Barbara Guest (2002); *A Poetry Handbook* by Mary Oliver (1995); *The Sounds of Poetry: A Brief Guide* by Robert Pinsky (1999); *A Poet's Guide to Poetry* by Mary Kinzie (1999); and *Poets Teaching the Creative Process*, edited by Alberta Turner (1980).

Finally, texts such as Mihaly Csikszentmihalyi's enormously important *Creativity: Flow and the Psychology of Discovery and Invention* (1997) and Margaret Boden's *The Creative Mind: Myths and Mechanisms* (2004) help to contextualize the poet's work within larger frameworks of artistic production and creative process. We encourage our students to read widely outside of their chosen genre and to investigate and incorporate varied approaches to creativity. Such texts stress the interconnectedness of arts and remain invaluable to teaching poetry writing.

4. FAVOURITE STRATEGIES FOR UNDERSTANDING THE MAKING OF POEMS

A. Diastolic-systolic method

Students are sometimes hoodwinked by the relative brevity of poetry in comparison to fiction, creative non-fiction, and drama. Poems, usually being shorter, are often assumed to require less time to compose. A myth persists that a sudden burst of creative energy – charged by a powerful emotion, vision, or image – will do just fine. In 'Of Modern Poetry', Wallace Stevens notes that poetry 'has to find what will suffice' in the modern world. As workshop instructors, we need to think through 'what will suffice' for poetry – how much time and effort we can expect our students to put into their productions and how we can best help them to develop in the craft.

Our experience has taught us that learning to overwrite is a vital part of learning to make 'sufficient' poems. With that in mind, we emphasize what might be called a 'diastolic-systolic method' of composition, in which poets are asked to run through several rounds of expansion and contraction on the page. In the expansive, diastolic mode, we urge students to let language, sound and imagery lead. We talk about an inductive, Darwinian gathering of copious data before any conclusions, any major conceptual or structural decisions, are reached. Diastolic strategies come in many forms: pure brainstorming and journaling; improv-ing and riffing on published lines; question-and-response strategies where students are instructed to answer mundane questions in wildly associative and unexpected ways; ekphrastic exercises in which students respond to artworks, photographs, music, and so forth; show vs tell callisthenics; the list goes on and on. Above all, the goal in this Dionysian phase of the process is to build a huge reserve of raw material – to create the clay out of which some statue, some rough figure, might begin to be shaped.

Students are frequently shocked to learn that practising poets sometimes develop a dozen or more pages of overwriting before even gesturing towards a poem. This is the phase of exploration for its own sake – of letting in the random, opening the unconscious, and entering uncharted waters. We like to encourage this kind of explosive, unruly, boundary-breaking 'burst' at the outset, in contrast to the short, singular burst that has become associated with the way poems are made. We need to teach a radical open-endedness at the start of the writing process, where the student does not think of herself as 'writing a poem', but as gathering the necessary language that might lead to a poem – often after several tours of the diastolic-systolic process. Students are naturally inclined to try to 'write the poem as they go', meaning that they start at the beginning with a clear-cut idea and then work their way down the page. That might prove fruitful as an initial brainstorming or language-gathering process, but it rarely produces strong final poems. We can't emphasize enough that most apprenticing poets want to end the process too soon; they want the finished product too quickly. We suggest that they have to be willing to dwell in incompletion and see what it can yield.

The diastolic-systolic process urges students to overwrite and then to use contraction strategies in search of a possible poem. In the systolic phase, the student seeks out the 'rough shape of a poem' and tries to apply some kind of organizing principle, some Apollonian logic or unifying device. Again, however, we advise students not to commit too soon, but instead to defer until a legitimate 'aha!' experience occurs. And such a revelation may require several run-throughs of diastolic expansions and systolic compressions. Systolic strategies are infinite, but here are some of our favourites.

Radical arrangement

Ask students to locate the strongest piece of language in their diastolic overwrite. Have them place a 1 next to that passage and then go searching within the diastolic overwrite for a line that interestingly follows. Have them place a 2 there, and proceed. This encourages leaping, mobility, and unlikely associations.

Creative erasure

The line 'I paid the December rent' might be considered a bit prosy. Creative erasure invites students to perform radical cuts that often change the sense of the line and yield more evocation notions and images. Working with the example above (which emerged in a diastolic overwrite), one of our students lopped off the words 'the' and 'rent' and ended up with 'I paid December'. This seems much more suggestive; the language takes a greater risk.

Guided imagery

After the expansive overwrite, it's sometimes fruitful to 'guide' the systolic contraction by focusing on a specific historical, mythical, cultural, or natural figure or situation. This may be a tactic as simple as arbitrarily writing 'Waterloo' at the top of the page, and then shaping the diastolic overwrite to gesture towards Napoleonic defeat, or a certain brand of hubris. This can't be forced, of course, but such a strategy can sometimes serve as a Virgilian usher into the underworld of systolic contraction. It typically produces unexpected results.

Rarely does an initial systolic contraction yield a poem, or even a solid means of organizing a poem. That being the case, we tell students that it is simply time to expand again. Here is where we ask them to dip again into their junkyards of imagery and lines produced in daily improv sessions and to search for possible insertions into the systolic contraction. Research can help, too. We also encourage them to return to the diastolic mode and to try to enlarge particular opportunities that may have surfaced in the first systolic contraction. The idea is to 'bulge' the text some more, to 'burst' a second time, and then to contract again into something – perhaps – closer to a text that can be submitted to the workshop.

B. Recursive method

Eliot famously remarked that contemporary writers – those involved in the 'tradition' of writing – are in constant exchange with history, that they may affect the past as much as they are affected by it. Eliot had an entire theory of influence in mind, a broad trans-historical and trans-cultural recycling process whereby a writer in the twentieth century may 're-invent' Dante or Homer. Certainly, Eliot's type of recursivity relies on the supposition that art is (re)cyclical, that it re-invents and feeds off itself. As a method of both generating and refining poetic material, however, recursivity may also work more locally, suggesting that writers may not only draw upon what has already been written by other poets in the past, but they may also immediately draw upon what they have just written. Using the recursive method, students need look no further than what they have just finished writing on the page, letting the poem generate its own lexicon and auditory textures. In a sense, this is nothing new. Localized recursivity accounts for many of poetry's mainstay structural achievements. Rhyme and metre both demand a strong degree of retrospect, where a certain stress or sound then dictates a later entry. Even closed forms – the villanelle, the sestina, and the pantoum, for example – rely on recursivity, the power of repetition.

In keeping with committed detachment, however, recursive strategies need not be as inelastic and unforgiving as, say, a villanelle's refrains or as predictably regular as rhyming patterns. Recursivity may be simply lexical in nature, where a word or group of words is repeated throughout the poem, each time in a slightly different context or with different associative powers. Writers as diverse as Lydia Davis, Carolyn Forché, Galway Kinnell and Mark Strand have benefited from the powers of lexical recursivity, but what we're talking about here is more the use of recursive strategies in the classroom with untrained writers. Lexical recursivity offers instructors of poetry writing a key way of showing just how powerful 'non-originality' can be, just how forcefully repetition may affect us. What is fresh in language does not necessarily always have to be sparkling new. When Seamus Heaney spoke in a lecture to the Royal Society of Literature of poetry writing as more an act of excavation, he was talking about the idea of 'foundness', that poetry is found as much as it is invented (Heaney, 1974). We are, in Barthes's thinking as well, scriptors rather than makers, pastiche artists using the language lying around us every day. Recursivity reminds students that emotional force and intellectual significance may indeed have roots in non-originality, in knowing when to repeat oneself.

Below is an example of an exercise in which students were asked to write four or five full sentences freely. Then they were asked to continue the exercise using as many possible words from the first part. Like good recyclers, they were to reuse what they had chosen first:

> The man with the high-powered rifle
> does not use swear words. The tower
> on which the man stands leans a little
> to the left. The man can't stand it,
> swears he will take them out
> from his position on the tower.
> He swears he will take them out
> with the high-powered rifle, if they swear.
> The left-leaning tower rides towards
> those he will take out. The out-takes
> don't quite swear but the high-powered rifle
> swears, swears it
> will take out the tower,
> and the man, and the lean.
> They all ride.
> They face the tower, riding hard.
> The words ride, leaning left, and tower
> towards something like swearing, but not quite.
> The man rides his high-powered rifle hard, swearing,
> but not with swear words,
> not quite, not quiet.

Here, the recursive strategy used by the student gave her a 'palette' to return to. Also of note is the way in which the repetitions may be read as an enactment of the obsessions of the rifleman. In an advanced workshop, the instructor might even take the recursive method further and encourage syntactical recursivity. A line such as 'They all ride', for example, relies on the culminating force of all the previous instances of the mysterious and victimized 'they' and the odd verb 'ride'. But the bluntness of that line's syntax, after some of the richer phrases in this draft, seems to bring the poem to a significant halt. The instructor might then discuss with the class the ways in which syntactical recursivity is able to manipulate the poem's movement.

Recursivity may just as readily be a tool for revision. When students say that they are stuck on a revision, that they are interested in a poem so far but can't seem to take it any further in the revision process, we encourage them to try the recursive method. That is, they may attempt to backtrack through the poem and pick up any images or words that seem important enough to return to. Inevitably, each time we see a certain word or image in a poem, the significance increases or, at least for the writer of the poem, there is the opportunity for increased significance through repetition. 'Do it once, it's a mistake; do it twice, and it's jazz,' said Miles Davis in his typically tongue-in-cheek way. And we might say something similar about poetry writing. The imagination may lead one to unexpected turns and images. It is the artist, then, who learns which of those words and images call for repetition, for more significance. And the best way to learn that art, it seems, is to practise it.

Recursivity may also be auditory in nature, where a certain sound is revisited and becomes an architectural element. In *The Triggering Town*, Hugo (1992) talks obliquely of this type of auditory repetition when he discusses his first attempts at poetry. Early on, he writes, he made a pact with himself: if he uttered a sound he liked, he would repeat it in the next line. Such nonce rules are very often the kind of motivation for poems in their early stages. Auditory recursivity, though, in a broader sense allows for a change in the writer's navigational equipment. If we return briefly to the obstacle of a 'readerly' perspective, we remember that the linear (narrative or logical) progression students experience while reading a poem does not necessarily translate into a writerly process. In our experience, poems are not written linearly but behave like magnets, attracting stray material that seemed, until the writing of the poem, disparate. Recursivity, especially auditory recursivity, calls attention to the non-linear writerly process by letting pure sound dictate at least in part the course of the poem.

Recently in workshop, a student poem spoke of 'Ocala, Florida'. When asked what 'sounds' in the poem were most striking, most memorable, many students cited 'Ocala, Florida'. In much the same way as, say, a jazz musician might then 'riff' off a particular pattern of musical notes, the students then 'recursively' returned to this sound during a group brainstorming. A few of their responses were 'Coca-Cola days', 'florid laughter' and 'Okay, Flo'. Again, such subversive methods underscore our belief that poems are not merely containers of meaning, reservoirs into which we place preformed thoughts. Connotation and explication are not the only ways poems mean. Part of a poem's meaning (usually a very substantial part) remains embedded in the sonic texture, in the dance or (to use again the jazz analogy) the riffs, the playfulness of the language on the page. Ultimately, where a discovery such as 'Okay, Flo' will take a writer depends entirely on how open that writer is to blundering through possibilities.

We might even take recursivity one step further and say that it is ever present in poems, though maybe not in such explicit ways as rhyme or even as the repetition of certain key sounds, words, or phrases. We believe there's even an associative type of recursivity, where larger, more oblique or intangible items are being recycled (shapes of lines, metaphorical containers, moods, architectural apparatuses, and so on). Our sense is that for each technique that works well for untrained writers, there exists a counterpart for more trained writers. Stafford says that the major distinction between those who write and those who don't is that writers naïvely trust that their imaginations will lead them to interesting material, that they have blind faith that something will come of the play of language. Hugo reinforces this idea by saying that a writer must believe a certain word or auditory texture belongs, that it is meaningful, because she put it there. Arrogant? Yes and no. A little ego is probably required in the writing of a poem, the belief that writing is important enough not to be doing something else (like studying medicine or even washing a car). But there is also a good deal of egalitarianism in the recursive process, the will to say that some cluster of words is important, some sound, purely because it echoes a former sound. And it is in the stressing of these ever-present and seemingly contradictory impulses (diastolic/systolic, readerly/writerly, the self/the world) that poetry finally means.

Chapter 3

The Novel

Graeme Harper
University of Portsmouth

1. SPACE TRAVEL

Ah, I hate talking about writing a novel. But I know I have to do it. It's in the remit; and I promised to say something meaningful. So I'm stuck with what many consider the impossible, and it serves me right. I guess it's a bit like talking about my space travel. I mean, of course I've done it. But every time I take off I get this feeling in my gut like I'm just not going to make it.

The thing about space travel, of course, is that no journey is the same as the one before. So, no matter how many times ground control tells you 'We have it in hand, Neil' you don't quite believe it.

So you panic, and on every trial run for the next two weeks your helmet steams up, you feel your LTA go sweaty and, no matter how much spandex and long water-tubed underwear they have you wearing, there is no way back. You stomp around at work. You stomp around at home. Your wife thinks you're angry because the Dolphins lost last week, or the Pirates went down in the play-off, or the kids don't appreciate the pressure you're under. But that surely isn't it. A day before you're about to blast, you finally turn to your Mission Specialist and you say:

'Frank ... Frank, you know, I got a bad feeling about this one.'

And Frank, Frank who's been out there what must be almost twenty times now, Frank who just looks like you met him out in Indiana somewhere – And, if things had been different, maybe you would have. Just back home out there jockeying a tractor, husking corn. Frank says:

'Neil, it's OK. It's OK, aright?'

Maybe.

Maybe it's just that when you look up there, to the novel, or into the vastness of universe, stand in your back yard with a decent Mai Tai and a couple of your friends from the Cape and shoot the breeze, the stars in their right ascension and the moon on the wane, you know that somehow it's going to be you who's going to have to fill it up.

I don't mean entirely.

Shoot, I'm not *that* conceited! But I do mean you're going to have to fill up that cabin with something, some kind of response to it all, and that someone is going to see that and, ultimately, you're going to have to explain.

The average guy, maybe someone like Johnson or McCormack or big Clem Bilkington-Pensell – they're good guys – the average guy like that, who knows his stuff, but doesn't have thoughts to creating some new thing, maybe getting into mission strategy or target outcomes, doesn't seem to sweat it. They don't seem to tie themselves up in knots. You don't see *their* wives calling their sisters in Pensacola at all hours of the night talking about Hell knows what and telling you next morning that 'Herb doesn't get stressed like you do, Neil'.

Not even considering that that's because Herb works at *Tyremaster*, Marion, and the last big deal Herbie had to face was whether some guy wanted Dunlop or the special offer on Bridgestone.

You can go through like that, keeping your head down, following others, reading what's written down, playing it safe. And that's fine. But once you become a command pilot then all that – and I mean *all* of that – changes.

I realize I'm supposed to be talking about writing a novel. I'm *aware* that's the case. But, there's a problem.

The fact is, I can start talking about one thing, and end up talking about another. It's a fault in my personality, and I'll be the first to admit it. A minute goes by and I just don't know what new topic might take my fancy. It could be space travel or, for all I can tell, it could just as easily end up being my poor old mother's veruccas. It could be the state of the peanut industry in Northern Australia, or the subsidence I hear is happening around all the great and magnificent monuments of England. I never know what it's going to be until the thought grabs me; and then, when it's got ahold, there's no chance in this world of it letting me go – for a while, at least.

So, not so long ago I was talking about space travel, but now I truly feel inclined to stop. It's not that I think you're bored with space travel, and I apologize for that. It's just that *I* get bored with talking about one thing, and just want to change the subject. It's probably quite the opposite for you, listening to all that stuff about Commanders and Mission Specialists and payloads and so on. Actually, I'm pretty sure you'd really enjoy hearing about how the Earth appears from up there, with the continents spread out beneath you like old leather patches on a pair of brand-new blue jeans. How clouds become as solid and as homey as the front drive of your home, even though logic tells you straight up that this is impossible. Or how, when you can see beyond the horizon, and the Earth is showing its curve like the ridge of an eyeball, it feels like you are nowhere at all: not in space, not on Earth, not in your suit, nowhere. It's like looking into the heart of a person and finding in there just this little fly buzzing around. You're just an ordinary house fly, buzzing around a jar or something. That's how it feels.

Yes, you'd probably enjoy reading about that. And, I guess, to stick to the point for one minute at least, that's something your average novelist has to think about too: about what you'd enjoy reading. But I just can't do it. I can't go on and on about the excitement and the desolation, the love, the loneliness, the sense of achievement and the sense of utter failure. I'd rather chew razor-blades, or eat a plate of worms.

When I was a kid – before things got serious and I had to decide on a career, or something that might masquerade as one – I took up surfing. Surfboard riding, I mean, not the other kind where you just have your body or some kind of soft rubber mat or a hunk of foam.

The real deal: the fibreglass board, the shorts, the leash, the sun-bleached hair. I was out there in the ocean sometimes eight hours a day. It was like becoming a dolphin.

We were living at the time up near Port Moreton and my folks were trying to make a go out of a decorator's business. You know the kind of thing: my dad would go around people's homes and tell them they had real good taste, except for their problem with carpeting and maybe something that needed doing with the window facings. Then my mom would follow up and talk to the woman of the house. That was always a bit of a trauma for Mom, because she is more of a man's woman. She can talk about all that stuff to do with curtaining and vanity cabinets and how men never put their socks away, no matter how much you had built-ins, but when it comes down to it she'd rather be out in the garage working on her Ford.

Anyway, Port Moreton was no home renovation capital, that's for sure. Mostly it was just a big shipping port with a few half-moon beaches and a banana factory. So Mom and Dad had it tough at first. I think that's why I spent so much time out of the house. It wasn't just the surfing; I kind of liked my own space. When I was out there bobbing around just beyond the break, I could be anywhere, instead of just out past Blue Rock, on the left-hander off the headland, with a view of the caravan parks and the car dealerships, their cars all colourful and shiny along the beach front, as if they'd just been washed up, and the Northside Mall, packed as always, and the great big yellow tin sheds of the banana factory, huge among the deep green of the hillside. The real world didn't matter so much. I didn't have to hear Mom complain that they didn't have enough money even to recondition her Edelbrock carburettors, or to hear Dad crying in the kitchen. He loved Mom; he would have bought her chrome tailpipes if they'd had the cash.

When, gradually, my folks started to make a proper living – mostly from the city types who had moved north, school teachers, pharmacists, middle management in banana exporting, retirees, who figured they had class and just because they'd moved to a hick port town in the north was no reason not to decorate it – when finally my folks started to make a proper living from these people, I'd already caught the surfing bug for life, and there was no turning back.

I think the thing with surfing is that it's a combination of natural acts and developed skills. You heard all this kind of stuff from guys who got into it back in the sixties; but, as much as it sounds like hippie talk, it's entirely true. When you first start out, all knees and no sign of balance, your head just trying to work out what you do first, you can't even get a good flow going. The wave starts up, you paddle onto it. You have this picture of what you're going to look like, going along. It all makes perfect sense; except that you're not doing it yet. As the swell jacks up you feel the surge under you. By now your heart's in your mouth and your arms have gone to jelly. But still you keep going.

It's precisely at that point that no other person in the universe can help. You can ask any of the guys in the water how they get to their feet, how they work out where to make their first turn, where they place their weight, what happens when they feel the surge. But, no matter what they say, you won't be able to decipher anything from it that's of any use to you. It comes down to something more personal. You can describe it, but no one actually means the same thing when they do. It's like a crazy-paving conversation.

One guy will say 'I leant right into it and jammed the rail' and the other guy will say 'Yeah, man, that's heavy'. But they're probably talking about entirely different things. One probably means he hates wiping out on the face, and the other figures he's talking about an insane re-entry. The whole is not just about manoeuvring a piece of fibreglass. It's not something they can teach you at Surf School. You might as well try to learn what gives some people great taste and lets other poor folk – and there's a bigger bunch of them than you'd think – go around decorating their homes in purple faux fur and gilded lampshades.

I'm running out of space. And I guess it seems that I still haven't talked much about writing a novel. The thing is, even though I loved my dad, and everyone said he was a great guy, I suppose in most things I take my lead from my mom. It's not just that Dad's been gone for a while now. It was always that way. When a problem comes along Mom's the kind that, rather than blurt out some rubbish, is more likely to look you in the eye and smile and say nothing for a while – 'cause it's all ticking over inside. Then she'll address the situation, and it'll be perfect. That's why she's so good with mechanical things – cars mostly. She doesn't expect immediate results, and she doesn't dive in without preparation. I mean, it takes a pretty special person to bore out a 283 block to 305, install Dynomax H-style crossover heads and Delta 43 chamber Flowmasters, replace the distributor with a Penetronix Flameflower II, tube it up to Moroso wires and A/C Delco plugs, and sit the only fancy business on a set of 22-inch Ferrini rims and 265 Goodyear Eagles. It's a skill that doesn't bear too narrow analysis, and it needs to have space to grow and be tinkered with, and thought through. That's why Dad left the garage to her and parked his old Impala in the street so that she could do whatever she liked in there. And that's why, when Dad died, diving for lobsters off Fischer's Point, she didn't immediately react. Instead, she just kind of stayed out in the garage, all that first day and night, working, trying to figure how to fit a Lokar floor shift into her Baja Bug. All up, it was a week before she came out of there. By then she'd replaced the transmission on a Thunderbird, installed a Roadrunner supercharger on her Pantera and stripped down the head on her 968. I guess you could say she'd been working things through, placing one element against the next, inching forward. When she finally came out, covered in grease and ready for sleep, she'd already made the decision never to speak about Dad again. I thought, at first, that she was just upset, and that eventually she'd relent. But, after six years, she still hasn't mentioned his name. Of course, his old Impala has never looked better. She's stripped it right down and rebuilt it from the bottom up. With its cherry red paint and snow-white leather interior, it's just like new. It's running 400 horsepower at 5500 rpm, and can pull at standing start to 60 mph in 5.7 seconds. Knowing Dad, I don't suppose he'd ever have pushed it that far; but I think, if he saw it, he'd appreciate where Mom is coming from.

Man, I sure would feel guilty now, if I thought I'd led you down the garden path! But, of course, I know I'm innocent.

While there's no doubt writing a novel is a personal experience, born of personal circumstances, most often constructed somewhere between truth and a lie (my Mom and Dad above, bless them both, are mostly figments), and often founded on a combination of formal learning and informal discovery, there are also some things about it that can be exchanged.

Maybe I've exchanged them already. It certainly feels to me like I've been talking about writing a novel, about how it might be explained and, perhaps, about how it might be understood. It's something, for me, that combines space travel with surfing and surfing with several different kinds of mechanics, tuning, polishing and a 'fair amount of detailing'.

In order to discuss, or provide, information on the writing of the novel, it seems entirely spurious to do so as if it is the same experience for each individual. It seems equally spurious to teach anything in relation to the novel *solely* as a matter of learning a skills-based craft. Talking productively about writing longer prose fiction, of which the novel is the primary example, involves:

- approaching some sense of the techniques involved, absolutely;
- also exploring the history and background to the novel's approach to the world, which is varied, but distinctive;
- considering a mindset, or a way of expressing a thought, an idea, a feeling, through the writing of a novel;
- avoiding either solely individual or solely holist discussion (i.e. considering the individual writer, but also a sense of genre, its past and contemporary guise and reception);
- encouraging a sense of empowerment, plain and simple.

2. KEY POINTS

The novel presents itself as a long distance effort, a Moon shot all on your own (mostly, that is, ignoring the relatively unusual situation of a collaborative writing effort, and the less unusual, but increasingly unlikely, position of the publisher's editor, or literary agent, who will spend a great deal of their own time 'working with you' on your novel).

Therefore, like successful space travel, a lot depends on personally holding it all together, even when it appears that it's just not going right, and even when the possibility looms of someone, somewhere, eventually showing some interest in what you're doing. Like surfing, it depends on following the natural rhythms, while working out in a way that is vigorous and exhausting, physically and mentally. Each novelist has their own experience of novel writing, no doubt; but, it is at least generally true that no one views the novel as a light paddle through a warm lapping shore wash. Finally, the novel involves a sense of working with the mechanics of prose, of making these elements come together in a way that dissolves any sense that this actually *has* a mechanics.

The metaphorical overload might best end there, as I blast off in the direction of Canaveral in my Corvette, my surfboard tied on the roof, imagining Mom and Dad in their overalls, standing by the roadside waving goodbye, as they have done on many occasions.

A. The novel in time and space

It's unavoidable that someone will want to say something like the following in a book entitled *Teaching Creative Writing*. It might as well be me.

To my mind, one of the worst crimes in the contemporary university is a lack of willingness to push the boundaries of human creativity and thought. Not that I'm holding myself up as an exemplar of boundary pushing! But it seems to me the modern university, at its worst, finds itself more concerned with the detailed management of economic and social performance and the accumulation of corporate 'learning resources', and less concerned with the simple but spectacular human act of *thinking and acting creatively*.

One of the 'chestnuts' found lying on the ground around any active discussion of creative writing is that grown from the seed of whether it can be taught; whether, in fact, creative writing classes in university and college are largely a waste of time, possibly even an elaborate educational hoax.

And maybe that's right.

Maybe, because of what contemporary academe has become in some instances, the teaching of creative writing on many campuses is well-nigh impossible – a kind of hopeful, but doomed, activity. That is, rather than teaching it, university employees (call them professors, lecturers, teachers, writer-teachers, or what you will) merely manage the discipline's existence. And the word here is very precisely 'discipline', even if that might not be the word, to many minds, that best fits the way creative writing practice works or how its results are viewed.

The history of academe has increasingly seen its activities marshalled according to principles first drawn from the four faculties recognized in the medieval university, Theology, Medicine, Jurisprudence and Arts, and from the subjects of the *trivium* and *quadrivium*, which provided the model for scholastic thought, and defined key notions regarding 'disciplines' or fields of study.

Affected, firstly, by social changes in the eighteenth and nineteenth centuries that saw universities opened up a little beyond their previous class boundaries, and then increasingly by economic forces, by the late twentieth century the corporate identities and intentions of universities far exceeded the sense of them being communities of thinkers and creators.

Thus – depending on your feelings about what higher learning involves – it could be said that the positive aspects of personal mentorship have been replaced by a form of teaching management that makes the meeting of mentor and protégé a minor part, if it is one at all, of contemporary higher education.

And yet, in the history of academe, there's ample evidence of a different ethos, an ethos based on close creative and intellectual exchange.

What has this got to do with the novel? Simply, that the novel also has existed in time, and it too has borne the brunt of changes in social and economic worth and, as history would have it, has survived the impact of these changes perhaps far better than the ideal of higher learning that once drove Plato to create his Academy. As J. Paul Hunter writes in *Before Novels: The Cultural Contexts of Eighteenth-century English Fiction*:

> Not everything in novels – even in good novels – goes the way critics and critical theorists think it should, and some of the 'failures' are characteristic of the species, even definitive. Novels, especially early novels, often bear features that do not 'fit' later conceptions of what the novel is or ought to be, and even the most sophisticated later novels often have features that embarrass readers who bring to them rigid formal expectations. (1990: 29)

Hunter is talking here of novels 'early' in the history of the novel genre, rather than 'early' in the history of any one writer's career, but the same point might be made in the latter instance. Novels, for writers and for readers, come with their own history. In order for anyone to learn something about them it seems prudent to point them towards the history of genre, and towards the history of any one novel in the history of each novel in the novel writer's life.

The history of the novel genre is already well considered by literary critics. But how much do we really know about the history of each novel in the context of each novelist's life? Do we know generally, for example, if one novel felt easier or harder to write than another? If we occasionally know how many pages each novelist might write in a day, do we always know how these pages are composed, when and where and with what impeding or assisting their composition?

In 1923 Virginia Woolf, writing to Gerald Brenan, writer and fellow Bloomsbury Group member, wrote this:

> I have had only 4 days writing at my novel since I got back. Tomorrow, I say to myself, I shall plunge into the thick of it. But how does one make people talk about everything in the whole of life, so that one's hair stands on end, in a drawing room? How can one weight and sharpen dialogue till each sentence tears its way like a harpoon and grapples with the shingles at the bottom of the reader's soul? (Woolf, 1977: 36)

The novel Woolf was working on was *Mrs Dalloway*. Woolf's letters and diaries are extensive; in this letter, writing to Brenan, she talks of the impact of her and her husband's publishing activities on her opportunities for writing, and goes on to reveal the undercurrent of writing life that often is, and certainly was for her, the meetings that occur between writers, the mix of personal life with writing practice, the interest in new works of creative writing getting their first public airing.

Not every writer leaves such evidence as Woolf, nor would they want to. And yet, somehow, if anyone is to understand the nature of novel writing, there's a need to have some access to this inaccessible history, to know at least something of the time and space of the novel, in all senses. This sometimes is found in journals and diaries and miscellaneous writings by creative writers. In 1931 André Gide, writing in his journal, shows his novelist's concern with the mode of connecting to readers:

> Allow only the indispensable to subsist was the rule I imposed on myself – nowhere more difficult and dangerous to apply than for the novel. This amounts to counting too much on that collaboration which the reader will supply only when the writer has already been able to secure it. (Gide, 1984: 512)

Gide spends some time talking about his desire to encourage a reader's imagination. At other points in his journals he talks about what other writers have said about the imagination, about reading sentences in his dreams, about the 'shrewdness' of Stendhal, about spirituality, about what he is currently reading, and much more.

Recorded elements of personal practice are grounded in the lives of individual writers, but also in societal and historical location. Nadine Gordimer, in conversation with critic and biographer Hermione Lee in 2003, says this:

> What is a writer? To be a writer, what is the essential quality? Unusual perception and observation; a lot of it comes from childhood. Having your ears open to hear what people say. Looking at people and really seeing what they say and how they move and sensing also what they haven't said. That is your training. (Gordimer, 2004: 326)

These comments of Nadine Gordimer's are very far from literary criticism, as it's commonly understood. And yet they fundamentally represent the disposition and intentions, the feelings and psychology of this Nobel Prize fiction writer, suggesting her behaviour patterns, alerting us to her human agency in the writing of her works, and giving considerable insight into the individual act and social circumstance that produce them.

B. Starting and finishing

The simple or not-so-simple labour of starting and finishing the writing of a novel is a subject that arises in most formal classes concerned with the writing of them. In casual conversation between novelists, anecdotal evidence suggests, the subject is not so prevalent. Why?

'The inability of fiction to stare at itself goes back to the earliest novels of the eighteenth century and arises, I like to think,' writes the late contemporary novelist Carol Shields, 'from the twinning of embarrassment and innocence' (2001: 215). Perhaps this is part of it. To talk of making fiction, somewhat baldly in conversations between the makers of it, tempts both embarrassment and innocence. Embarrassment at what Shields calls 'lying, inventing, daydreaming', but what might more broadly simply be called a life 'creating with words'. Innocence, in that the fiction writer is guilty of nothing more than using the tools they feel are there for them to use, and almost never would claim to know everything there is to know about fiction writing. So the fiction writer, using what is the relatively common language of prose, is potentially struck by innocence on two counts, and embarrassed on at least one. No wonder novelists talking casually together about a day's work is uncommon!

That said, two things seem at least some comfort to any novelist. Firstly, that to write a novel you have to begin one. Secondly, that to publish a novel you have to eventually finish one. Fortunately, these facts are not as trite as I've first made them appear. Henry James, writing in his Notebooks on 8 September 1895, notes his frustration at the idea of starting out:

> I am face to face with several little alternatives of work, and am in fact in something of a predicament with things promised and retarded. I must thresh out my solutions, must settle down to my jobs. (James, 1987: 129)

At the time James had agreed to write two novels for the publishers Heinemann and complete a story for a well-known magazine. Quite a few beginning fiction writers would sell their souls to be in such a predicament. And yet, even with a writer as experienced as James – he'd published his first short story thirty years earlier, and his first novel only five years after that – the idea of setting out was as a 'predicament'. Finishing a novel is no better. Hilary Spurling, in her biography of Paul Scott, writes:

> Paul finished the *Birds* at 4 a.m. on 1 March after a ten hour stint at the desk, staggered into bed 'drunk with success, horny with fulfilment', and slept for twelve hours, only to find himself assailed on waking with his usual doubts: 'it was all wrong. I knew it was wrong when I typed it'. (1990: 244)

That novel, *The Birds of Paradise*, was published in 1962. Scott's first novel, *Johnnie Sahib*, had been rejected by 17 publishers before being published in 1952, while *Staying On*, the final novel of his published in his lifetime, won the Booker Prize in 1977. While Scott's experience of the highs and lows of publishing might be a little extreme compared to some, there's little doubt that the history of any one novelist's career is itself a matter of following a pattern from a career's beginnings to its conclusion, and that there are highs and lows along the way. When teaching creative writing, and focusing on what are often long-term projects (e.g. novels), it seems reasonable to give new writers a sense not only of the difficulties encountered in writing the first word of a book, or the last one, but also to give personal dimension to the idea that the writing arts, like any other of the arts, rarely see a writer experiencing a straight, upward trajectory, artistically, in terms of learning and knowledge of the field, and even economically. Here, moving away from artistic or critical responses and towards those of political economy, we might indeed remind ourselves, and others, of the common economic shape of any artist's career:

> The artist's willingness to sacrifice in order to devote herself to creative work (*art for art's sake*) implies several properties of artists' incomes and activity patterns. Given the elastic supply of would-be artists, their competition will depress the average wage earned from the creative work below the wage of hum-drum labour, by an amount reflecting the strength of their preferences for creative labour. (Spurling, 1990: 78)

Very few novelists work solely as novelists. This has always been the case, and this is most often linked to financial imperatives. Equally, there are good writerly reasons for creative writers to venture beyond their desks. Albert Camus, in his Banquet Speech when accepting the Nobel Prize for Literature, talked of not placing his art above everything and of not separating it from his 'fellow men'. Richard Ford talks, more lightly but in a similar vein, of 'Goofing Off While the Muse Recharges' (2001: 65).

The ability to complete a long project, which the novel most often is, sometimes with the pressure of competing activities, monetary concerns and self-doubt, is at least partly enhanced by the simple, far from trite, observation that once the first word is written, and a degree of effort applied, the last one will eventually follow.

C. Patterning

To return to my fictitious parents – I've missed their company these last two thousand words or so. If my Dad was invited into a home in his professional capacity, then the first thing he would notice would be the style of the place. You could see his brows twitching as he stepped into their yard. He was eyeing up the lawn, looking at whether folks had to jump over a bunch of kids' toys to get to the front door, checking out the kind and colour of the vehicle they were driving.

Once inside, he'd straight away say something that would set those potential clients back on their haunches. Something like: 'Incidentally, I see you're from Chester County.' Or, 'You know, my sister never liked spiders either.' Or 'How did you manage to go and catch a 60 lb blue wrasse on just a 5 lb line?' It was a thing he did that went way beyond observation. I think it had its origins in mathematics, or something that equated to biology in a way. He operated like some kind of detector. You couldn't even always see what he was looking at. But he could see it, and he could describe it, though not always in a way that made immediate sense. He might say:

'Mr and Mrs Pinchlin are green. They'll go for a tangle.'

Or: 'In each corner of that house there's a big fat nub. 84 in all, actually.'

Or: 'Though they don't realize it, they'd be happier in a bungalow.'

I think that was what originally drew my dad to my mom. They both appreciated the hidden intricacies of one thing with another, the connections, what might be called patterning. You couldn't decorate a house without a sense of it, Dad said. As to Mom: she could rebuild a Dino Ferrari on the back of studying its shape.

Writing a novel is not far removed from this. It involves a personal sense of patterning, of shaping, and there's no fixed list of alternative ways of doing this. One writer might benefit from viewing a novel as a construction, a set of rooms or even planks of wood to be put together to make an entire house – a novel, in this case. Another writer might benefit from seeing a novel as the vehicle for his or her ideas, and imagine (as my mom might do) that each component adds to the viability of the final vehicle, its potential speed, comfort also perhaps. Another might find mathematics an entirely viable way of thinking about their novel: chapters of a certain length, certain geometry, parts of books within the novel of a certain size, and so on. Another writer still might see the novel as a journey to be undertaken, so that each point in the novel becomes a place on a map and the journey can be traced, literally or metaphorically, from start to finish.

The alternative notions of patterning are infinite, and no one writer necessarily views the shape of their novel in the same way. But the idea of patterns, or of constructing and observing patterns, is seen in many parts of the natural world, and it seems at very worst to be a way of working through ideas, and at very best to be the clue to ensuring each component of the book is considered for where it fits in among the rest.

3. NOTABLE READINGS

'Impossible!' Frank calls, from the Command Mobile. And he might well be right.

The more I think on it, the more readings I want to include. Suddenly notable readings on the novel, and the writing of it, are taking up the whole of another book. So I'd best stick to a 'Top Five'. In the intriguing world of numerology, number five is apparently connected with an openness to new experiences and new ideas. Thus, it seems a worthy number; certainly as worthy as the love and commitment I feel for my fine, fictitious parents.

Keep on revving, Mom.

1. Serge Brunier, *Space Odyssey: The First Forty Years of Space Exploration*, trans. Stephen Lyle (Cambridge: Cambridge University Press), 2002

It makes me feel more significant in the world than I am, and makes the task of writing a new novel less significant than it feels. Both responses seem to me to be useful for a novelist setting out to write a novel. I feel the same way about: a road map; an atlas; a big biographical dictionary; those books that set out the timelines of history; a good work of historical geography; looking over someone's family tree in detail; reading the world population statistics, nation by nation, or looking at the number of works of fiction published in every language every month.

It's not so much a 'tool of trade' as a somewhat magical instrument for maintaining perspective.

2. Paul Feyerabend, *Against Method* (London: Verso), 1978

There's a few things to disagree with in this book. But it haunts me. It's not a book about the novel; in fact, it's mostly a book about science. And yet, the suggestions it makes seem to me to be fundamental to understanding the construction of a novel. To wildly para-phrase: essentially what Feyerabend notes is the 'anarchist' nature of discovery, what might just as easily be called 'openness'. He does not throw out the idea that it is possible to learn the techniques, construct methodologies, explore things in a structured way. What he says, however, is that people chase these discoveries along many paths and in many ways, not simply according to strict methodologies (in a way often suggested in discussions of science or even by science's exalted position in society as 'truth provider').

A sense that there is always a 'maze of interactions', as Feyerabend outlines it, seems an ideal starting point for considering, and attempting to write, any novel.

3. Margaret Atwood, *Negotiating with the Dead: A Writer on Writing* (Cambridge: Cambridge University Press), 2002

In mid-2000 Atwood gave a series of lectures at the University of Cambridge's Lady Mitchell Hall. They became this book. You can hear Atwood in here; she's like a guest who's come to dinner at your place so well prepared for a good chat that you just offer her a seat and she gets right on in and starts chatting. Brilliant!

Sure, on occasions, you'd like to say 'Margaret, listen, but what's it really like putting your socks on in winter?' But that's fine: you're not going to get the nitty-gritty on her personal life, and you probably don't mind. The book is full of Atwood, the writer, and Atwood the person – just don't expect to join her family by the time you've finished it.

Atwood's birthday is 18 November, by the way, the same day as astronaut Alan Shepard's, the first American in space. Shepard's gone, unfortunately: he died of leukaemia in 1998. But, like Atwood's neat control of her prose and careful creative sense, he too had a handle on his world.

In the early 1970s, and by then the oldest astronaut in the Apollo programme, Shepard led the Apollo XIV mission to the Moon. When he landed there on 9 February 1971 with fellow astronaut Edgar Mitchell, Shepard took out a golf ball and, with due aplomb, promptly hit it across the lunar surface.

So, while Neil Armstrong was the first human on the Moon, Alan Shepard made himself the first to try that difficult dogleg off the front nine out past the Fra Mauro Formation. Like Atwood, whose success has been quietly considerable, he too might well be remembered for playing one of the fine shots that takes both a big hunk of knowledge and a large supply of gumption.

4. Henry James, *The Complete Notebooks of Henry James*, ed. Leon Edel and Lyall H. Powers (New York and Oxford: Oxford University Press), 1987

You go into this book and you find James talking to himself. So, taken by surprise, you step back out. But this is a big book and a big book is attractive: its weight makes it so, and so does that sound the pages make when you flick them through with your thumb. So you go back in, and James is still doing it – over and over again.

In fact, Henry James talks to himself and others right through this book. There's the Pocket Diaries, where you find out with whom Mr James was lunching, and the Notebooks, where you find Mr James worrying, deciding, re-considering, fixing things, dealing with thoughts that do, and don't, become actions. And there's more.

Best suggestion is to buy a copy of this from a second hand shop: not because it's expensive, but just so you can smell the thing as well. It's a full sensory experience, this book.

5. Brian Boyd, *Vladimir Nabokov: The Russian Years* (London: Vintage), 1990

All of Boyd's biographical work on Nabokov is first rate. That's a personal opinion, not a critical assessment. I'd even more highly recommend *Vladimir Nabokov: The American Years*, except I don't want anyone to buy the copies floating around out there. It seems I've begun accumulating them, and I want to go for a world record. I have six copies so far, in hardback and paperback. At various points I haven't known what I have in my library so, when seeing a copy of *American Years*, I've excitedly bought it – six times over!

I'd probably do the same with Matthew Bruccoli's biography of F. Scott Fitzgerald, *Some Sort of Epic Grandeur* (2002), and David Marr's biography of Patrick White, *Patrick White: A Life* (1992), and Douglas Day's biography of Malcolm Lowry (1973) and half a dozen others.

4. SPECULATIONS

It's evening and, outside the building, a green neon sign flickers: *..v.l's Gym*.

The thought has crossed my mind that this is actually the Devil's playground, the *Devil's Gym*. Sure, it fits. Frankly, it's that kind of neighbourhood. Where else can a writer and astronaut get a decent apartment at decent rent these days? But let's be Devil's advocates instead and imagine the word is actually *Novel*.

The Novel Gym: upstairs, a whole bunch of novelists in the hall, all of them dressed in sweatshirts and trainers, sweaty streaks down their backs, looks of despair and distain, a slight aroma of rebellion in the air. I'd rather not go in there; but it's my session and I'm supposed to offer them something. Assuming they let me in the door, I'll go for something like this:

Exercise One

The world is made of shapes. One of the most interesting exercises, toning the biceps or something, is to consider the relationship between form and function. That is, are there discernible relationships between natural and human-made things? Can we look at form as a concept already well represented in what is around us, and therefore feel comfortable with employing it? It might be productive to select perhaps three human-made and three natural things and consider the relationship between form and function (e.g. a bicycle and its function; a petal and its function). The final, sweat-stained, act is to think about how that might relate to formal thoughts on your next novel.

Exercise Two

This exercise worked with a bunch of screenwriters. They're a different crowd to novelists, of course. For one thing, the really successful ones are obviously Californian. So a lot of them get around in Volkswagen vans with surfboards on the roof. For another thing, quite a few work in teams; so they're more inclined to go drinking Mango Margaritas and Watermelon Coolers after work and then need to take off a few pounds afterwards. Anyway, take a breath, and let's give it a shot.

Voice is an essential tool to writers. In a long novel, establishing and maintaining voice is a mighty task. Many novelists do it extremely well; some don't. Not every voice is as self-determining as, say, the voice of the narrator in Salman Rushdie's *Midnight's Children* (1995). Some are more subtle. Some are more like their authors than others. The exercise presented to screenwriters goes like this:

Come up with a simple, generic point-by-point plan of a novel. Come up with three different voices. Determine how the different voices will potentially change not only the sound of the novel, but perhaps even what is presented in its plot, the kinds of characters that emerge, the overall structure, and so forth. Once having tried this from the plan 'outward' to the voice, then try it the other way around, from the voice back to the plan. To take Paul Feyerabend's lead, this is an exercise looking at the 'maze of interactions' that create a novel, but starting at a point in the process that is easily discernible, thus giving the new writer an initial way into the process. Using voice as the starting point appears to also assist new writers to think about 'address to the reader'. Certainly the screenwriters started to think of their films having a way of speaking to their audience, and that made them distinctive in a way that they had not seemingly considered previously.

Chapter 4

Writing for Children and Young Adults

Jeri Kroll
Flinders University, Adelaide

1. THE WRITER-TEACHER'S VIEW OF WRITING, THE UNIVERSE AND EVERYTHING (INCLUDING THEORY)

> This is what we remember: What we do for children, how we approach them, what we tell them ... it is all in the vision. Whether our story affirms or denies the child's innocence, protects or exposes the child, informs or deceives the reader, depends on how we see children. (Provoost, 2004: 17)

The Belgian young adult novelist, Anne Provoost, views the culture of developed nations as child-oriented, yet believes that young people are still largely powerless. They yearn for knowledge but are mostly denied it by a split adult mentality that, on the one hand, believes in childhood innocence and, on the other, realizes that children must grow up to become productive human beings. The writer must be two-faced, hearing the demands, laughter and pleas from both sides, because the production and dissemination of children's literature is controlled by often conflicting ideological, aesthetic and commercial agendas.

Children's and young adult literature[1] is like an undeclared war zone. It might seem strange to begin this chapter with such an assertion, yet anyone working in the field is aware of a series of flash points that given the right circumstances can explode into conflict. Where minors are concerned, passions run high. Guardians and gatekeepers want to protect the vulnerable, but protect them from what and from whom? Debates that flare concern literacy (the whole language versus phonics debate, for example); the crass commercialization of 'kid lit'; the evils of the global market and the perils of free trade agreements that barter with a nation's cultural heritage;[2] the temptations of new technology; the dominance of the series and bestsellers (Harry Potter, *et al.*); and political, social and religious correctness of all kinds that want more or less sex, drugs and lifestyle roles. Hostages are taken in the form of books that, if published at all, are kept hidden in libraries, only to be borrowed with written parental consent. The censorship or selection debate reveals the land-mines planted by liberal as well as conservative pressure groups that plague the professional lives of teachers, booksellers and librarians.

At the beginning, rather than the end, of this chain is the lone writer, who must produce his or her brainchild and then send it unprotected to be inspected, evaluated, prodded, reshaped and packaged in order for it to take its first hesitant steps to reach its audience – initially not even its primary one, the child, but the gatekeepers who review, purchase and select books for young people. As in any battle zone, adrenalin fuels the Fight or Flight instinct, but for those who choose to face the challenges, the experience can be rewarding, especially when a writer connects with the triumvirate of children, reviewers and critics.

The writer-teacher in a university performs multiple roles, because they have to keep up to date with critical and commercial developments. They need to be 'embedded', to borrow recent war jargon, in all camps, to observe what's happening to report back to their students so that when they venture out they have a sense of the risks as well as opportunities. Writer-teachers evaluate work in newspapers or journals and at the same time devise new plans of attack on the market, negotiating with agents and publishers, testing the lie of the land. In other words, to break out of the metaphor, writers in a university context are aware of the critical and theoretical environment that receives literature for young people while they experience the stresses and rewards firsthand of creating for this amorphous group.

Let's begin at the beginning

> Children's books ... are books chosen for us by others; either because they pleased us when we were young; or because we have reason for thinking that they please children today; or because we have read them lately, and believe that our adult enjoyment of them is one which younger people can share. Unfortunately, none of these reasons is in itself a sure guide. (Milne, 1994: 1)

At the beginning of the semester I give my students a questionnaire that encourages them to think about the nature of the adventure on which they are about to embark. It asks them to verbalize their assumptions (which are neither right nor wrong, simply theirs) that then become a reference point to gauge their intellectual and artistic journey when they complete the semester; in other words, they self-evaluate what they believe they have learned. Four of these questions are:

1. What is literature?
2. What is children's literature?
3. How old is a child?
4. Do you think it is easier to write for children than for adults? (Be honest.)

These questions lead into a discussion of the complex world of children's literature in the twenty-first century. A nexus of competing agendas, the field offers myriad opportunities in the form of clearly defined markets, promising commercial success, yet many writers also desire adult acclaim for the quality of their work. There is certainly a bias against writers for young people among their adult peers and the community at large, as if they were suffering 'arrested development' (Disher, 1997: 3), not yet mature enough as artists to produce a grown-up book.[3]

There have been advances, however, helped by the cultural-critical revolution, led by Marxists, Feminists, Poststructuralists, et al., which exploded the Anglo-American canon's monopoly on quality. The fact that we pair the two terms now in an academic context – 'children' and 'literature' – ensures the discipline's increasing richness; critics apply their favourite literary or cultural theories, reading traditional and contemporary texts in innovative, radical or subversive ways.

As one of the foremost critics of children's literature, Peter Hunt, has argued, children's books, like their adult counterparts, are never innocent; they have an agenda.

> We read literature in a different way from non-literature; we extract from the text certain feelings or responses. Yet with children's books, we cannot escape from the fact that they are written by adults; that there is going to be control, and that it is going to involve moral decisions. Equally, the book is going to be used not to entertain or modify *our* views, but to form the views of a child. (Hunt, 1991: 51)

So children's books always have a functional purpose to some degree, even if the function is simply to entertain. There might in fact be a 'poetics of childhood' (Garrett, 1995–96: 2), based on alternate criteria, but can adults ever truly understand them or only observe from afar? The establishment of Children's Choice Awards, roughly from the mid-1970s onwards, in Australia, Canada, New Zealand, the UK and the US,[4] acknowledges that young people might assess differently, although all awards exhibit some degree of adult control in administration, structure and text selection.

Adults realize, then, that children have their own agendas. To return to Anne Provoost: ' . . . we thought it was all in the perspective, how you look at children, but we overlooked the fact that children look at us, too' (2004: 19). Maurice Sendak has commented that the young 'know exactly what's going to frighten their parents, and they don't ask questions that will upset mommy and daddy' (1998: 23). Like adults, they read for pleasure and information, but maybe not the information that adults want to make available. So children discover alternate sources, not always the best or most reliable. 'Isn't it kinder', Sendak remarks, 'to give children the bitter pill in a work of art' (p. 23)?

When does childhood begin and end, however, so that guardians know what kind of pill the young can easily swallow? When does young adulthood begin, for that matter, a time when presumably most of the barriers between books and their audience should crumble? In *Literature for Today's Young Adults*, Kenneth Donelson and Alleen Pace Nilsen admit that educational bodies, university teachers and critics use the term inconsistently.[5] Psychologists and sociologists also debate age parameters, but their research is far too complex for me to introduce here. Students need to be aware, however, that those questions have been asked and that answers might change over time and from culture to culture.

What we can assert is that educators, carers, parents, politicians, booksellers and religious leaders all have a stake in what publishers produce for the 0 to 15-plus age range. Those publishers select manuscripts for a multitude of reasons: ' . . . when the book is an end in itself' and when 'books are means to ends' (Kirk, 1992: 149). Since the seventeenth century, the urge to teach has been evident, the picture dictionary identified as the first children's book – 'Comenius's Orbis Pictus (circa 1657)' (Nodelman, 1988: 2) – with moral tracts, 'fairy tales, ballads or nursery rhymes' (Scott-Mitchell, 1991: 75) following soon after, adding a modicum of pleasure to the mix. These chapbooks were illustrated, appealing to parents as well as their progeny. From the beginning, then, 'instruction' had to be mixed 'with delight', as publisher John Newberry said, adding the third element – commercial acumen (quoted in Susina, 1993: v).

In our century, books as 'means to ends' covers a broad territory, from Basal Readers, to picture books to support literature-based approaches to the teaching of reading, to texts to encourage aesthetic appreciation, to those dealing with crises or problems (for example, bullying, gay parenthood, family death, etc.); the latter is known as 'the biliotherapeutic approach to literature' (Sheahan-Bright, 1999: 13).

Of course, any work can be used to teach given the right context, since books reflect the society in which they are created. Morris Lurie suggests this view in his novel *Madness*, where his protagonist, a children's author, bursts out at a 'Kiddie Lit' conference: 'A children's book is a primer. It's a guidebook. It's a standard of behaviour. It's a map. It's welcome to society, kids, here's how it works' (Lurie, 1991: 70). Children's stories deal with the preoccupations of a culture but employ direct strategies. Joan Aitken describes the approach in this way: writing for the young 'should come out with the force of a Niagara, ought to be concentrated; it needs to have everything that's in adult writing squeezed into a smaller compass . . . in a form adapted to children's capacities . . .' (quoted in Saxby, 1993: 4).

We can see that these myriad attitudes underlie the Educational and Trade divide in children's books, which are produced for different markets and distributed by different means. Educational publishers service school and community libraries, which buy in bulk and demand that the materials are tightly controlled (often bland and inoffensive, catering to a national or international audience). Trade books are sold from bookstores, are reviewed more widely and can be subject to more rigorous literary judgement. There are areas of overlap, however, with some educational books praised for literary merit and trade books (especially lowest common denominator series such as Goosebumps) criticized for paucity of vocabulary and characterization or plot predictability. Students need to be aware that these divides exist, however, and will condition what they create.

I have space merely for an overview of the complexity of children's literature, but the point needs to be made that writers should be aware at some stage in creation or revision of that dual audience – adults and young people – for their texts, and the attendant pressures. This is especially true of picture books, which do not really exist until they become physical objects. Those who are not illustrators but solely writers own the concept and develop it, but until the illustrator adds the visual narrative, the book remains an embryo. It is not truly born until it exists in print, and after the additional input of the designer, too.

In summary, my approach to the teaching of writing for young people is both practical and theoretical. I endeavour to make students aware of those cultural, political and social pressures discussed above, as well as of the technical constraints of genre and format. So far I have not mentioned craft, which most books about writing purport to foreground. I said recently in an article about 'How To' books that no text that purports to teach writing can be solely practical: 'If "no text is innocent", then *ipso facto* "no textbook is innocent"' (Kroll and Evans, 2005), and hence 'theory-free'. A philosophy or set of assumptions underlies every approach: 'Writers engage with theory even if they do so unwittingly' (Kroll and Evans, 2005). According to another recent analysis, writing texts in the US and the UK privilege the idea of a common universal experience; without acknowledging their assumptions, they are based on 'contradictory and problematic notions of the "self"' (Wandor, 2004: 115) and hence replicate the pattern in Australasian books. What are my assumptions? I am still working them out, trying to excavate them from underneath years of exercises and strategies, but below are some tentative ideas.

Reinstating authorial intent in a workshop context does not mean that writers, in a classical or Romantic sense, 'having drunk the milk of paradise' (Coleridge, 1951: 45), can tap into some unwavering universal or mystical truth. It suggests that authors, aware of culture and tradition in T. S. Eliot's sense, or necessarily affected by it in Roland Barthes's sense (Kroll, 2004: 94–5), must listen to the texts of the past as well as to the voices around them. They can also allow voices that have been silenced to speak. Some writers for young people have consciously adopted this approach, hence the late twentieth-century movement to produce texts from Feminist, Indigenous, Black and Hispanic positions, among others.

Consider this focus in twentieth-century children's writing – empowerment, the actualization of the self – which can be rejuvenated when it signifies in fresh ways for diverse groups or cultures. The experience of an Anglo girl coming of age in Sydney will be both like and unlike that of a Puerto Rican boy coming of age in New York; the same can be said for an Indigenous boy in Alice Springs or a lesbian girl in Canada. Their special perspectives can be embodied in texts.

I find this aspect of modernism and postmodernism pedagogically useful; the suggestion that multiple viewpoints exist and that questioning rather than asserting is a viable strategy for seeking after truth. Much contemporary young adult fiction exemplifies this proposition. The plethora of formats available in children's publishing reflects the reality of a volatile cultural context, too. Stories can be born simply because writers want to explore ideas, but when it comes to choosing a format or targeting an audience, they have particular creative and technical decisions to make.

Workshopping thus has a number of options. For example, teachers can encourage students to:

1. Try out a range of styles and formats, including poetry.
2. Speak in other voices (male/female/Anglo/Indigenous, etc.).
3. Interrogate the ethics of doing 2.
4. Consider the effectiveness of texts in meeting the needs of target groups.

At this juncture, it is worth saying that most students taking a Writing for Young People topic will not go on to become professionals in any meaningful sense. So what can they gain, aside from polishing their writing and sharpening their editorial eye? They will come away with an understanding of the dynamics between author, text, publisher and reader, as well as between children's literature in general and the society that both conditions and consumes it.

2. KEY POINTS IN TEACHING: STUDENTS DON'T ALWAYS GET WHAT THEY WANT, BUT TEACHERS HOPE THEY GET WHAT THEY NEED

For more than a century now society has looked to the artists, including writers, for reports on how the society is going. It doesn't matter which metaphor you use, but artists have consistently been expected to measure the temperature, shine the spotlight, give the barometer reading, reflect the culture. (Marsden, 2005)

The book [The Cat in the Hat] took Theodore Geisel – Dr. Seuss – more than a year to finish; he described the experience as 'being lost with a witch in the tunnel of love,' an analogy it is probably best to leave unpacked. (Menand, 1997: 112)

The text [of a picture book] is akin to a sonnet: small, powerful and tightly disciplined. It's like a short, smooth plank of wood when seen beside the luxuriant oak-tree effect of a novel. (Fox, 1990: 149)

The above remarks suggest that writers for young people around the world agree that their task is challenging and frustrating, albeit rewarding, because they are judged as entertainers, educators, artists and cultural guardians. Teachers entering a classroom have, therefore, two challenges initially. One is to communicate what they believe students need to learn in order to work effectively in the field as well as to enjoy the experience. The second is to encourage the airing of preconceptions that might prevent the first from happening. This section of the chapter will engage, therefore, with the sometimes conflicting agendas of students, teachers and markets.

My topic description explains that students will learn about the craft of writing and its cultural environment. But what does this mean, and how in particular does it relate to what students already believe? This is where the questionnaire previously mentioned elicits some standard preconceptions. One is that if they remember their childhood, they will be able to write more or less from recall. This attitude colours a student's ability to knuckle down to pay attention to craft. Rosemary Wells deals with this 'misperception that children's books are a sort of muzzy and not-quite-serious art form' (1998: 46) that anyone who enjoys them or knows children can create. For Wells, it is 'the most difficult discipline I know' (p. 46); its rules must be learned (p. 47).

The second preconception is that young people's stories always need to be happy and playful, reflecting childhood innocence. This stems from an underlying belief that the world 'out there' is haunted by goblins, or child molesters, or used-car salesmen, and soon enough these innocents will have to deal with its unsavoury side – as if TV, film and computer games did not introduce them to social, sexual and political realities already. Students who favour this approach might not remember their past too well, or don't want to examine closely the lives of their own children.

At this juncture it is worth introducing Maurice Sendak, certainly one of the single most influential creators of children's books in English in the last half-century, who produces multidimensional texts that do not oversimplify childhood. Sendak has wondered how children somehow 'manage to grow up', or 'to get through childhood, defeating "boredom, fear, pain, and anxiety"' (Lukens, 1999: 66). His verbal and visual narratives incorporate honesty and humour, enabling him to treat the psychological challenges of youth.

In my topic handbook, I include Sendak's description of the origins of *Where the Wild Things Are*, which captures the child's point of view, the child beset by relatives whom he is powerless to withstand, hampered by the restrictions that age and size entail. These relatives provided pictorial models for his 'monsters'.

> It wasn't that they were monstrous people; it was simply that I didn't care for them when I was a child because they were rude, and because they ruined every Sunday, and because they ate all our food. They pinched us and poked us and said those tedious, boring things that grown-ups say, and my sister and my brother and I sat there in total dismay and rage. The only fun we had was later, giggling over their grotesque faces ... (Sendak, 1963: 20–1)

Employing a familiar 'There and Back Again' structure, within which the child becomes the hero, Sendak allows readers to acknowledge emotions such as rage and feelings of frustration and powerlessness. Max saves himself through his own imagination in a wild verbal and pictorial caper where he rebels safely before returning home to find that maternal love still accepts him. Its conclusion is psychologically comforting and artistically satisfying without being unrealistic. *Where the Wild Things Are* exhibits harmony between words and pictures and expert text placement that enhances suspense;

in its entirety it demonstrates how sophisticated the picture book can be, appealing to an intergenerational audience.

Beginning with picture books, then, allows me to focus on aspects of the topic that students must understand: the craft of writing itself; the technical aspect of genre; and the concept of audience. The first can be addressed under the heading 'Language Matters'. In a picture book, as in a poem, rhythm, pace and nuance contribute to the overall effect. The second addresses elements as specific as the function of the peritext or the number of pages in the standard trade version (32 pages, because of the way in which the paper has to be folded).[6]

The third discusses appropriate language and subject matter for particular age groups. Although 'appropriate' or 'suitable' are terms trotted out to praise or damn books, they have their uses that do not involve attempts to censor content. For example, a picture book about 'Career Day' for four-year-olds at a childcare centre is not appropriate for a host of reasons, as I pointed out to a class (where the idea was suggested). The target audience is occupied with acquiring skills to help them to cope with their immediate environment, not with what skills they might acquire in future to create an adult identity (although Lion Tamer and Candy Maker might just grab their attention). A story about what a particular parent did for a living has an entirely different emphasis.

Generating story ideas might be the obvious starting point, but the next step is communicating with the intended audience. And should the focus be on 'ideas', or on 'story'? A mature-age student with teenagers might want to investigate intergenerational conflict, but if they begin with a concept instead of a situation, or simply an intriguing piece of dialogue, they will probably wind up with something fit for a parenting manual. A young adult student who only wants to write books like their recent favourites has enthusiasm and openness, but they are usually not competent to attempt a full-length work; their short stories can suffer from the drawbacks of slavish imitation and/or genre fiction (horror or romance, for example).

Sharing scenarios generated in small groups, and developing individual responses to those scenarios, is one strategy that allows a class to concentrate on the text itself, on issues of structure, language and characterization, rather than on the personal dimension. Attention to what the story demands encourages them as well to believe that they have more than one personality as a writer. They can learn general lessons about text construction, manipulation of language and (visual) narrative from exploring the diversity of picture book types (the wordless story, 'the picture book of ideas' (Saxby, 1993: 86), for example), which they might later apply to other forms such as the chapter book, short story or narrative poem. As professional writers realize, experimenting with another genre or strategy can open up possibilities and refresh their practice.

In addition, beginning with picture books facilitates discussion not only of technical issues, but cultural, educational and commercial ones. Some knowledge of how children learn to read, what types of language appeal to them and how adult and child interact with texts can inform the revision of a promising draft. The picture book as physical entity foregrounds both an understanding of plot development and the reading experience itself when each page is turned.

I have considered what skills and overview of the field teachers might want to convey, and what students' goals might be. Of course, another critical factor in the equation exists: the market. But who or what comprises the market? Teachers can begin by identifying trade and educational publishers; drawing attention to corporate families, with linkages to entertainment or food conglomerates (see *International Book Publishing: An Encyclopedia* (Altbach and Hoshino, 1995) for background information) and discussing the interaction between publishers, book chains and pressure groups. Providing selected readings and, in particular, a regional or national case study, are ways to raise student consciousness. For example, series are often a direct response to a perceived need or gap in the market. In Australia, the push to help children to read more effectively gave birth to a specific form, a 1,000-word chapter book with a Lexile rating called the SOLO (Omnibus/Scholastic Group), which was then copied by Penguin (the Aussie Nibbles series).

When I introduce the SOLO form I begin by saying that writers don't wake up one morning with a burning desire to write a 1,000-word chapter book for a 6-year-old reading level. They might want to write a story to explore what happens to a heavyweight pony which isn't appreciated by a snobby little prince (Kroll, 2001); or one to reflect their disgust with the rubbish contaminating our environment (Brian, 2001). Once a workable draft exits, then other aspects of the template (word count, sentence construction, vocabulary, number of chapters) can be addressed at the revision stage.

Publisher and author Dyan Blacklock, who conceived of the SOLO, describes the gap in the market she discovered and how the Omnibus team made the necessary innovations to produce a highly successful series that allowed 'a publisher ... to walk a fine line between real worth in a book and economic sense' (Blacklock, 1997: 24). She considered length, reading level, structure, cover design, print size, type of paper and author and illustrator biographies. The goal was to publish 'books that were engaging, pacy and, best of all, readable' (p. 25), which would give beginners a sense of achievement at having completed their first 'real' book solo.

Blacklock's article suggests the multiple functions that most children's books must perform in the marketplace and hence the myriad ways creators need to understand what can be both their vocation and their occupation. Whether aspiring children's authors are fuelled by something as amorphous as their initial passion for childhood favourites or as specific as their off-springs' complaint about lack of decent reading material, they will inevitably be affected by the actual world in which the production and dissemination of children's books happens. A classroom can highlight these interconnections and suggest strategies for writers to juggle their skills and talents as well as cultural and economic imperatives.

3. NOTABLE READINGS: WHO DO WE LISTEN TO AND WHO SHOULD WE READ?

> We need to share our stories in order to work out who we are and where we are going. Cultures across the world have always used stories to regulate themselves. Right now I believe that our own culture is turning its back on stories. Never have we had so many badly told, trivial, gratuitous tales served up to us. And children are the main sufferers. (Jennings, 2003: 297)

Developed nations have classic stories that contribute to their cultural heritage. I make this statement at the beginning because it is, in the twenty-first century, problematic. Evaluators of a tradition are conditioned by personal preference, theoretical perspective and socio-economic background. As a writer competing in a marketplace, where being reviewed in a major publication can begin to seem like winning an award, and as an academic selecting texts for topics, those qualifications make me ask questions:

1. What does 'classic' mean and what or who determines whether books stay in print?

2. Who decides what is notable? (What is the background of judges, reviewers, critics and teachers?)

3. How do publishers select manuscripts and how much influence do marketing people have?

4. How far can we trust critical judgement that evaluates texts, when this decade's fashionable theory might become as outmoded as shoulder pads or mini-skirts (which have made a comeback)?

5. If a text is hugely popular, does this mean it is necessarily 'good' in a literary sense?

I raise these somewhat obvious questions as they impact on my life as a writer and teacher, rather than a critic. Number 5 is behind requests for comments from journalists whenever a new Harry Potter novel hits the stands; they want to turn the series phenomenon into some form of simple equation: Passion for Potter equals passion for reading, or popular text equals great text. Jack Zipes's recent book, *Sticks and Stones: The Troublesome Success of Children's Literature from Slovenly Peter to Harry Potter* (2002), contains a provocative analysis of Potter as a market commodity that has suggested responses to some of the above questions.

In a postmodern world, questions about ideology, ethics, quality, popularity and viability buzz around a writer's head like flies in an Australian summer; they are irritating, relentless, impossible to ignore. You swat one away with what seems a reasonable response (a theory, a positive review, a healthy royalty statement) and another zooms past your ear. Worst of all, they are not seasonal.

The late twentieth century has seen an increase in texts applying a range of literary, cultural, linguistic, educational and psychological theories to children's literature. The economics of publishing has now become a research focus, too. It would be hard for an active writer to be unaware of this complex milieu. The cult of the author places many in the spotlight at festivals and readings; many write 'How To' books or anecdotal accounts of the creation of particular works. Frequently they step outside their author's role to comment 'as a parent' or 'a teacher', acknowledging their multiple personalities.

Some of the texts mentioned below are only a few that have helped me to comprehend this diversity and to enrich the teaching of children's writing. Peter Hunt's groundbreaking work traces the development of the field's history and criticism (see 'References and Some Additional Sources'); his critique of Aidan Chambers's (1990) notion of the implied reader ('The Reader in the Book') and those who followed him leads to an enlightening discussion of the complex relationship between readers and texts. In addition, Hunt's classification of the main factors influencing children's books in the twenty-first century (according to Hunt, the new era began in 1970, rather than 2000) engenders useful debates about such overarching concepts as culture, childhood, colonialism and commerce, among others (Hunt, 1994: 12).

Peter Hollindale's 'Ideology and the Children's Book' (1998) analyses the primary adult camps – 'book people' and 'child people' – with stakes in children's literature. From discussing the myth of 'the average child' (p. 7) and the possibility of a 'good literary text' that exists outside the notion of readership (p. 9), Hollindale moves to the pervasiveness of ideology. He does not see this as good or bad, merely a condition of all texts. Therefore the ways in which children read (and can be taught to read) are critical. John Stephens carries this area of study forward in *Language and Ideology in Children's Fiction* (1992) by applying linguistic and narrative theory to investigate how fiction of all types (from picture books to novels – historical, realistic, fantastic) works on young readers.

Utilizing a 'shamelessly eclectic' (p. x) blend of the work of semioticians, reader-response theorists and others, Perry Nodelman's *Words About Pictures: The Narrative Art of Children's Picture Books* (1988), offers innovative analyses of the genre's visual dimension. Jane Doonan's *Looking at Pictures in Picture Books* postulates the concept of 'the beholder' (1993: 8), which can help students to grasp how we do not 'read' pictures in the same way as text, but absorb them at a different pace. One strategy for revising a picture book text is in fact anticipating possible visual strategies; for an author to realize what they do *not* need to say; to apprehend how the verbal and visual can play off against each other.

Critical texts both by and about ethnic and Indigenous groups is another developing area. In Australia, Anita M. Heiss has published *Dhuuluu-Yala (To Talk Straight)* (2003), which presents for the first time a history of Australian Indigenous publishing (including chapters on Canadian First Nations' and Maori Literature) and canvasses the ethical issues and protocols, making it a necessary source for non-Indigenous authors. Clare Bradford's *Reading Race: Aboriginality in Australian Children's Literature* (2001), considers representations of Aboriginality, particularly analysing the ideologies under-pinning them from the nineteenth century to the present, and how they support socio-cultural values. In the United States, many textbooks include primary multicultural and indigenous materials, but not specifically for young people, although bibliographies in the field exist. *Reclaiming the Vision: Past, Present, and Future: Native Voices for the Eighth Generation* (an anthology of conference papers – the result of a conference of North American Native writers) does concern itself with literature for the young (Francis and Bruchac, 1996).

The proliferation of good book guides and read-aloud handbooks testifies to the confusion among parents, schools and librarians with limited time and budgets. Written by journalists, educators and high-profile authors (Jim Trelease, Mem Fox, Paul Jennings, *et al.*), their message is the same: the nation's future is involved in the literacy stakes as well as the emotional and psychological health of families. Sometimes the market gets it wrong and entertaining, aesthetically satisfying books disappear. Valerie V. Lewis and Walter M. Mayers's *Best Books for Children* (2004) includes a section entitled 'The Out-of-Print Hall of Shame'. These guides provide an overview of what some educators and writers believe constitute worthwhile texts.

The issue of 'what must not be missed' clearly has different meanings depending on our personal, regional, national or international perspective. Hilary McPhee, former pub-lisher and Chair of the Australia Council, analyses the impact of globalization on any nation's artists in this way: '. . . only strong local cultures have a chance to thrive in a globalised world' (2004). Economist Richard Florida's *The Rise of the Creative Class* (2002) makes the case for US regional cultures (Mcphee, 2004), but how feasible is their survival in smaller nations? McPhee argues that vibrant local cultures might always need some non-commercial or governmental support to survive.

Clearly, global monopolies have impacted not so much on writers' abilities to be published in the first place but to reach the widest audience without having to compro-mise their texts. Educational publishers restrict local content routinely; I copy their guidelines to show students that for this market, cricket and vegemite are out, let alone overtly rebellious children and slang. Trade publishers are not as heavy-handed in editing, but they will also demand changes from country to country. According to Arthur Levine, an editor and publisher with an international list (J. K. Rowling, Roddy Doyle, Philip

Pullman, *et al.*), he does not 'Americanize' but 'translates' (Levine, 2000: 20) in order to give young American readers an experience similar to a native British or Irish reader's. He worked on the Harry Potter books with Rowling in this manner. Text alteration is frequently debated by non-American English-speaking authors who sell rights overseas.

I began this section by talking about a concept of national literary heritage, which usually includes some children's books. Teachers, critics and reviewers would no doubt nominate contemporaries whose work they believed was worthy of inclusion. Superstars are already visible in the global sky and I do not need to point them out. Teachers will have their own favourites. In the following exercise section, I will only name some texts, therefore, because they have worked successfully for me in a specific pedagogical context.

4. STRATEGIES AND EXERCISES: WORKSHOPS THAT TEACH MORE THAN WRITING

The workshop

Writing for Children and Young Adults should address both the craft and the culture of children's literature. Supplying a Reading Handbook (containing essays from critical texts; articles from magazines and newspapers; recommendations of books that illustrate trends or provide models) supports the learning process. Workshops can then focus on student efforts. Teachers might want to bring in their own drafts to demonstrate how a manuscript moves from initial idea, through revision, to published text. I find this especially useful when discussing the nuts and bolts of picture book production, which entails negotiation between author, illustrator, designer and editor.

The portfolio: background

Each year I ask students to set goals for themselves in the questionnaire they fill out on day one and instruct them to evaluate their progress at semester's end. The majority want to enrich their understanding of children's books and simply to learn new writing techniques. Older students might want to create something for their own children or gain insights to help them select reading. Only a few believe they will go on to publish in the field. So what can teachers assess?

The majority would accept this truism: they cannot teach talent. That has never been the point of a creative writing workshop, however. Students can demonstrate assessable skills in many ways. The Portfolio is one form I have devised that asks them to perform a number of specific tasks; it demonstrates commitment to the topic and documents the learning that has taken place.

The portfolio: content

Students need to include: all the set exercises, including the original questionnaire and final analysis; annotated drafts of two other students' work; their evaluation of class feedback on one of their exercises; and responses to three guest writers and/or industry professionals who come regularly to our university. In addition, they can add a journal/scrapbook section where they comment on related reading (literary; critical; newspaper and magazine articles; cartoons; and Internet sources). I always learn something new from the best Portfolios.

Exercise 1: How do we begin?

Preliminaries

When students take a Writing for Young People topic, they believe that they already know something about its content. After all, they were once children and they read books. They have also studied literature. Hence I begin with the questionnaire previously discussed. The following task builds on our airing of assumptions about childhood, literary worth and the place of the children's author in the cultural hierarchy.

Exercise

Bring to class a children's book that you liked (or disliked) as a child. Answer briefly:

> Why did you like this book?
> Was it popular with other children?
> Have you reread it since and when?
> Do you still like (or dislike) it and why?

The ensuing discussion allows the class to look at how and why children react to texts. For example, was it content (horse, ballet, truck story or film tie-in) that made it enjoyable? Was it the reading context (shared at home with a favourite relative or at school or playgroup)? Was it the illustrations that they loved (i.e. fairies, animals, heroes)? Perhaps they still respond to it for any or all of the above reasons, but the ideological subtext (gender or ethnic stereotyping, for example) interferes now with their enjoyment. Alternatively, why didn't they like the text?

The most telling insights come when students realize why they might or might not want to share their choice with a child today. What is it about the book that still makes it effective or powerful; or why is it no longer a desirable read? Sometimes students realize that the text remains meaningful only because of nostalgia. At others, they rediscover their delight in the language or the clarity and potency of the characterizations.

Exercise 2: The picture book narrative: how the verbal and visual interact

Preliminaries

First, I provide samples of a variety of styles and approaches. Then students classify them according to audience and type (i.e. infant and preschool; wordless; picture book for older readers). We focus on plot, linguistic patterns and interaction between verbal and visual texts of the standard 32-page trade picture book.

Exercise

Your Handbook contains the texts of two published picture books. Each has been typed as a block of prose with no paragraphs. Choose one and break it into what you believe are appropriate units; in other words, divide it so that the text becomes a workable narrative. Now consider how you would illustrate the text. Write brief descriptions of the pictures.

Students bring their versions to class, where the texts are projected onto a screen. I use an erasable projection pen to break the narratives up based on student suggestions. Considering illustration ideas and text placement allow us to focus on the book as a physical object, which requires readers to turn the pages frequently. Narrative pace can be controlled in this way. When the class is satisfied with the divisions, we look at the published books.

Jenny Wagner and Ron Brooks's *John Brown, Rose and the Midnight Cat* (1977) and Pat Hutchins's *The Very Worst Monster* (1985) are my choices. The first book focuses on two relationships: that between the dog, John Brown, and Rose, and the other between John Brown and the Cat. The narrative works to move all three into the same space at the end, verbally, visually and emotionally. The second book, through animal (or monster) fantasy, treats sibling rivalry. Hutchins employs clear linguistic and pictorial patterns to embody Hazel's jealousy of her baby brother.

Additional books

Teachers can use these to focus on some of the following: the artist's media and style; overall book design; metafictive techniques and intertextuality.

- *Fox* by Margaret Wild (2000), illustrated by Ron Brooks – use of colour and mixed media; text placement (some of the narrative has to be read sideways, for instance).
- *Possum Magic* by Mem Fox (1983), illustrated by Julie Vivas – rendering of invisibility.
- *Greetings from Sandy Beach* by Bob Graham (1990) – breezy cartoon style and adult subtext.
- *Zoo* by Anthony Browne (1992) – perspective, satire.
- *Window* by Jeannie Baker (1991) – wordless picture book for all ages (three-dimensional collage artwork).
- *Aunt Isabel Tells a Good One* by Kate Duke (1992) – metafiction.
- Janet and Allan Ahlberg's *It Was a Dark and Stormy Night* (1994; hybrid illustrated book) – postmodern playfulness, intertextuality, metafiction.

Exercises 3 and 4: The picture book narrative: verbal and visual extension

Preliminaries

The text that introduces these exercises is pedagogically useful in more than one way (see exercise 5). Margaret Mahy's *The Man Whose Mother was a Pirate* (illustrated by Brian Froud in 1972) was revised and republished in 1985 with new illustrations by Margaret Chamberlain. The difference between the two visual texts is remarkable (Mahy also tightened and refined her words). The original, dull collage illustrations, which depict a lumpy pirate mother and son and a static sea, contrast sharply with the vibrant primary colours and freewheeling style favoured by Chamberlain. Not only does she bring out the inherent humour in the story with her visual play, but her flowing lines and use of space underpin the book's themes: that the power and poetry of the imagination can free individuals, helping them to break out of stereotyped roles.

Mahy's comments about her work reveal why Chamberlain's art complemented her story so well: 'I do think I can claim that my stories suggest that there are times when it's appropriate for any individual, male or female, to surrender to the amazement of the moment and to break away from the forms necessarily that control our day to day life and enter upon a rather freer and more anarchic type of existence' (quoted in Kroll, 1987: 64).

Exercise 3

Break into groups. You will each be given a copy of an original and re-executed illustration of a portion of text. Discuss the differences and how they affect reader response and the book's overall impact. A summary of the discussion should be included in your Portfolio.

Exercise 4

Generate a picture book draft of no more than 500–600 words. Type your draft so that it reflects the page divisions. On a separate page, type the text again and include ideas for illustrations.

For workshopping: Break into groups and discuss your drafts. Now swap texts so that another student pencils in illustration ideas. Compare the results. How might the differing visual interpretation affect the story?

Exercise 5: The picture book narrative as non-rhyming poetic text

Preliminaries

Define image, simile and metaphor. Discuss and **read aloud** passages of *The Man Whose Mother was a Pirate* either as a class or in groups and identify the figurative language. Is it effective, or do you find it overdone? Where does this type of language appear in the book? How does it support the book's themes? For example:

> The little man could only stare. He hadn't dreamed of the BIGNESS of the sea. He hadn't dreamed of the blueness of it. He hadn't thought it would roll like kettledrums, and swish itself on to the beach. He opened his mouth, and the drift and the dream of it, the weave and the wave of it, the fume and foam of it never left him again. At his feet the sea stroked the sand with soft little paws. (Mahy, 1985)

Exercise

Generate your own similes and/or metaphors, extending Mahy's description of the sea or, if you wish, use figurative language to describe another natural phenomenon.

Exercise 6: Newspaper sources – focus on point of view

Preliminaries

Often writers collect clippings from newspapers or magazines. Recently a student of mine for this assignment clipped out an article (*Sunday Mail*, Adelaide, 24 April 2005) that reported how Florida police were called to a school on 14 March in order to deal with a misbehaving kindergarten girl. They handcuffed the five-year-old.

The story behind this story (and the motivations and emotions behind the facts) might be accessed from a variety of viewpoints: those of the teachers, the policemen, the girl, the principal, the parents, an older sister who was exasperated by her sibling's behaviour. Consequently, this could be the basis for a serious adult story about a dysfunctional family or a satiric exposé of over-enthusiastic police, a young adult story about sibling jealousy or a chapter book about learning to control anger.

Make sure students understand the various narrative points of view.

Exercise

Clip out a provocative article from a magazine or newspaper, preferably one that gives only a factual skeleton with not much background. Write a story based on this clipping that explains the motivations that underlie the event, particularly offering an insight into a young protagonist. Hand in the article with the draft to be workshopped.

Teachers can also provide students with an article or articles. A variation on this exercise asks students to write three openings to a story from different points of view or from a different time or place in the narrative.

Exercise 7: Short story and gender

Preliminaries

Discuss some of Paul Jennings's stories, whose central characters are almost always Anglo-Celtic males about 14 to 16 years old. Are there any other similarities in characterization or plot? Do Jennings's stories, especially the conclusions, imply a value system or world view? (For more on Paul Jennings, visit www.pauljennings.com.au)

Exercise

Suggest a way of rewriting one story from a female point of view. Can this be done easily or would the story's emphasis or significant plot elements have to change? Write your own story from whatever point of view you choose and try for a Paul Jennings quirky twist at the end. Does your end 'pay back' the central character at all? Why?

Exercise 8: In-class – packaging the product for multiple audiences

Teachers can display novels that have been republished with a new cover or that appear in more than one imprint (i.e. child, young adult, adult, fantasy). Well-known examples are Philip Pullman's His Dark Materials trilogy, Lian Hearn's Tales of the Otori (a trilogy with a prequel and sequel to come) and John Marsden's Tomorrow, When the War Began. These books not only have alternate covers and designs aimed at different age groups but covers and titles vary from country to country.

Exercise

Compare the covers and note the differences. Why do you think these changes have been made? What assumptions seem to underlie them? How might you update or retarget a book with a new design? If you have an idea for a book, what kind of cover do you envisage for it? Why do you believe that this will appeal to your target audience?

Exercise 9: Sending your child into the world – submitting a manuscript

Preliminaries

Discuss the markets for children's poetry and fiction in your region or country: for example, school magazines, publishers that accept unsolicited manuscripts, literary agents. Supply a list of potential outlets and indicate the type of work in which they specialize. Supply the template of a submission letter that can be individualized by students and discuss submission strategies.

Exercise

After you have completed your final creative project (picture book, poetry, chapter book, short story, etc.), prepare it as though you were going to submit it to a magazine, agent or publisher. Include the covering letter and submit the project for assessment.

Conclusion: being intimate with everybody

> There's an intimacy between the reader and a printed page that is probably more intimate than any other form and I think parents get nervous seeing their kids intimate with anybody else outside the family, even in a metaphorical sense. (Morris Gleitzman, quoted in Kroll, 1998: 7)

Morris Gleitzman, who specializes in books for the preteen audience on the cusp of puberty, tackles cutting-edge moral and social issues such as sibling death, AIDS, euthanasia and contraception. He cannot help but be aware, therefore, of the potential reaction to his material, but his words about the intimacy of the act of reading should reverberate with anyone wanting to reach a young audience. 'Reach' is the operative word. As Colin Thiele remarks, 'The important message for writers is that they do not work in a vacuum. I believe that authors of children's books are much closer to their audience than are writers for adults. They get feedback more quickly. Many are even called on to read or tell or perform their stories in public. ... It is a living experience ... ' (Thiele, 2002: 3).

In summary, what Gleitzman and Thiele suggest is that children's authors are evaluated by adult guardians, but also by their readers, who apply their own critical and aesthetic judgement. Their performance has to satisfy complex criteria. As Katharine Paterson believes, the ideal children's book, like a theory to explain the universe, needs to be beautiful: 'What are the properties of beauty to a physicist? ... simplicity, harmony and brilliance' (1998: 152). How many students taking a prose or poetry writing topic begin by thinking that they will need to be responsible, not only to themselves and their own artistic standards but to their audience and to the wider community as well? This is the challenge that professional writers for young people acknowledge and that students entering the field need to understand.

Chapter 5

Creative Non-fiction

Martin Lammon
Georgia College & State University

1.

I first became interested in writing non-fiction during the 1980s. Back then, I'd never heard of 'creative' non-fiction, a term that, according to Lee Gutkind (of late, the so-called 'Godfather' of the genre), was first used by the United States' National Endowment for the Arts to describe the non-fiction category for its creative writing fellowships. Unaware of a 'new' genre, I published two essays in 1986 and 1987. Both were linked to the American poet James Wright, born and raised in Ohio, my own home state. In those days, as a young poet, I felt simultaneously inspired and intimidated by the older poet, who had died in the spring of 1980, much too young at 52 years old.

That spring I was just 21 years old, still in college, about to turn 22.

The 1987 essay, published in *The Iowa Review*, was more of a critical look inside Wright's work, based on books he had owned in the early 1960s in which he'd scribbled notes along the margins and on scraps of paper slipped between pages. Now a graduate student, in the summer of 1983 I examined those books in the Ohio University Library's Special Collections. Although hardly a work of Creative Non-fiction, that project taught me a crucial early lesson: Research is essential to non-fiction writing, no matter how personal one's story may be. And that essay was not completely scholarly, however; I chose to include several anecdotes and personal asides. Even then, I knew that I could not write solely from a critical perspective. I wanted narrative, personal insight, a *connection* to my subject.

The other essay was most like what we now call Creative Non-fiction. In the spring of 1981, just a year after his death, Wright's hometown public library hosted the first 'James Wright Poetry Festival' in Martins Ferry, just across the Ohio River from Wheeling, West Virginia. Robert Bly and Dave Smith were the featured poets, but for me the real story became a woman I met there, a reporter from the *Wheeling Intelligencer* who was covering the festival. Together we ditched those poets, and she showed me James Wright's landscape, the dingy houses, diners and factories of Martins Ferry and Wheeling. I saw tall smokestacks lit up at the top like giant candles. She showed me the Ohio River and long barges hauling coal from Pittsburgh to Cincinnati. At 3:00 in the morning, she dropped me off back at the library, where I waited until morning, hearing gunshots in the distance.

Here was a story my poetry couldn't tell. Here was something new to write.

A poet's story: telling the truth (slant)

Here is Creative Non-fiction's secret appeal: how *true* stories can be both compelling and unsettling. I remember that the woman I'd met at the James Wright Poetry Festival was a little pleased but even more unnerved when she found out I was publishing the story of our day together in Martins Ferry, even though I never identified her and the essay was to be published in a staple-bound literary journal (*Northeast*) with scarcely a few hundred readers. Her feelings resembled what the reader of good Creative Non-fiction experiences, a voyeuristic blend of pleasure and anxiety that comes from being granted an insider's view. The writer is also both eager and anxious, motivated to tell the whole truth, but worried about divulging too much.

Lesson 1: That line between what to include and what to leave out is perhaps the hardest yet most crucial decision a writer of Creative Non-fiction must confront
A common impulse when writing non-fiction is to include everything that happened within the space of time one is writing about. An equally common impulse, however, is to censor some details that might prove embarrassing or even painful for the people involved, including the writer. The first impulse can clutter a scene with extraneous facts, such as trying to identify everyone at a party, interrupting a conversation when someone takes a bathroom break, or including a description of the hostess's cocktail dress (when what she's wearing has nothing to do with the story you are telling). The second impulse can drain a work's emotional energy. For example, I might wish to write about my mother's high school days, but to protect her reputation in our small hometown, I leave out any explicit (or even implicit) sexual references.

What I must do, of course, is choose what to include (and what to exclude) that will express the *essential* story, as well as the meaning I would relate through that story. I may not want to describe in lurid detail my mother's 18-year-old love life, but if what I'm trying to express is a moment where a mother perceives her adult son for the first time as someone other than her little boy, I will probably need to divulge to some degree what she confides to him, and what he confides to her.

I'm writing now as a poet who only recently has turned more seriously to Creative Non-fiction. I confess that my poetry has almost always been biographical – poems of firsthand experience or poems of witness – and when readers ask me whether or not my poems are 'true', I admit that they are – for the most part. When I write poems about trying to corral a cow grazing in my front yard, or about how my father proposed to my mother, I'm not making up stories. In fact, I tell my students that I lack the imagination for fiction, and that I need to go looking for my poems wherever I can find them. For me, writing purely imaginative short stories or novels was never an option.

On the other hand, in my poems I sometimes do fabricate or smudge facts. In my poem 'Stories a Mother Could Tell', I imagine my factual mother telling me the story of how my father proposed to her, a true story I'd known for years, but in the poem she also remarks how the proposal was on her eighteenth birthday, a detail I made up for the sake of the poem's dramatic energy. I also have the mother in my poem revealing private (even subtly sexual) details that my real mother would surely never speak out loud. The poem ends (in my mother's voice):

> The stories I might tell you
> I could not speak out loud. How one night your father
> wanted all of me, how I knew
> what he wanted, and what to do.
>
> When you lie down with a woman, curtains closed, your face
> so near she feels you breathing, I know what she feels
> is the story a woman keeps to herself.

When I showed my mother the poem, she told me that she liked it, then added: 'But of course no one else can ever read it.' I suspect that I'd described at least some of those 'private details' more accurately than my mother would have liked. Clearly, her mixed feelings about the poem expressed those sentiments I mentioned before, that condition suspended somewhere between flattery and anxiety. More surprising to me, however, was when I tried to rationalize to her why I'd manipulated facts and made my father's proposal occur on her birthday.

'But it was my eighteenth birthday,' she said, and I was delighted that somehow art had anticipated reality beyond mere implication. For me, having this fact deepened the truth of the poem. Of course, years later, after I'd told this art-imitates-life story half a hundred times, I mentioned the poem to my mother again.

'Well, it *was* around my birthday,' she said. I told her it was too late to change her mind. For me, and for the poem, it *was* her birthday when my father proposed, no matter what she said now.

Luckily, poets find their truths wherever and however they can.

Lesson 2: Creative Non-fiction writers seek a different kind of truth that's founded on facts. The only dilemma is in defining just what a 'fact' may be

I remember the first time that I taught a Creative Non-fiction writing class to undergraduates. I'd taught poetry before, of course, and also fiction, but this was an experiment for me, a chance to learn along with my students a new way of writing. I talked to the students about telling the truth, and then one student raised his hand. 'But how will the reader *know* you're telling the truth?' he asked. I explained how intimate details about the writer's topic, and how the well-crafted writing's emotional intensity, would establish authenticity and credibility, what in rhetorical terms is called by scholars the text's *ethos*.

'But how will the reader know *for sure*?' my student insisted.

He was right of course. The reader is at the mercy of the writer.

But the writer will know, and the more truthful the writer is, I believe, the more meaningful and evocative the writing will be. While I may allow myself some factual latitude in my poetry, I don't try to stretch the truth when I write Creative Non-fiction, even if I think I might patch up a weak scene with a fabricated detail or two. However, if I adhere to the *truth* in my Creative Non-fiction, I also understand that there's a *creative* imperative to the genre.

I seriously turned my attention to writing Creative Non-fiction after I'd returned from living in Costa Rica in the autumn of 1995. I'd taken a leave of absence from my teaching job. I'd sold my house and most of my possessions to finance the trip, travelling with the woman who would, less than a year later, become my wife. Libby and I studied Spanish, lived in a ramshackle house near the Caribbean beach just north of the tiny seaside town of Cahuita. Our house had electricity, a toilet, even a rusty refrigerator. But we had no car, no phone, no television, no radio. We washed our clothes by hand in a five-gallon plastic tub, wringing out the soap from our shirts and jeans and towels in our kitchen sink. Three days a week, we taught English in a farming community a few miles inland. We rode up the gravel mountain in the back of a pickup truck, the only motor vehicle in the tiny town of San Rafael. The owner of the truck's name was Jesus. Our contact in San Rafael was a man named Macho. All of this, including their names, is true.

Although I'd written some poems when I was living in Costa Rica, I realized when I returned to the United States that I could only write the story of this adventure in prose. There were too many people we encountered whose lives mattered to me, our own lives had been so fundamentally changed, and I had so many questions I needed to answer. Only the larger canvas of a Creative Non-fiction memoir would serve the purpose of the story I felt compelled to tell, even the parts that were unsettling to me. But although I knew that I needed to turn my head from poetry to prose, knowing what I needed to do was not the same as actually writing my way into the story I wanted to tell.

For the next three years, I followed a trial and error method, experimenting with point of view, characterization, plot, dialogue – all the fictional ('creative') techniques one tries to apply to non-fiction memoir. I tried working out a strategy for using the present tense, which might make my narrative more immediate and intense. I tried shifting between past and present tenses. I tried working with alternating flashbacks. I even tried telling some of the story in the third person. Nothing worked for me.

Another impediment for me was revision. As a poet, I was accustomed to a writing process of drafting followed by persistent revision. Whenever I returned to a poem, I'd always reread and revise, even if all I changed were a word, or a comma. When I began writing my prose memoir about living in Costa Rica, I could not break my revision habit, and as the book would grow longer, I'd have to read and revise all that I'd written up to that point. By the time I got to 30 or 40 pages, I'd usually reached the limit of whatever scant writing time I could spare that morning.

For all these reasons, my efforts to tell that story kept stalling out.

Lesson 3: For me, how I wrote the story was as important as the story itself
Finally, I determined to seek complexity through simplicity. I would write in the simple first person, past tense, of the reminiscent narrator. I would write short 'chapters' of around ten pages, *más o menos* ('more or less' … that Spanish phrase I used so much in this land where *la pura vida* was a catch-phrase for tourists and locals alike), each chapter designed to stand alone, much the way an essay would. I would follow a simple chronological arrangement for the chapters, and focus on the classical unities of time, place and action. Although we'd visited and even lived in other parts of Costa Rica, I would focus the narrative only on our main residence in Cahuita and what happened while we lived there.

Most of all, these simple strategies allowed me to focus on the writing itself, as I set out to tell this story in what I would call a 'poet's prose'. And for me, that attention to craft and style also taught me how Creative Non-fiction could be faithful to the *truth* but also to one's aesthetic principles, essential to one's artistic and literary tastes.

Living in Cahuita, I wrote almost daily in a notebook, describing phosphorescent blue *morfos* butterflies, assembly lines of leaf-cutter ants, and the fruit of the ackee tree which (so I was told) could kill you if you ate the plant before it was ripe. I wrote about our bumpy ride up the mountain where we taught Basic English to about 30 men, women and children and where we found out that our new friend Macho's real name was Omar. I wrote about the ocean's incessant surf, and how we lived 'under the weather' of torrential rain, an equatorial sun, and mysterious illnesses for which we had no names. With no medical facility or pharmacy (with no bank, no petrol station, no supermarket), Cahuita was a place as far away from home as I'd ever known.

Over the next two and a half months, I filled about 220 pages in my journal. Back in the United States, I actually numbered the pages and created a simple index for events, names and subjects I'd recorded in my black, hardbound sketchbook. When I sat down to write the memoir, having that notebook was a godsend.

Lesson 4: While mining one's memory is certainly part of writing a memoir, having access to a journal, letters, books, or any other such pertinent documents will trump memory every time

So in the summer of 1999, confronted by the onset of the new millennium, I was ready to devote myself to this project. I had a story to tell. I had a strategy. I had my journal full of firsthand accounts of what I'd seen and what had happened almost four years earlier. I had books about Costa Rica that would help me with facts about places and events, flora and fauna. I was ready to write.

What I wasn't ready for, of course, were the times when fact and truth collided, where competing personal and aesthetic motives threatened to undermine my decisions about what details to include and what stories to leave out. I was face to face with this genre's greatest dilemma: How to tell the truth, even when the author knows that some scenes will require a 'creative' writer's concession to the limits of memory and history. But most of all, I wasn't ready for the emotional upheaval – both thrilling and disheartening – of remembering those days my beloved and I lived just nine degrees north of the equator.

2. WHAT CREATIVE NON-FICTION IS (AND WHAT IT ISN'T): TAKING A STAND

No matter what you read – here or in another book – the best lessons you'll learn are the ones you'll find while you're sitting at your desk or keyboard, writing, revising, and revising again. In this way, all of us are students of creative writing, and our best teacher is our devotion to a process that does not happen between one's ears, but only when we actually begin putting words down on paper or computer screen.

That said, we *can* learn lessons from other teachers.

Not that long ago, there was one fundamental question: *What is Creative Non-fiction?* Traditionally, non-fiction was biography and autobiography, journalism, the personal essay (with a lineage we could trace to Montaigne). Was Creative Non-fiction something new?

In 1993, Lee Gutkind published the first issue of *Creative Nonfiction*, the first journal devoted exclusively to this new genre. In his introductory essay, Gutkind recalls starting to write non-fiction in the 1970s, how back then works by Tom Wolfe, John McPhee, and Gay Talese were being called 'The New Journalism'. For 20 years, Gutkind had been writing and teaching a genre that many of his colleagues did not appreciate or even accept. But each year, new books and essays appeared that clearly were stretching the limits of what used to be called simply 'non-fiction'.

Gutkind claims that all the works collected in that first issue of his journal would be examples of what had come to be known as *Creative Non-fiction*. He identifies two key elements of this new genre: First there is a 'strong element of reportage, which is the anchor and foundation of the highest quality of journalism and of creative nonfiction'. The element of 'reportage' (which Gutkind has also referred to sometimes as a 'teaching' element) obviously relates to the 'non-fiction' part of the genre. The second element is where Gutkind opens Pandora's Box:

> The word 'creative' refers to the unique and subjective focus, concept, context and point of view in which the information is presented and defined, which may be partially obtained through the writer's own voice, as in a personal essay. (Gutkind, 1993)

There it was, the nemesis of all respected journalists, historians and biographers: licence for writers to apply their own 'unique and subjective focus' to whatever factual topics they were writing about. Although for years authors, editors and critics had already begun the discussion (now and then more like a barroom brawl) over what to do with this 'New Journalism' and its misshapen progeny, it was Gutkind's journal that fuelled the debate over what Creative Non-fiction was and whether or not one could even call it a 'genre'.

Five years later, in his journal's tenth issue, Gutkind responded to James Wolcott's scathing *Vanity Fair* article (October 1997) that refers to writers such as Gutkind, Phillip Lopate, Tobias Wolff and John McPhee as 'navel gazers'. Wolcott reserved a special rebuke for Gutkind, dubbing him the 'Godfather' of Creative Non-fiction. Wolcott considered such writing to be 'civic journalism for the soul', and even worse, a 'sickly transfusion, whereby the weakling personal voice of sensitive fiction is inserted into the beery carcass of nonfiction' (Gutkind, 1998).

The ongoing fight had escalated, and Lee Gutkind has been the most outspoken proponent for the genre ever since, even taking on (with a wicked sense of irony) the 'Godfather' role that Wolcott had sought to saddle upon him.

Now, antagonists debate over what is fact and what is fiction, whether or not 'composite' characters are allowable, and if for the sake of narrative focus a writer might compress different events into one dramatic scene. Some philosophize that all writing is fiction, and that there is no such thing as objective truth or facts. We live in an era where a Pulitzer Prize winning historian-biographer, Edmund Morris, faced with an inscrutable yet mesmerizing subject, Ronald Reagan, resorts to creating fictional characters – including making himself an imagined eye-witness to events before he was even born – in order to illuminate the often opaque life of a President. In writing *Dutch*, Morris acknowledges on the book's jacket cover that he has created what 'amounts to a new biographical style', a strategy he shaped 'directly from Ronald Reagan's own way of looking at his life'. An article in *The American Historical Review*, echoing many other critical commentaries about *Dutch*, calls Morris's book the 'first harlequin historical romance to be reviewed in the *ARH* ...'

Sigh. Arguments about what is and what isn't allowed for Creative Non-fiction (or even what distinction, if any, exists between fiction and non-fiction) express little more than academic exercises. Writers with stories to tell aren't really listening.

Finally, none of these arguments really matters. Writers are pushing the limits of the genre further and further, and we can't close Pandora's Box.

But I do believe each writer has to look inside that box and search for whatever 'hope' one can find there, and thus determine how to write his or her particular brand of Creative Non-fiction. What matters to me – especially addressing writers and teachers new to this genre – is to first establish and respect certain traditions inherent to Creative Non-fiction. I remember when I invited author Dinty W. Moore (yes, that's his real name) to my classroom, and a student asked him what was the difference between fiction and non-fiction. Moore did not hesitate with his answer.

'Fiction lies. Creative Non-fiction doesn't,' he said.

The first and most important principle of Creative Non-fiction is that the writer does not change the basic facts of what happened. There's no need to wax philosophically about this. I remember one occasion when a student of mine had written a scene in which he accidentally ran over a long-eared, long-whiskered rabbit. I don't remember why, but I questioned him about what had happened, and he confessed that he'd actually hit a possum, but that he thought a rabbit would be a more sympathetic creature.

The only Creative Non-fiction principle I live by: Possums are not rabbits; your Great Aunt Mary, Third Cousin Marla and Grandma Magda are not the same person

In her essay 'Everything But the Truth', Fern Kupfer (2004) recalls how she found out that a student in her non-fiction seminar at Iowa State University had made up stories that he passed off as 'non-fiction'. Kupfer had given him an 'A' for the course. Discovering her student's duplicity, she felt angry, betrayed. When she retrieved the young man's final examination, she encountered his answer to a question about defining what Creative Non-fiction was. His rather jaded view noted how the economics of books determine genre, and how publishers like to 'keep things straight'. He concluded: 'Some people want to read true things. Some people don't. Me, I don't give a shit. True, false, fiction, non-fiction, journalism – it all ends up as fiction in the end' (p. 292).

Kupfer doesn't say how old this student is, but I wonder if he has ever been married for 20 years, faced divorce, or a child's colic, or worse, a spouse or child battling a mortal illness, like leukaemia, the slow hope and the slow death that the long-married will often and, to be honest, inevitably face. I'd be surprised if he had. Such abstract theorizing about the difference between fiction and non-fiction is easy when one is innocent. The best writers of Creative Non-fiction transcend that innocence, whether they are 23 or 43 or 83 years old.

Kupfer does not accept her student's answer, nor do I, but she does describe three kinds of 'lies' that she considers 'acceptable'. And recalling Lee Gutkind's (1993) notion of what's 'creative' about Creative Non-fiction (the 'unique and subjective focus, concept, context and point of view in which the information is presented and defined'), I certainly agree that the 'truth' we try to convey in our writing cannot match the truth of empirical reality. But I think there is a difference between 'telling lies' and 'subjective' truth.

First, Kupfer accepts those 'little white lies' we make when 'memory has blurred the details' (2004: 292). There's no getting around the limitations of memory. What was the weather like on a particular day? What colour was your lover's shirt? The most common concession to memory is when we recreate dialogue. Perhaps Dustin Hoffman's character in the film *Rain Man* could repeat word for word what he heard, or what he read. Most of us, of course, don't possess such peculiar gifts of recollection.

What I recommend is that writers restrict what they can't remember and focus instead on what they can (or mostly can) recall. I remember my first Boy Scout camping trip, when I was 11 years old, how it snowed that night, how I slept with my clothes on, and how I pulled the sleeping bag over my head. I remember in the morning, when I poked my head out from under the sleeping bag, how the cold took my breath away. When I finally looked outside the tent, I saw that our campsite was fully covered in snow. When we tried to make breakfast, our orange juice had frozen solid. Even the eggs we'd brought had frozen inside their shells.

I don't remember what colour my sleeping bag was. I don't remember the name of the boy with whom I shared that tent. I don't remember what the colour of my shirt was. But I do remember that I'd brought the wrong shoes to wear, black leather loafers, and that I could barely pull them over the two pairs of socks I wore. I remember how frigid my toes felt.

Start with what you *do* remember, and limit imagined details to what you *feel* is essential but also faithful to the scene you are recreating, even if you couldn't swear in court that your great aunt's feather boa was lavender or pink.

Kupfer connects her second set of acceptable lies to those that 'narrative structure often demands: composite characterization, compression of time, omission of unnecessary detail' (p. 292). Here I think Kupfer accepts too much on behalf of 'narrative structure'. I agree that creative strategies from fiction are essential to the non-fiction stories we would tell – especially establishing scenes that frame narrative action – and that the writer needs to exclude extraneous details. But I would rank sins of omission well below sins of commission. Kupfer admits to deleting scenes that introduced new people in her already over-populated memoir *Before and After Zachariah* (1988), and to me, such excisions are acceptable. She also admits to omitting 'details that clogged the narrative' (2004: 293). And as I've said before, such decisions about what details to include and exclude define the Creative Non-fiction writer's aesthetic process.

But Kupfer goes on to confess that she compressed three friends into one person, 'a sort of paradigmatic friend who was always there for me'. She also 'compressed time to move the narrative along at a more energetic rate' (p. 293). For example, a week in the hospital is 'compressed' to an afternoon.

Such composites and compressions are, for me, what fiction writers do with reality. Kupfer provides a disclaimer in her acknowledgements that for the 'sake of privacy and clarity, some characters in this book have been fictionalized and some names and places have been changed'. Kupfer (and many others, of course, including Pulitzer Prize winning biographers) have resorted to such tactics. But before you start 'fictionalizing' your non-fiction, try telling the truth first. You may have to work harder to maintain the integrity of your 'narrative structure', but perhaps your writing will be better for that effort.

Finally, Kupfer identifies a 'kind of conjecture' that she calls 'the gift of perhaps', and which is perhaps the most problematic of the three acceptable 'lies' she identifies (p. 293). When you look at a family photograph album, and see old portraits of people you've never met, Kupfer explains, why not imagine 'what if?' The writer's conjecture about those ancestors in the photographs – the writer's feelings, impressions, yearnings – are the reality of that particular 'non-fiction'.

Such conjecture can be tricky. I've written quite factually about how, in Costa Rica, rats had nested in the attic crawlspace just above our bedroom's ceiling. Our neighbour and landlord, Winston McCloud, told us he would look into the matter. One evening we came home, and McCloud was in the yard. He looked disturbed, almost in shock. 'I take care of the rats,' he said. He told us he'd taken a wooden board and clubbed the rats, but when we asked him to tell us what happened in more detail, he couldn't. 'It was bad, very bad,' was all he could say. After writing that scene, I allowed myself to conjecture what McCloud might have encountered up in that dark loft:

> Winston would not give us details of what happened in the crawlspace above our bedroom. I imagined two or three mature rats, a half dozen immature siblings, nesting in shredded paper, hair, banana leaves, and plastic bags. I imagined excrement, urine, and coffee grinds, rotting fruit and stillborn pups, perhaps the mangled feathers of a bird, the mutilated bodies of

lizards, the ripe mash of papaya and mango distilling in the attic heat. I imagined stench, flies buzzing, baby rats sucking at their mother's teats. I imagined Winston crawling forward, his club stunning one rat, then two. I imagined the mother rat hissing at Winston, baring a rodent's long, sharp teeth, before he swung his club across her body. I imagined one rat's naked tail slipping down a hole, escaping. I imagined Winston bringing down his club again and again on the limp bodies of the rats he had stunned or wounded, their bones cracking under his blows.

Employing a poet's strategy, I slipped into a litany founded on the phrase 'I imagined', and in repeating that phrase, I reassured my reader (and myself) that what I was describing was not McCloud's empirical reality but my own subjective conjecture based on what I knew, and what I imagined. The nightmare of my imagination was certainly the truth as I could envision it.

Kupfer ends her essay on another kind of conjecture, how you may remember a day so clearly, but it's only your memories of those events, filtered by your emotions and the passage of time. Kupfer tells us the story of a perfect day when she was 20 years old. Her English teacher read her paper to the class and called it a 'sterling example' and called Kupfer a 'real writer'. It was a day when, riding on her motorcycle, her long hair blowing in the breeze, she thought: 'It will never get any better than this.' But then she confides to us what she *knows* is true:

> I had a motorcycle in college. I used to iron my hair. I did once write an English paper that my professor read to the class. I remember being twenty on a beautiful spring day and thinking, 'It will never get any better than this.' But did all this happen on the same day? Were the jeans white? Were those the professor's exact words of praise? And does it matter? The truth of the story is the narrator's perception of youth, of fleeting time, of the longing to capture a golden moment. And that's the truth I've told. No lie. (Kupfer, 2004: 293)

Here Kupfer presents the dilemma that all writers of Creative Non-fiction face: What do we remember and what do we *think* we remember. I recall interviewing David McKain in the spring of 1990, who expressed essentially the same sentiments as Kupfer. He talks about his memoir *Spellbound: Growing Up in God's Country* and discusses how, in the chapter 'Exposure', the ending 'hinges on the fact that there's a winter storm, the first of the season'. But responding to my question about 'compressing' facts, he admits that he wasn't 'sure if it [his father physically abusing his mother] happened during winter .... But it *could* have happened in winter' (Lammon, 1991: 5) He continues:

> To tell you the truth, I'm not sure that everything didn't happen just the way I wrote it. I mean, people have often said to me, 'Where did you change this or add that?' You hear such questions so often that after awhile you begin to think that maybe you did change the experience. I'm not really 100% sure, but it's pretty much what my memory had done to that aspect of my childhood over the years. Before writing it down, at some point I had structured the moment for the inner theater of my own mind, so I could play it over and watch the performance again and again, so that it had a structure, a shape. I mean, art is not something we arbitrarily make for others, it's something we need in order to understand our own lives. (p. 7)

Each new writer of Creative Non-fiction will face the uncertainty of memory, and each of us must look in the mirror and ask one fundamental question: *Is what I'm writing true?* Others can debate what truth is, and what's the difference between fiction and non-fiction. While I disagree with some of Kupfer's 'acceptable lies', I do respect her choices. They're just not the choices that I could look in the mirror and live with.

Finally, in taking my own stand for what I think Creative Non-fiction is, I like what McKain had to say near the end of our interview:

> At its best, what you write should be the essence of the experience. It's not that you add this or that to render it more presentable. You don't change an experience for effect just for its own sake. You alter and change over the history of your memory to render the experience as *truthful* as possible. (p. 7)

Let your possums be possums. Let your Grandma Magda wear her apron, your Great Aunt Mary wear her feather boa. And when those two women need to talk to each other, create dialogue and description that will dazzle us, as long as you don't impose upon us any language or images that, when you look in the mirror, you couldn't accept yourself.

3. NOTABLE READINGS

For such a 'new' genre, Creative Non-fiction has more of a history than one might suspect. Of course, the provocative essays, autobiographies and biographies of the past were harbingers of what was to come. *The Autobiography of Frederick Douglass* and *The Education of Henry Adams* are two early examples of what one might call today 'Creative Non-fiction'.

More recent books, some of which were representative of the so-called 'New Journalism', might be considered the immediate progenitors of this future new genre, even if some of these authors resist the loose handling of facts found in more recent books. But one certainly finds the roots of Creative Non-fiction in books such as Truman Capote's *In Cold Blood* (1966), Tom Wolfe's *Electric Kool-Aid Acid Test* (1967), Frank Conroy's *Stop-Time* (1967), Joan Didion's collection of essays *Slouching Towards Bethlehem* (1968), John McPhee's *The Pine Barrens* (1968), Annie Dillard's *Pilgrim at Tinker Creek* (1974), Maxine Hong Kingston's *The Woman Warrior* (1976), Norman Mailer's *Executioner's Song* (1979), and Gay Talese's *Thy Neighbor's Wife* (1980). These books and other titles by these authors should be on anyone's reading list that is interested in Creative Non-fiction.

Contemporary readings: one writer's list

Since the early 1980s, thousands of books have been published that belong to the new category of Creative Non-fiction, and it would be impossible for anyone to provide an exclusive 'who's who' list of must-read books. So instead I offer up a sometimes personal, sometimes random abecedarian list of Creative Non-fiction works that explore a variety of approaches, strategies, experiments and styles. Researching authors for such a list proved to be daunting. How to choose between David McKain, Ethelbert Miller (*Fathering Words: The Making of an African American Writer*), Nancy Mairs (*Waist-high in the World: A Life Among the Nondisabled*), Dinty Moore, and all the other 'M' authors I could choose from. How to choose between Phillip Lopate (*Portrait of My Body*), William Least Heat-Moon (*Blue Highways*), Anne Lamott (*Operating Instructions: A Journal of My Son's First Year*), and Barry Lopez? (One way, of course, was to slip in just now a few extra names and titles.)

So remember, this is just one writer's list, selected in part to reflect how many authors one will find, both well known and relatively unknown, who are writing compelling Creative Non-fiction. Not so many whose names begin with Q, X, Y and Z, perhaps, but that's another story.

- Diane Ackerman, *A Natural History of the Senses.*
- Janet Burroway, *Embalming Mom: Essays in Life.*
- Judith Ortiz Cofer, *Silent Dancing: A Partial Remembrance of a Puerto Rican Childhood.*
- Rosemary Daniell, *Fatal Flowers: On Sin, Sex, and Suicide in the Deep South.*
- James Ellroy, *My Dark Places.*
- Patricia Foster, *Just Beneath My Skin: Autobiography and Self-Discovery.*
- Melissa Fay Greene, *Praying for Sheetrock: A Work of Nonfiction.*
- Robin Hemley, *Nola: A Memoir of Faith, Art, and Madness.*
- Pico Iyer, *The Global Soul: Jet Lag, Shopping Malls, and the Search for Home.*
- June Jordan, *Soldier: A Poet's Childhood.*
- Tracy Kidder, *Mountains Beyond Mountains: The Quest of Dr. Paul Farmer, a Man Who Would Cure the World.*
- Barry Lopez, *Arctic Dreams.*
- Dinty W. Moore, *The Accidental Buddhist: Mindfulness, Enlightenment, and Sitting Still.*
- Kathleen Norris, *Dakota: A Spiritual Geography.*
- Mary Rose O'Reilley, *The Barn at the End of the World: The Apprenticeship of a Quaker, Buddhist Shepherd.*
- Lia Purpura, *Increase.*
- Molly McQuade (all right, a stretch for the 'Q'), *Stealing Glimpses: Of Poetry, Poets, and Things in Between.*
- Janisse Ray, *Ecology of a Cracker Childhood.*
- Karen Salyer McElmurray, *Surrendered Child: A Birth Mother's Journey.*
- Amy Tan, *The Opposite of Fate: A Book of Musings.*
- John Updike, *Self-Consciousness: Memoirs.*
- Frank Vertosick, *Why We Hurt: The Natural History of Pain.*
- Terry Tempest Williams, *Refuge: An Unnatural History of Family and Place.*
- Malcolm X, *The Autobiography of Malcolm X* (as told to Alex Haley).
- Ray E. Young Bear, *Black Eagle Child: The Facepaint Narratives.*
- William Zinsser, *Spring Training.*

Such an eclectic list owes as much to my own tastes as to the limitations of my selection process. But below you'll find the means to access much more thorough reading lists. Happy hunting.

Learning the craft: anthologies, teaching texts, journals

I recommend three websites devoted to Creative Non-fiction that provide ample information for students and teachers both. Creative Non-fiction writer Sue William Silverman (*Because I Remember Terror, Father, I Remember You*; *Love Sick: A Woman's Journey through Sexual Addiction*) provides a wonderful list of books (arranged topically), journals, and websites: www.english.uiowa.edu/nonfiction/SilvermanCNFReadingList.pdf

Another useful Internet source is Bruce Dobler's Creative Non-fiction Compendium: www.pitt.edu/~bdobler/readingnf.html

Dobler (University of Pittsburgh) offers a brief introduction to the genre, then provides several lists of authors and their works, including four anthologies useful for classroom adaptation.

Perhaps the most essential on-line source is the website for Lee Gutkind's journal *Creative Nonfiction*, the first literary journal devoted to the genre: www.creative nonfiction.org

Although this is a commercial site, promoting the journal, these web pages provide many free articles and essays (sometimes excerpted) from past issues of *Creative Non-fiction*. The website includes a page called 'What Is Creative Nonfiction?' that features a CSPAN interview with Gutkind (audio files) and five of his *CNF* essays, including 'The 5 R's of Creative Nonfiction'. In this essay, Lee Gutkind (*Many Sleepless Nights: The World of Organ Transplantation*; *One Children's Place: A Profile of Pediatric Medicine*; *Stuck in Time: The Tragedy of Childhood Mental Illness*) lays down a modern-day primer for writing Creative Non-fiction.

These on-line resources will help any student or teacher navigate the expanding landscape of books, journals, anthologies, textbooks and other publications relating to Creative Non-fiction. Here, I'll offer three titles that I have found useful.

1. *Writing Creative Nonfiction: Instruction and Insights from the Teachers of the Associated Writing Programs* (edited by Carolyn Forché and Philip Gerard, 2001). This book offers essays on the art, craft and business of Creative Non-fiction, as well as 17 essays by such authors as Alan Cheuse, Annie Dillard, Martin Espada, and several others who I included on my own list above.

2. *The Fourth Genre: Contemporary Writers of/on Creative Nonfiction* (edited by Robert L. Root, Jr, and Michael Steinberg, 2004). This book (whose authors are associated with the literary journal *Fourth Genre* at Michigan State University) is divided into three sections of essays: 'Writing Creative Nonfiction' (actual examples of the genre), 'Talking about Creative Nonfiction' (essays on the genre) and 'Composing Creative Nonfiction' (essays about writing strategies).

3. *Tell It Slant: Writing and Shaping Creative Nonfiction* (Brenda Miller and Suzanne Paola, 2003). This textbook provides useful introductions, strategies and exercises for students of Creative Non-fiction and is ideal for the college classroom. The book also includes an anthology of over 30 essays by older writers (Virginia Woolf, E. B. White, James Baldwin) and by such contemporaries as David Sedaris and Paisley Rekdal.

Finally, perhaps the best way to keep up with contemporary Creative Non-fiction (not to mention find venues for publishing one's own efforts) is by reading literary journals. As I've mentioned already, *Creative Nonfiction* and *Fourth Genre* are two of the best examples of literary journals devoted entirely to the genre. *River Teeth* (Ashland University, Ohio) is another. Of course, most of the best literary journals in the world publish essays, many of which would fall into the category of 'Creative Non-fiction'. Some that come to mind are *Arts & Letters* (which is the journal that my colleagues and I at Georgia College & State University edit), *The Gettysburg Review*, *The Georgia Review*, *Granta*, *The Iowa Review*, *The Kenyon Review*, *Michigan Quarterly Review* and *The Missouri Review*, just to name a few.

I tell my students: *great writers are great readers*. If your goal is to write Creative Non-fiction, read as much as you can.

4. DOWN TO WORK: STRATEGIES AND EXERCISES

In the special issue of *Creative Nonfiction* (No. 6, *The Essayist at Work*), Lee Gutkind writes about 'The 5 R's of Creative Nonfiction', which are 'Real Life' (the writer's *immersion* in a topic), 'Reflection', 'Research', 'Reading' and 'Riting'. As I note earlier, that essay is available on-line at www.creativenonfiction.org, and I urge you to read Gutkind's 'primer' on writing Creative Non-fiction.

So now it's time to get down to work. Here are some essential strategies to keep in mind for writing Creative Non-fiction and some helpful examples and exercises.

Scene. Perhaps the most important element of effective Creative Non-fiction, 'scene' is moment(ous), focused in time, place, event, and is usually limited to a few 'characters' (people). Scene is the means by which we frame our Creative Non-fiction, and avoid dull lapses into blow-by-blow, minute-by-minute recreations of an afternoon, a day, a week, a year, a life. Scenes need 'action' and blend narrative, description, dialogue and commentary. Anecdote is related to scene, usually only a paragraph or two, those 'little stories' that more meditative Creative Non-fiction writers use to avoid the 'talking head' syndrome of television news. Transition or 'narrative leap' reflects the writer's sense of rhythm between scenes and sections of an essay. Often a 'leap' in time or place, such transitions move the essay from one eventful scene to the next, jumping past irrelevant or unremarkable details to reach the next important scene. Or sometimes such transitions mark a shift from action to a pause in the narrative for relevant, essential commentary. For a powerful example of 'scene', see Margaret Gibson's essay 'Thou Shalt Not Kill' at the *Creative Nonfiction* website (Issue 2), where she develops into a sustained scene a vivid memory about 'killing chickens' at her house in 'Amelia County, away from the city of Richmond', Virginia.

> Exercise
> *Recall an experience that was for you a 'first time' (for example, the first time you rode a two-wheeled bicycle, the first time you hooked a worm and unhooked the fish you caught, the first time you cooked dinner for your significant other, or some other 'first'). Write a scene in which you focus on the time and place when that 'first time' happened. Focus on the 'essential event', what happened in less than 30 minutes. Try starting 'in medias res' (in the middle of things) rather than building up the moment with a lengthy explanation or preamble.*

Story. Even essays that rely more on factual or historical commentary need to tell a story. Like good fictional stories, Creative Non-fiction needs to have a sense of unity (time, place, action, character, conflict), and something needs to *happen*. For a good example of a more meditative essay that uses a simple story (digging up a lilac bush) to 'frame' larger ideas and commentary, as well as anecdotes that maintain the element of story in a reflective essay, see Dinty W. Moore's 'By My Own Hands' (*Arts & Letters*, Issue 3, available on-line at http://al.gcsu.edu).

> **Exercise**
> *Write about an important relationship (parent–child, best friend, spouse, college room-mate, etc.) in which you shape the essay about that relationship with a 'framing story', the way Moore does in his essay about his father.*

> **Exercise**
> *Visit a local institution to which you have reasonable access (your child's school, a hospital where a friend works, the nursing home or other facility where your grandparent lives, etc.) and for several days, or even weeks, observe what you find there: Take notes, talk to the people affiliated with the institution. Find the 'story' that frames the reality (that you perceive) of this place. For example, after talking to the nursing staff at the assisted living facility where your grandmother lives, you might discover that the nurse your grandmother thinks is the 'best' has a story to tell that might frame an essay that's not only about your relationship with your grandmother but, more universally, about such institutions and the people who live and work there.*

Description. All good writing needs images, detailed descriptions that evoke the senses and make impressions without relying on exposition or commentary. Although commentary may well depend on descriptions, usually strong images precede comment. Finally, effective descriptions depend on precise nouns and verbs, not adjectives or adverbs. Words such as *gnaw* or *mug* or *slip* don't need such modifiers as 'voraciously' or 'ugly' or 'carelessly'.

> **Exercise**
> *Take one of the scenes you've worked on and create what's called a 'lexicon', that is, a list of specific words related to a place or activity. For example, a kitchen scene would suggest words like 'boil', 'oregano', 'steam', or 'mustard'. Revise that scene for detail, using nouns and verbs from your lexicon.*

Dialogue and character. Even if your essay depends more on description, narrative, exposition and commentary, good Creative Non-fiction 'stories' need to establish the key 'characters' (people), and we need to hear those people speak, even if only briefly. Indeed, the best dialogue *is* brief. With dialogue, try to focus on only two people at a time. Avoid speeches (longer expressions can be handled with a combination of direct and indirect dialogue, interspersed with description or exposition). Also, avoid excessive 'tags' for dialogue (*he exclaimed, she lamented,* etc.).

Exercise

Create an imagined scene and practise writing dialogue that expresses an emotional tension between two people. Your aim is to recreate the essence of what someone says, to create the verisimilitude of authentic speech. For example:

'I'm here for the dog,' I say.

'The lab or the spaniel?' The woman looks at me as if she wonders why I'm really here. I'm wondering the same thing. The name tag on her blouse reads 'Sandra'.

'The Black Labrador. It's for my son.' I hope Sandra will accept this reason, a father buying a gift for his son, a beloved pet for a little boy.

'How old is he?' she asks.

But I pause too long, panic, and then I say too much. 'He's seven, but he's a mature seven, and he's big for his age, and . . .'

'Let's go inside,' Sandra says. 'Let's talk.'

Topic: personal vs impersonal. All Creative Non-fiction includes at least some personal element, but there's a wide range of personal involvement, from intimate author (memoir, personal essay, autobiography) to an objective but invested, observant writer (immersion journalism, writer as 'witness'). In all cases, it's better that your subject be something important to you rather than merely topically current.

Exercise

Write two versions of a scene that addresses an important event in your life that involved another person (for example, a funeral for a best friend, where both you and the friend's parent or spouse are grieving), one in which you are the central person in the scene, and one in which the other person is the focus. Each version is a first-person narrative, but in the second, your new focus will be on the other person, and how you interact with that person.

Facts and commentary: personal. All good Creative Non-fiction depends on 'facts' and how you address those facts. *Personal* facts are details related to your own life, what you learn directly by experience or indirectly from others. Your commentary on personal facts may take the form of reflection, meditation, musing – your emotional or intellectual response to these experiences. Of course, sometimes it's best just to let the 'facts' speak for themselves.

Exercise

When you visit that institution (see earlier exercise), write daily about your visits in a journal. Try to write at the end of the day, when you're home, or first thing the next morning, before your next visit. Date your entries. Write about what happened that day, about what you perceived through your senses (sight, sound, taste, touch, smell), but also now, upon reflection, about what you are feeling and thinking. This journal will become your personal resource for the longer writing project that develops from this immersion experience.

Facts and commentary: historical. Most (if not all) Creative Non-fiction includes facts that teach readers something about the world in which they live. Usually, such facts require research, whether from primary sources (interviews, excursions to a place) or secondary sources (books, almanacs, encyclopaedias, etc.). *Historical* facts may lead to commentary (analysis, social or cultural observation), but again often it's better to let these facts speak for themselves without any commentary.

Exercise

Link an event in your own life to a historical event, and write an essay in which you converge the two events. For example, a student of mine wrote about how her difficult and life-threatening pregnancy finally ended with an emergency Caesarean section on 12 September 2001 – the day after terrorists attacked the Twin Towers in New York City and other sites in the United States. Your own story, of course, need not be so dramatic. If nothing obvious occurs to you, then first think of several personal stories you'd like to tell. After you have three or four potential stories, go to your library and find old newspapers from the days when each of those experiences happened. Perhaps you'll find a historical event that might resonate with your personal story.

Whether your writing depends on personal or historical facts (or more likely, a combination of both), be wary of lapsing into simplistic polemical or pedantic commentary about those facts. That said, don't be afraid to take risks, to speak from your mind and from your heart.

Exercise

Find a personal scene you've already written and research the etymology of a key word or words from that scene. See if you can incorporate a word's 'history' into commentary relevant to your personal experience. For example:

In Costa Rica, maybe the secrets I learned were only old secrets after all. Maybe all mysteries are like that, hand-me-downs, well-worn, but new to us when we are young.

Singing, dancing. Saying poems and saying grace. These customs belong to the language of what the body yearns for, the language that supersedes basic needs. The word desire comes from the latin *sidus*, which means 'constellation' or 'star', hence 'sidereal motion' refers to the motion of the stars. To 'consider' means 'to observe the stars closely'. To *desire* means 'to long for the stars', to hold them in your hands.

That night, nearly ten o'clock, it was very late for us. We climbed upstairs, got into bed, and read our books for a little while – one of life's other great pleasures – but soon we were falling asleep.

I turned out the light. There was just enough moonlight and starlight that I could see Libby's face. It did not matter to me that, in the history of humankind, billions of people had been in love before us. That night, we slept soundly. In the morning, we held each other close again, warming our bodies against the chill that was so common here, yet so strange to me, knowing the earth's bulging equator lay just a little more than nine degrees south of our bed.

Martin Lammon, 'My Name Is', The Iowa Review *(Winter 2003/04)*

Exercise

Find a scene you've already written and research whatever activity might be related to that scene (cooking, working on cars, fly fishing, running a marathon, mountain climbing, running a hospital emergency room, watching cable television, etc.). Revise the scene to include factual/historical details. For example:

Work has changed, obviously, inevitably, and so have our tools. The current Craftsman catalog offers a 1,197-piece professional tool set – included are 311 wrenches, 72 screwdrivers, 415 sockets, 36 pliers – for roughly $5,000. Sanders' grandfather built a house with little more than a hammer and a saw, and I'm guessing his entire budget was well under that figure.

And this massive modern tool set offered by Craftsman is just hand tools. Power tools in the same catalog include drills, drill presses, edge banders, fasteners, finishers, sander/grinders, sander/polishers, buffers, power hammers, jigsaws, biscuit joiners, lathes, planers, routers, band saws, circular saws, miter saws, chop saws, radial saws, reciprocal saws, scroll saws, table saws, and precision laser levels to replace the plumb line on a string.

Such is progress. We are an affluent people, and our smorgasbord of specialized tools reflects that. More and more we no longer even hold our tools – we push the wood through them, or attach the wood to clamps, and just stand back.

Dinty W. Moore, 'By My Own Hands',
Arts & Letters *(Spring 2000)*

Finally, as you hunt for facts about the stories you have to tell, whether personal or historical, always remember to tell the truth. Don't forget: *Possums are not rabbits.*

Chapter 6

Playwriting

Michelene Wandor

DRAMA QUEEN: PREPARING TO WRITE THE TEXT DRAMATIC

1.

I first taught an ongoing creative writing course in the early 1980s. Until then, I had done one-off workshops in all sorts of places, but nothing over a longer period of time. Colin Chambers, then dramaturg with the Royal Shakespeare Company, suggested I should teach playwriting to first-year acting students at the Guildhall School of Music and Drama, and the experiment was welcomed with enthusiasm by Tony Church, then actor-director of the drama school.

Their reasons were not that some students might want to write plays; rather, they thought it would be useful for performers-to-be if they had some kind of insight into the playwriting process. In their second year the students did some group-improvised and devised work, and I would – in effect – be preparing them (softening them up, as it were) for the writing part of that exercise.

I knew no one then who was teaching creative writing in higher education. I was a professional writer, earning my living from plays, poetry and journalism; I never sought a career in academia, and had no interest in teaching literature, even though my two Literature degrees and subsequent work attested to my passion for language, fictions of all kinds, research and cultural analysis. Teaching literature is a very special skill, as I know from my excellent teachers at school and university; but it was not a skill which interested me. My interests, insofar as drama is concerned, were always in performance. I was, after university, very briefly a professional actress, before having children and turning to writing.

I have always followed academic developments in cultural theory which blossomed (or spread like weeds, depending on whether I thought I understood the stuff), sometimes with great interest, and sometimes with great scepticism. I benefited hugely from other people's academic research – for example, when I dramatized Elizabeth Barrett Browning's verse-novel, *Aurora Leigh*, performed at the National Theatre and on Radio 3 –

knowing that in my approach to writing drama, I shared similar ideological and cultural approaches with academics, across different discourses.

Although writers have a long and honourable history of presence on campus, there is also something of an ongoing tension between academics and professional writers. It isn't just the faint aura of implied two-way jealousy: from academics, that we writers somehow not only have it lucky because we don't have to teach for a living, and from writers that academics bamboozle us with jargon, while using our work as raw material for exegesis. In the past few years, while teaching creative writing at a university, I became used to people sidling up to me and telling me about the novels they were also writing, about how they wished they could have time to write as I did. As if I lived some kind of mythical life of leisure, scribbling between social calls, instead of the constant insecurity of the free-lance writer's life, and the sheer hard work of it.

As writers, while we may be sceptical of theoretical discourse, we know the importance of being sanctioned by the academy: our books, once on reading lists, sell, are more likely to remain in print, are more likely to become embedded in the contemporary canon. I was very aggrieved a couple of years ago because I had not been included in an anthology of Anglo-Jewish poets – not simply because of the implied slur on my poetic visibility, but because I knew that functionally it would help sales of my books, and circulate knowledge of my work more widely. This form of dependence on distanced academic patronage is not always easy to accept and approve. The new presence of writer-teachers in the academy is raising interesting questions about the relationship between the two; sometimes giving rise to the same old suspicions, sometimes leading to new ways of working together.

I began writing professionally at a fortuitous time for British culture, and was – quite literally – able both to earn my living and to acquire my skills on the job. My first plays were produced in the early 1970s in the wake of the repeal of theatre censorship in 1968. I also worked as Poetry Editor and theatre reviewer on the (then) new *Time Out* magazine, developing different journalistic styles along with other people who were often directly involved with the phenomena on which they were reporting – their own 'making' as well as reviewing the making of other people. *Time Out*'s importance as a cultural networking guide cannot be underestimated, either then or now. The post-1968 enthusiasm for theatre was nationwide, and still is. One of the June 2005 issues of *Time Out* lists 110 plays and 30 musicals on offer in London alone.

During the 1970s and 1980s, I was writing plays, poetry, short stories, reviewing and writing books about the new theatre. I knew writers and poets who occasionally worked in schools, but I was not in touch with the English Literature academics who were beginning to explore the uses of creative writing in the academy. So even as I agreed enthusiastically to take on the job at the Guildhall, I knew I was going to have to make it up as I went along.

And so, Reader, I did. I had no idea then about whether I would (a) like teaching dramatic writing, or (b) do it effectively (leaving aside for the moment what 'effectively' might mean). However, I found that developing ways of teaching creative writing generated enthusiasm both for the practical process and for developing cultural and theoretical analyses of what it is, how it is taught and how I think it can be taught.

During the two decades in which I've taught playwriting, I have developed a methodology, enhanced and expanded by the fact that over the past decade I have also been teaching poetry and prose fiction writing. I write in all three genres myself, and teaching has enabled me to formulate a theoretical/aesthetic backdrop to my teaching (its pedagogy), to be interested in what is significantly distinctive about the imaginative and practical processes of writing in different genres, and, as an interesting by-product, to sharpen my understanding of my own writing.

The teaching of playwriting/drama arrived in the academy later than its more senior fellows, prose fiction and poetry.[1] Drama writing courses are often elided with screenwriting, scriptwriting, and other variants on the various performance media. This is, at best, confusing, and at worst ignores the fact that to write in an informed way for the technologically intensive performance media of film, TV and radio, it is essential to learn about the ways in which a production is put together. It is hard enough to teach playwriting to students who are often ignorant of, and even have little interest in, theatre, but at least it is a live medium, and some of its conditions can be minimally replicated in the classroom.

The aesthetic and technical conventions of the other media are too important and too complex to be understood from books. Part of the problem here is that, for their vocational potential, screenwriting courses tend to be popular, and universities want to run them. I really believe that screenwriting is, in any real way, unteachable simply as a classroom-based study. There is, however, a great deal to be said for a course in drama writing *per se* as a foundation from which students can go on and study the film/TV/radio drama making process.

For theatre, the watershed date of 1968 is particularly significant. After the repeal of official theatre censorship in Britain, plays no longer had to be submitted to the Lord Chamberlain for approval, before they could be rehearsed and staged.[2] Even after a script had been approved, representatives from the Lord Chamberlain's office might well visit the theatre incognito, to make sure no untoward ad libs or other changes had crept into the production.

Until 1968, therefore, there were strict controls applied to representations of royalty onstage, of important historical figures, explicit references to sexuality, nudity, potentially blasphemous content, and the censorship of 'bad' language. It is extraordinary (and salutary?) to realize that writing for the theatre has only had the same freedoms accorded to the novel and poetry for less than half a century. The post-censorship theatrical landscape not only helped transform who wrote and performed what, where it was performed and to whom, but tacitly now made it possible to teach dramatic writing in ways which were very different from the years before 1968.

During the 1970s a whole range of new dramatic phenomena emerged: writing, venues, studio spaces, touring companies who performed plays in community halls, in schools, pubs, basements – anywhere with a space and an audience. The range and vibrancy of this theatre has been chronicled elsewhere.[3] Alternatively called 'fringe', 'alternative', 'underground', 'political', it was closely linked with the cultural and political movements of the time: socialism, feminism, the gay movement, avant-garde artistic experiments, in poetry, performance art and theatre, often incorporating moves to democratize theatre-making and theatre-going. An academic counterpart generated new thinking in psychoanalysis, structuralism, postmodernism – the increasing presence of cultural and literary theory – or, as some would have it, 'Theory'. [4]

As I developed my approaches to teaching dramatic writing, I found that I had to embed within the process correctives to widespread assumptions of what a dramatic text is, and where the writer's focus and responsibility lies. I was articulating and explaining ideas which were colloquial versions of theoretical formulations, and challenging some unthinking clichés about writing drama.

This was not at all calculated; it just happened. In the moment-to-moment experience of the class, I was almost constantly negotiating between theory and praxis without the fact ever being articulated. In any case, referring to theory in conceptual language would have made no sense to students who were not required to read and study this kind of material. Even when students were taking courses in critical theory, it made no impact on their approach to writing.

2.

In this chapter, a half-way house between fully amplified theoretical/aesthetic discussion and practical guidance, my account is necessarily presented in a different discourse from the way it happens in the classroom; in the way I work, everything emerges in relation to the writing done in class (I don't call this work 'exercises', because they are not – see later). However, no matter what the differences are and however minimally conceptual this account is, the issues raised need to be seriously considered by teachers and students of dramatic writing alike.

The clichéd assumptions with which students and many teachers approach dramatic writing are widespread. They appear in practical books about acting and directing, they appear in performance theory, postmodern and semiological analyses of theatre. I call them clichés because they seem to have taken root in ways which are not questioned. They need institutional, practical and theoretical deconstruction.

The first, most misleading cliché is that the dramatic text on the page is only a 'blueprint' for performance. The rest of this chapter could be taken up with an extensive bibliography in which this cliché is taken for granted; by virtue of its constant assertion, the cliché is elevated to quasi-theoretical status, or to a 'universal truth'.

It follows from the 'blueprint' idea that the text does not exist adequately as an object for scrutiny, until it has been lifted off the page and embodied in performance – on stage, in film, TV or radio. Because performance-based theory in part arose in reaction against the historical convention of studying plays-on-the-page, the degree of academic over-compensation has now created a definition of the dramatist who necessarily writes an incomplete text: 'It is because the playtext is such a strange – incomplete – object – that it seems useful to have a guide as to how someone might get the most out of dealing with this object.'[5]

The dramatist is thus immediately corralled. S/he supposedly provides inherently incomplete work: the blueprint, which is always secondary, always lesser and offering only the starting point, a signpost for the 'real thing', for which the director and the rest of the team are responsible. This is a profoundly ironic state of affairs, given that theatre history is still often studied in terms of its playwrights, and in which (performance-based theatre apart) there can be no performance and therefore no theatre without a text. Performance theory, interesting as it always is, is also inherently unstable and provisional: no one theatre performance is ever identical to any another – there is never a performance 'object' which can be reliably identified. This in itself is a fascinating condition of live performance, but it is its problematic impact on dramatist and written text which concerns me here.

The analytically useful distinction between 'dramatic text' and 'performance text' has produced notions about drama as an incomplete written text, and about the dramatist as a writer of the incomplete – a diminished value is thus accorded to the working dramatist. If the writer produces the 'incomplete' dramatic text rather than the 'completed' performance text, as characterized by Keir Elam and others, the relative value judgement is clear.[6] The writer is clearly ascribed lesser importance. One might at this point legit-imately wonder why any writer should ever bother to sit down and write something which is inherently incomplete? Because they're star struck, or just plain masochistic?

Paradoxically, then, while the published, performed and/or canonical (live or dead) dramatist is privileged, as a working writer s/he is theoretically diminished. The notion that the only good (because never troublesome) writer is a dead writer has a particularly resonant irony for the dramatist. The Death of the Author is far more than a sophisticated piece of postmodern analysis: it encapsulates with painful poignancy the way many dramatists experience their involvement in production.

There is an institutional corollary to this – or perhaps it is the institutional cause which gives rise to the theory? If we analyse the relationship between the dramatist and the power and authority structures as they operate in the dramatic media, we can see other versions of this situation. I am referring here to 'power' and 'authority' as institutionally defined, not as attributes which are desirable or not.

In all dramatic forms of production, there are clearly demarcated skills – a division of labour: who does what, and how the skills are linked. The writer writes, the director directs. Sounds simple. The writer acquires skills to do one thing well, the director acquires skills to do another thing well. Each refines their expertise during the course of their cultural practice as part of the production of the dramatic event – whether it is theatre, film, TV, radio or video.

However, institutionally there are further important distinctions. Whereas the writer's job begins and ends with the act of producing the written text (writers may be consulted on casting, set, etc., but even when consultation is enshrined in a contract, it doesn't guarantee full consultation, participation or agreement), the director's responsibility extends over a wider field. S/he not only puts together the final artefact in performance, but also co-ordinates all the artistic and technical skills, and is ultimately accountable to the management/producer. This gives the director overarching responsibility, and an inevitable degree of power. This is the predominant model we have across the perfor-mance industry.

The closest working relationship a dramatist is likely to have is with the director. A dramatic text will stand or fall on its first showing, depending on the director's achievement. Good direction and performance (begging the detailed question of what that is!) can cover weaknesses in the writing. Bad direction (ditto) can destroy a brilliant text. A director who has commissioning power can make the reputation of a new dramatist by ensuring that they continue to have their plays produced.

When a dramatic text in any medium goes into production, however welcome the writer may be, however many changes might be made to the text during the process, the writer's job is essentially done. The writer becomes an informed spectator, but never-theless no more than that: a spectator with special interests, but not a central participant. Production can as easily (some might say more easily) take place without the writer as with him/her. During the 1970s, the Writers' Guild and the Theatre Writers' Union spent a great deal of time putting in place a contract which asserted and protected theatre writers' rights. The right to presence in rehearsal was a hard-won principle – and one for which the writer is rarely, if at all, paid. BBC radio drama contracts have a participation clause in the writer's contract, with a pitifully tiny payment for a day's attendance. In film, the writer has an even tougher time. This is not likely to encourage any writer to believe their presence (or, indeed, their work, perhaps) is really taken seriously or fully acknowledged.

It is a rare thing to find fully harmonious relationships between writers and directors in any medium. Of course, it does happen, and generally this is because there is (a) familiarity with each other's work, (b) genuine and mutual understanding about the nature of each other's skills and an acknowledgement that each must be allowed to 'author' only their own work, (c) each likes and approves the other's contribution, (d) there is some kind of *modus operandi* which allows for communication between and across skills.

The more common case is the situation where the writer thinks/feels that their work is not understood and/or wants to intervene in the directorial process: don't, you can't, it's not your job and no one will let you anyway. Or there is the situation where the director thinks they perceive textual problems, and think they know exactly what rewriting needs to be done; in some cases, they may even think they can rewrite lines better than the writer can. Don't; you are not a writer, and even if you do identify something in the dialogue which may need attention, that doesn't mean you know what the solution is.

Writing and directing are intrinsically different skills. To be able to do the one is rarely to be able to do the other. It takes a professional lifetime to do both well. Some writers do direct and some directors do write, but this doesn't affect the basic point. Directors (for institutional and skills-based reasons) are always going to be in a position to alter texts, while writers can have absolutely no significant impact on direction/performance. Nor should they, perhaps. In many ways, one of the most exciting things about writing a dramatic text is that others bring to it amazing skills, and reveal things in your text which are new and exciting. It is always a risk, because it may go the other way. But those of us who write drama like living dangerously – up to a point, anyway.

The second cliché is that the director is only there to realize the 'vision' of the writer, to be a handmaid (*sic*) to the greater glory of the text. This sounds good; this sounds like revering the writer, like having the greatest respect for the writing. But even where this is a sincerely held approach, institutional imperatives mean that if the director wants to go another way, s/he can; the dramatist does not have the structural power (ultimately) to influence seriously, insist or veto. The respect and reverence are always in the director's gift or patronage. The director giveth and the director can also take away.

The third cliché is that the performance media are 'collaborative' arts. What this simply means is that lots of people work together on the same production, but it does not (in our conventional working structures) mean that all have the same decision-making power, or the same creative options. Teamwork, democratic or otherwise, only fully happens when it is structured in such a way that everyone contributes their own skill, while acknowledging the skills within the existing power structure. As far as dramatists go, this is another shibboleth which is bandied around to keep writers in their 'incomplete' box. On the surface it suggests cosy and/or stimulating artistic interaction, and at times, indeed, this is what it's like, but only within the constraints of the working structure. The problem with the cliché is that it serves to mask the authority structure and keep the writer in their constrained place.

The fourth cliché, applied particularly to film, but often used in relation to the other performance media, is that film (or whatever it is) is a 'visual' medium. In film and TV (visually-technologically weighted as they are) this leads to the assumption that 'stage directions' are – effectively – more important than dialogue. The dramatist, goes the cliché, needs to be able to visualize, i.e. think/write pictures, descriptions of place, setting, and/or matter about the emotions and motivations of the 'characters'. In radio this takes the form of suggesting lots of sound 'effects'. In fact, to write dramatically for either of these media is based on knowing how to utilize the technical possibilities within the dialogue-based structure of the work, not on whether one can write clever 'effects' or 'shots'. Again there is a confusion between the dramatic text proper and the performance text which follows.

Cliché number five is related to the above: that a dramatic text is hard to read, and that training is needed to make sense of what is on the page. This may have some surface truth, but is actually about something quite different, not the mystique of the performance form. Any idea that reading dramatic texts is harder than reading a novel is less a comment on the nature of the dramatic text than on the fact that in our culture the novel is still the dominant fictional form.

Within the novel, the overarching, singular fictional narrative voice sets the terms of reading. Without this, and the conventional elements of 'description', etc., the dramatic text appears to be lacking, to be relatively empty. This is yet another rationalization of the relative inferiority of the dramatic form itself: again, it is seen as an 'incomplete' piece of fiction with the important bits missing. After all, dialogue in the novel is generally a minor element. So a dramatic text continues to carry an extended 'minority' status. The argument goes that first of all, the writer must (as part of their craft) learn to visualize (i.e. to provide all those elements to which others in the production process contribute), and secondly, that stage directions help untrained people to read the text more easily. More easily, that is, because then it can feel more like a novel (albeit still seriously 'lacking').

These five major clichés lead to the pivotal issue of stage directions. These highlight three important issues: aesthetic, institutional and writerly. The nature and function of stage directions is historically determined. If one compares the minimal stage directions in a play by Shakespeare with their fulsome presence in the plays of George Bernard Shaw, and then again in plays by Harold Pinter or Caryl Churchill, one can see how variable and disposable the phenomenon of the stage direction is.

British 'high art' drama came back into literary prominence around the end of the nineteenth century. Until well into the twentieth century plays carried a transitional legacy (from the dominance of the novel in the nineteenth century) in the way stage directions appeared: with a single-voiced narrator dipping in and out of the dialogue. But even though, as in the case of Shaw, the written texts themselves sometimes appear to be hybrid novel/dramas, the dominance of the dialogue as determinant of narrative, relationships, themes, etc., defines them as dramas rather than novels. Stage directions are aesthetically on the cusp between novel and drama, and from the writerly perspective involve crucially different ways of imagining and writing.

Dialogue has no built-in singular narrative voice. Or, to put it another way, ALL dialogue is, at the moment of its appearance on the page and on the stage, written in the directly articulating first person in the present moment of speaking, rather than in a first-person narrative of events which have happened or are happening elsewhere.

When one reads dialogue in a novel, even though there may be surrounding narrative, description and context, in the moment of dialogue there is nothing else. We read the exchange in its present-tenseness, the now-ness of the fictional people speaking. We are able to do this because we grasp the signs on the page which indicate an interactive exchange between people, through the convention/signs of dialogue-speech.

Reading a dramatic text is an expanded version of this – and more. In the reading of a dramatic text, then, we each draw implicitly on our understanding of novel-reading – not, necessarily, to 'fill in' the gaps, but to read across the gaps, to read what is not there (or what might not be there) from what is there. We are thus reading gaps and absences (pace Macherey) as we read the dialogue. By this I do not mean that we imagine what characters look like or how they are moving or where they are sitting – I mean that we do not need to know these things in order to read the dialogue. In dialogue we are 'reading' relationships, which is what drama is all about.

As I say in my classes, again and again, sometimes in jest, always in total, emphatic seriousness, in drama there is nothing but dialogue, there is only dialogue, and the dialogue is all. If the dramatist – for whatever medium – cannot imagine and create the whole fictional shebang through dialogue, forget it. This is not an easy matter. While everyone, in my experience, can sit down and write a short scene of dialogue (after all, we all know what talking is, what having a conversation is), the ability to work only with and through dialogue is a far more taxing imaginative task. For most people, the experience of writing prose fiction comes more easily – the single narrative voice is easier to grasp imaginatively, and to write within.

This can be tested with any play: take away the stage directions in a play by Shaw, and the text will still be complete and stageable. Take away the dialogue in the same play, leaving only the stage directions, and narrative, story, relationships have all gone. The dramatic, stageable, indeed readable text has gone. It may be worth also adding that, however wonderfully visualized, imagined and indicated in stage directions, no drama is ever accepted and staged on the basis that its visuals are good. The argument stands for film, too, although the issues here are more complexly intertwined. But, unless it is a silent movie, no screenplay is ultimately accepted on the basis that the visuals (in prose) are 'good', if the dialogue (i.e. the story, narrative, relationships, etc.) is not.

In any case, all dramatic texts, including film, the moment they become candidates for production, are immediately denuded, explicitly or otherwise, of their stage directions. Setting, design, subtleties of interpretation included by the dramatist for readability are not only the first to go out of the window, they MUST go out of the window, since no dramatist can ever really anticipate what direction and performance will bring.

Even someone wanting to realize the detail of stage directions will have huge problems. The subtly placed pauses and silences in Harold Pinter's plays are often held up as examples of stage directions vital to the text. And in the loosest sense, of course they are. He wrote them. But how long is a pause? How long is one pause compared to another? And even when this is decided, any production of the play might reveal either other ways of pacing the delivery to reduce a pause to almost nothing, and/or to discover other places where the pacing of the dialogue allows for new pauses.

Stage directions can never represent a dramatist's realizable intentions for how the play is to be staged, even if written with total conviction and enthusiasm. This applies as much to bracketed instructions for expression, such as (*smiles*) or (*tragically*), which seem to instruct performers how to perform or inflect a line or a word. This is not simply because our post-Stanislavski age has created rehearsal norms where director and cast enjoy exploring all sorts of psychological, emotional and gestural ways of delivering lines, but because it is inherent in the signifying conventions of the text itself that all 'directions' are misnomers. Not only are these directions patently imprecise at best (what does 'smiling' mean? How many different smiles are there?), but it is evident from the fact that each production of any play varies, that while the dialogue remains the same, the process of production – set, lighting and performances – may be very different. The only real 'directions' in any dramatic text lie in the dialogue: directions to the performers about what they have to say, not how they could/should/might say it. Actions, even when spelled out in stage directions, only ever need to be absolutely minimalist. The actions are always embedded within the dialogue.

There is an analogy in music texts, where much is made of the post-diatonic convention of including expression marks along with the notes on the page. This encourages the idea that playing a section marked 'forte' loudly is somehow realizing the composer's 'intentions'. Here impossible ambiguities of interpretation operate, similar to those relevant to the realization of stage directions. It is not that it is necessarily wrong to try, but no expression mark can ever be as precise as a crotchet, which, while it may be a slow or a fast crotchet, always has a set of reference points to which to relate (the breve, the semi-breve). At best, only approximations are feasible, and while interpretation is always relevant for dialogue too, the words, like the notes in the musical score, are the only signs which must, in the end, be read at face value.

Within the dominant conventions of musicology and music performance, much is still made of playing the music as the composer 'intended'. In the developing theorization of creative writing, the notion of authorial intentionality seems to be making a comeback (not, I suspect, that it ever really went away). After being debunked as the Intentional Fallacy, and being thrown out of court via the Death of the Author, large parts of creative writing pedagogy now/again insist that the writer's intentions are, after all, crucial in assessing the success of a piece of writing. While this chapter cannot be a comprehensive refutation of this last-ditch attempt to reinstate the unverifiable, my discussion of the impossibility of stage directions is one example of the way in which intentionality is at odds not only with the imperatives of the dramatic text, but also in relation to the process of dramatic production.

The development of a way of teaching dramatic writing led me into these theoretical formulations, and back into taking on clichés and assumptions with which normally I would never have bothered. But in the process of teaching, these matters come up in the minds of students, whether they have read theory or not, and have to be dealt with.

The dominant convention of 'how-to' creative writing books is the 'exercise'. Books and articles contain favourite exercises; teachers 'borrow' exercises from others. This is not how I work. During the course of a module, or across a whole year, I get students to build up a 15 to 20-minute drama in class. This is written scene by scene in each class, and works similar to the way music ensemble or fine art classes may be conducted. Each student accumulates a short number of scenes, which, by the end of the course, form a complete play. The experience of completing is vital to this, since all writing – it is often very useful to articulate the obvious – starts and ends, and the relationship between beginning and end, and therefore the nature of 'structure', can only really be understood in this way.

The plays are built up in a flexible fashion: they may begin at the beginning and proceed to the end, or they may not. They may be pre-planned or they may not. Everything about (a) the imaginative and technical processes of writing drama and (b) the implications in terms of words lifted off the page and into the three-dimensional conventions of performance, is dealt with out of issues which arise during the course of the classes. That is why it is impossible for me to represent a series of 'lesson plans' or discrete, or even developmental 'exercises'. I know the order in which I am likely to deal with certain issues, and everything is always covered.

There are two absolute rules which I impose all the way through:

1. No stage directions.
2. No monologues.

I have already spelled out in some detail the rationale behind the first 'rule'. The monologue, whether it carries the connotations of the Shakespearian soliloquy, the Restoration comedy aside, the Brechtian 'alienation' device, the polemical monologue of

1970s political theatre, or the narrative monologue in plays of the 1990s, like stage directions, also belongs to the writerly convention of prose fiction, rather than drama. In performance, a monologue can be extraordinarily gripping and dramatic – because it becomes dramatized story-telling, and the better the performer, the more gripping the dramatic event; but monologues are not drama. They are theatrical short stories. They are very popular among directors and performers, because they are cheap, they enable a single performer to control every aspect of the world of their narrative, and they're handy as audition speeches.

The enthusiasm for monologues, in both writing and performance, also relates to concepts of the fourth wall, that invisible divider between performers and audience. While it is undoubtedly the case that the interaction between the two is what makes each performance unique, it must be remembered that a performance can perfectly well take place without an audience (it's called rehearsal), and that the fourth wall never disappears (it never disappeared in Brechtian theatre, or in audience participation pieces, or even in music hall). It is, in fact, the constant explicit or implicit movements around the fourth wall which lends these apparently disruptive modes their excitement. The word 'apparently' is crucial.

The monologue appears to be addressed directly to the audience, rather than to someone onstage, 'as if' the fourth wall were not there. Of course, it always is. Even the (in his time) shocking devices Brecht incorporated, where 'characters' appeared to step out of 'character' and address the audience directly, with interpretations and messages, should be seen as a device within a device; compounding the levels of theatrical illusion, but never dismissing them. The appealing transparency of the first-person monologue is only another theatrical trick – since trickery and collusive illusion is what it's all about.

3. (4)

The emphasis in my teaching, then, is on the constantly shifting and changing relationship between: (1) The imagination and the page. (2) The page and the performance space. (3) Ways in which 2 might impact on 1.

This process involves continuous observation and close textual analysis, NEVER any kind of value judgement on the writing. This doesn't mean a woolly liberalism, in which anything goes. But in the context of a class and short, timed writing exercises, it takes all the time there is to analyse the dramatic implications of what is written. I have commented elsewhere about the relationship between value judgements and creative writing pedagogy.[7] By further analogy here, we enter into what the material is in a creative writing class; what the object (as against the objective) of study is. The students' writing is the raw material out of which aesthetic, linguistic and theoretical issues can be discussed.

4. (3)

My suggestions for other kinds of work is – and these should be done at the same time – first, to spend weeks reading nothing but stage plays, in order to internalize, through reading, what a dramatic text 'is'. Even for people interested in film, TV and radio, reading stage plays will far more easily enable the would-be dramatist to internalize what it means to imagine everything in terms of interactive dialogue. Reading published film scripts to see how other people have written film scripts is a different exercise, as much concerned with the formulae of presentation as the imaginative aspects of the genre.

In the nature of commercial things, only established dramatists are published in collected volumes. Read anything. Think about the cultural/racial/ethnic/gender provenance of the writers, and see how this may be part of their choices of subject matter and styles of writing. Start by reading every word of the plays, and after you have read a few, ignore the stage directions and read only the dialogue. Avoid reading novels while you do this, if you can.

At the same time, go and see as many stage plays as possible. It doesn't matter what you see (it may well depend on the cost of tickets anyway). It also doesn't matter whether you like what you see – except insofar as it may affect your enthusiasm! But the point of this is to take in the entire experience, the *mise-en-scène*, and distinguish/analyse your response to all the different elements which go to make up the experience. This will enable you to 'see' what is written text, what is performance, what the direction does, what the lighting is/does, what the set is/does. Ultimately, the most important analytical outcome is the ability to separate (after the event) the written text from each element which makes it into a three-dimensional performance. See a play, then read the text, if it is published. Or vice versa. But move in your reading between page and stage, just as your writing will do via a very different process.

EPILOGUE

I am revising this chapter after returning from one of my adult education Playwriting courses, at the City Literary Institute, in London. The group is varied, in age, amount of experience in writing, degrees of ambition. There is no accreditation attached to the class, which means that the process has a freedom about it which is rather different from the atmosphere of a university setting. I work in the same way; each student accumulates a number of scenes, and there are a series of preconceptions (not always conscious) which have to be demolished.

There is the fact that, once written, a scene must be lifted 'off the page'. For this, more than one copy of the text is necessary, so that each performer can have their own script, to read their own 'voice' in the dialogue. It is extraordinary how long it takes many students to realize why this is necessary – to make the transition from page to stage. In the class, I get students to 'move' their scenes at one end of the room, and as soon as they get up from their chairs, whether they have acting experience or not, the imperatives of performance take over. Now they are bodies in space, being watched. It often takes a number of sessions before they understand that any ad libs (e.g. 'am I in this scene?' or 'whoops, I've dropped my script') interrupt the world of the text. The distance travelled between imagination to the page to the stage is far greater than one might think, and it is that journey which has to be made, before any drama, for any medium, can be written.

Chapter 7

Scriptwriting for Radio

Steve May
Bath Spa University

1. INSTINCT AND ANALYSIS

Radio is my first love.[1] It's where I started as a writer. Unlike novel writing (which I still find excruciatingly hard) scriptwriting for radio came very easily to me. I'd listened to so many radio plays, my ideas seemed to form themselves into a radio identity very early in the creative process. I had an instinctive (or unconsciously acquired) feel for structure, dialogue, scene shape and scene linking. I automatically 'heard the play in my head'.

Did that make me a good teacher of radio writing? Far from it. There can hardly be a less helpful teacher than an 'instinctive' writer enjoining others to be instinctive too. I had never consciously thought through what I was doing and why I was doing it.

It was only when I began to teach writing at undergraduate level that I thought about what I did as a writer, and analysed the processes I went through at each stage of developing an idea into a finished piece.

For all my vaunted instinctive grasp of the medium, I have very rarely (successfully) written a play through from the beginning to the end. I know some writers who work exclusively in this way – they argue that they can't know where they're going, they have to surprise themselves in order to keep interested, etc. - but in my experience this method of writing is more or less fatal for a beginner, and often leads to torture and torment even for the most experienced practitioner. The beginner who refuses to analyse or plan usually gets stuck around page 5. You won't know why you got stuck. You'll say things like, 'it seemed to run out of steam', or (even less analytic) you'll preserve the glowing memory of that piece as it came to you as a bright idea, you'll refer to it as 'a play I'm working on', even though you haven't taken it out of the computer equivalent of the bottom drawer for five years, and the thought of looking at it again appals you. You have a remote comforting sense that one day you'll go back to it, and all will work out well.

You never do go back to it.

So what was my (unanalysed) method? Most plays started from snatches of dialogue, or characters – very rarely events. I'd jot things down, other characters would appear, and the piece would proceed by a mixture of compilation and rolling revision. So, I would write experimental bits and pieces from different parts of an idea, and then cut and paste them together, meanwhile editing, and filling in gaps. I would rearrange scenes, shortening, lengthening, changing, until the sequence 'felt right'. I would then find a beginning, and start there, physically rewriting each draft in longhand until I got to a point where it didn't work. Then I'd go back to overview, rearrange, write new bits, throw out old ones, and then start again at the beginning.

These days, I'd say I was working simultaneously in the two ways essential for any writer: on the one hand using intuitive writing to get to know the characters, find out who they are and what they want, what story they want to be involved in; on the other analysing, identifying key moments and linking them to build towards a climax and then resolution. Does it help for a writer to know this? Maybe not if a project is going well and easy. It's when it won't go right that the 'theory' really comes into its own. If applied properly, it will tell you why the thing isn't working. Now, that won't actually and necessarily enable you to put it right, but it is a good long step in that direction. Apply scene analysis to that moving sequence involving the little girl and the puppy, and you find that for all the delightful pathos of dialogue, nothing has actually happened. In short, you know why it's in the computer equivalent of the bottom drawer, and you know why the thought of pulling it out again appals you. You certainly need never refer to the myth of block.

So, while I can't personally go to the structural extremes of Syd Field (see Field (2003), for example) or Robert McKee (1999), I do believe structure is essential, and that (in whatever way suits you best) you should be thinking about structure from the earliest stages of composition. Because, although a well-structured piece of work may not be inspired, or original, an inspired and original piece of work must still be well structured (even if the writer is not aware of that structure). It does even the wildest original genius no harm to know general principles, if only to facilitate his or her revolt.

How does one get this across to students?

With some difficulty. Most (at least when they start their course) believe that writing depends entirely on 'inspiration', and simply involves sitting down and writing your inspiration as it appears in your head, until it runs out (which we have observed is usually around page 5). Anything other than this 'pure' act of writing is seen as unacceptable compromise. Planning is tedious and inhibiting, revision is downright dishonest. To quote one:

> I don't like editing my writing, because when I write it, that is what I think, and if you edit what you write, you are changing what you think, so it isn't true.[2]

The writing process is linear, and one-off. These students are like marathon runners who haven't done any training, trying to run an unmarked course the whereabouts and layout of which they have only the vaguest notion. They may get to the end, but it is a very long shot, and they're unlikely to break any records.

So, one of the key aims of any creative writing course, but particularly one devoted to scriptwriting (novelists can get away with waffle), is to get students out of this linear, one-off state of mind, to encourage them to see a play as a project, which has a definite shape and structure, and of which the words are only a small part. Inspiration, while welcome, is not necessary all the time, and can be sought, as well as waited on. Further, inspiration is not something that can appear in our learning contract. What they can learn are techniques, both of work and of structure. There are plenty of things a writer can do while not inspired which will serve to advance the project.

Put another way, the first aim of any writing course should be to make students better editors of their own work. This isn't as simple as it sounds. Often it is misguidedly thought that editing only means copy editing, that is, nit picking, word-by-word polishing. So, after workshopping, a student of the one-off linear persuasion might grudgingly agree to change the odd word here or there. The suggestion that they might need to actually chop some, move big parts, start in a different place, is greeted with blank incomprehension.

Word-by-word editing is only appropriate at a late stage in the writing process, and can be positively harmful if undertaken too early. How many students (and writers in general) waste their time agonizing over whether it should be 'sofa' or 'settee', when the whole scene in which the furniture occurs needs removal?

So, I include under the heading 'editing' all those skills involved in taking an idea, teasing it out, considering options, finding the story, structuring that story, developing a plot, research (of all kinds, for example into genre, length, markets), exploring characters, and (eventually) writing the dialogue. To quote Peter Brook:

> A word does not start as a word – it is an end product which begins as an impulse, stimulated by attitude and behaviour which dictates the need for expression. This process occurs inside the dramatist; it is repeated inside the actor. Both may be only conscious of the words, but both for the author and then for the actor the word is a small visible portion of a gigantic unseen formation. (1990: 15)

If your students grasp this picture of the business of the writer, if they accept that dialogue is only a small part of a play, that they may have to write 100 pages to find 100 good words, once they accustom themselves to interrogating any idea they have for its pre-ferred genre, length, market, once they abandon any thought of inspiration, and accept the fact that there is a good lot of work you can do when you aren't inspired, then they are some way to understanding what it is to be a writer, and perhaps becoming a writer themselves.

2. TEACHING AND LEARNING: KEY POINTS

It's usual for teachers of radio writing to say: 'In this medium you can go anywhere and do anything.' In principle, yes. But if we are talking about writing for radio which might get broadcast, then there are certain caveats. In the UK, the BBC has a virtual monopoly in the commissioning of radio drama (although up to 20 per cent of output is made by independent companies): although it is a cheap form compared to television, it is still horrendously expensive compared to chat or recorded music output. Only the BBC has the resources to make radio drama in bulk. This means, in effect, that the BBC defines the genre.

This raises a group of related questions: how far should industry conditions shape the teaching of radio writing? Should one teach a medium to the full extent of its artistic possibilities, or should one anchor oneself to the limits imposed by the 'real' world? Should one reference the real world at all at undergraduate degree level?

Some colleagues still look askance at any such pollution of the ivory tower. Surely, they argue, to allow the intrusion of mundane considerations of market, resources, and industry standard practices is a compromise, and a big slide on the slippery slope towards mere vocational 'utilitarianism'. But on the other hand, is it acceptable to teach students without at least some information about what they are likely to encounter outside the academy?

The point is even clearer regarding television. Given current opportunities in mainstream television drama, not just for new writers, but for any writers, are we justified in luring students into the complexities (and perhaps indulgences) of (say) Dennis Potter, when the best they are going to get a chance to write (to start with) is an episode of a day-time soap? Likewise in radio, should we encourage them to use fancy, subtle (and technically time-consuming) techniques, if those likely to buy their work give specific advice such as (about the 11:30–12 a.m. slot):

> Clear, simple plots and smaller casts should make it easy for listeners to follow the narrative, given that this is still quite a busy time of day.

Or (about the afternoon play, 2:15–3 p.m.):

> The dynamics of the storytelling should be clear and well signposted. Overuse of sound effects and playing with form will be less suitable for this daytime audience which is listening while engaged in light housework or driving. ... The slot will aim to increase the listening in cars by ensuring that the programmes are not too complex in their use of sound or storytelling.[3]

The best approach seems to me to be to define those elements of the 'real' world which aren't just incidental, but which actually shape the art of the possible, and are hence key in the development of a writer, whether they compromise or rebel.

A simple example: as a radio dramatist you might feel driven to write a full-length, 90-minute script. Unfortunately, since 1995, the BBC does not regularly commission 90-minute scripts (with the exception of a vanishing few on Radio 3, and on Radio 4 on special occasions). If you want the best chance to have your work broadcast, you should think in terms of 45 minutes, or at most one hour. If you insist on the 90, then you will either have to work very hard to sell your piece, or you will have to look for alternative methods of airing it. It surely does the student no harm to understand these conditions, and in fact puts them in a position to make an informed decision.

Likewise with content: since 1995 the BBC has become more and more command led, more and more prescriptive about what it wants in terms of tone and content in the various slots. Controllers are no longer content to sit back and let the programme makers make programmes; commissioners try and theme and match output to audience profile, and producer/directors increasingly want writers who will write to a brief rather than writers with ideas of their own.[4] In terms of the writing process, it is increasingly unlikely that the writer who locks himself away in a garret, writes a script, and sends it in, will hear it on air. If we want more Milk Wood, maybe we should send our students to the pub and caution them under no circumstances to deliver a commission on time. However, their chances of getting their wayward masterpiece on air will be very small.[5]

Therefore, it would be disingenuous to laud the medium's flexibility, range and capacity without adding this caveat: if you want your play broadcast, you may have to compromise somewhere along the line.

Collaboration

Like any script medium, radio drama is essentially collaborative. This affects the writer in many ways. Even if you are working on your own idea, there will inevitably be input from other people: from the producer/director/script editor, and then in studio, from the actors and studio staff. When I first started I wanted every word, every sound to be exactly as I had heard it in my head. I quickly learned that this was not only impossible, but undesirable. If your script is any good at all, it can be handled in an infinite variety of ways. Of course, your best can be ruined, but also what you secretly feel are weak bits can suddenly be transformed by a brilliant performance, or a good directorial note, or a good technical suggestion.

It is therefore essential to build this collaboration into the teaching process. The question remains, how far should one go in reproducing industry conditions?

Recently we experimented by splitting a radio writing class in half: one group (as is usual) both wrote and acted their pieces; the other teamed up with a group of actors. At first the control (no actor) group were suspicious of the extra benefits their colleagues were getting; but as the course developed, it was the actor group which beefed the most. Baldly, we had reproduced the industry role of the writer too exactly: namely, a lot of sitting around doing nothing while the director works with the actors and technicians. Meanwhile the control group had the benefit of acting out each other's work, and hence understanding it much more intimately and effectively.

This leads on to the related question, how much time should you spend on technicalities? Of course, a radio/audio writer must 'hear the play in his/her head', so it is essential to do some recording and playback (see the 'chase' exercise below), but given limited time, what kind of balance should be struck? To watch the elements of a radio drama being edited together on a digital editor is for many a mind expanding and inspiring experience – to actually see the sounds being orchestrated into visible patterns, to have the mix split up into identifiable factors. To *use* a digital editor is perhaps even more liberating (and great fun) – but given time constraints, at what point do we have to rename our course 'Radio writing and digital editing'?

So, if we aren't going to go very far down the technical line, maybe we can't afford the digital editor, or the technical expertise to use it properly – is it then pedagogically justified to use equipment that is either well below or different from current industry standards? For one thing, technology is changing so fast;[6] is it essential to keep up to date with latest developments? Or is old equipment satisfactory for pedagogic purposes?

I have no simple answer to these questions, other than to conclude that it is essential that students see their play as something other than words on a page. The larger context, both in terms of market and technical resources, will (or should) have an impact on how they think about their work, and what they eventually produce.

3. READINGS IN RADIO DRAMA

Radio drama is notoriously neglected as an art form, certainly in the English-speaking world.[7] There are a few 'How To' books,[8] fewer critical texts,[9] and virtually no scripts in print.[10] Plays in audio book form are also very thin on the ground.[11]

Most teachers of radio drama that I know rely on their private collections either of recorded output or scripts. If I hear a play which is of particular interest I will contact the producer, and ask very nicely for a CD (with the writer's permission). Very few writers will object to having their work studied at degree level. You may even manage to get a script.

So far as I know, only one PhD thesis in the UK is devoted to radio drama. What a wide-open and inviting field.

4. STRATEGIES FOR TEACHING RADIO WRITING

Listening

The term 'radio drama' has culturally specific implications in the UK. For persons over a certain age, it means a large wood box of a receiver with Hilversum, Sunday lunch and the Family (in the 1950s, pre-TV) gathered to be educated and entertained. For persons under that age, it probably means little, or nothing.[12]

It is exceptional among a group of twenty undergraduates to find more than one or two who have consciously listened to a radio play. When confronted with the term 'radio drama', their typical reaction is bewilderment ('I didn't know there was such a thing'). They may have overheard something that might have been a play on the radio in the kitchen, their parents might listen to *The Archers*. So, although younger people are used to aural entertainment, certainly in the form of increasingly sophisticated categories of music, and also in spoken word formats including popular book readings (many aimed at children), they probably have no concept of radio drama.

Given the task of going away and finding a radio play and listening to it (not that arduous in the UK, where there are plays on every day of the week, not to mention soap opera, sitcoms and serials), students can have problems. To start with, many can't tell the difference between a play and a reading, and in some cases will bring back a report on a documentary programme.

Further, once they've found a play, many also report difficulties in the act of listening: their attention wanders, they have trouble identifying characters, they can't tell what's going on, or where the action is set.

How, then, to introduce students to the listening experience? The fact is that only a minuscule proportion of the actual radio audience listens as a main activity, seated in a finely balanced acoustic with state of the art equipment (there are such people, but whether they constitute the 'proper' audience at which radio writers should be aiming is another question entirely). In the UK, according to BBC research, the audience profile for the afternoon play is as follows:

> There are currently around 400,000 listeners at 14.15. ... Most are listening at home, although the car audience is growing towards the end. ... The audience is mainly middle aged and retired women with very few retired men listening at this point. Some middle aged working men are listening in cars. The audience is less AB than is typical for Radio 4. Many listeners are resuming domestic activity (housework, gardening, shopping, etc.) after the lunch-time break ... some plan activities such as sewing/ironing/paperwork to fit the play.[13]

Should one, then, try and reproduce these conditions when playing exemplary drama in a scriptwriting course? Of course we can't magically age our students, but, given the commissioning guidelines, can one expect a play written as supplementary activity to grasp and hold the attention of a group of people artificially gathered together in a seminar room, with nothing else to do but listen?

Some students certainly don't appreciate the devotion of much workshop time to passive listening:

> [The tutor brought in] these scripts from radio 4, and one lesson, he just like played them for the whole two hours or whatever it was. There was no direction of this is how you do it, this is how you write it.[14]

The group factor is important in itself. It is very different to be in a large audience as opposed to being alone. A group dynamic will almost certainly take over: if you're the only person gripped while 20 others shuffle, sigh and yawn, it's difficult to maintain concentration or interest.

My own compromise is to play students the opening of a wide variety of plays. Students are encouraged to doodle, draw, and also to note their responses, especially if they mentally 'switch off', which fact they signal. We will listen to the piece until a majority have signalled switch off, then stop and analyse why the play failed to grip. Occasionally, by mutual consent, we will listen right through to the end of something, and (of course) analyse why we stuck with the piece. It is instructive to note that the 'best written' or most 'complex' or 'literary' of pieces are not necessarily or perhaps even regularly the most gripping. Many students report a dichotomy of reaction, on one level acknowledging that a piece is perhaps weak or predictable, but also being drawn to hear what happens next.

What is it that grips a listener to a play?

Structure: actions, not words

It's a common if not universal fallacy to suppose that radio plays are necessarily, essentially, 'wordy'. Radio plays are as much rooted in action as any other form of drama. The actions must be conveyed in sounds, but they are essential all the same.

Therefore I advise students to think primarily in terms of events. Don't start off by trying to write beautiful words. Write beautiful words by all means: I do myself, and I usually leave them in the script right up to rehearsal stage. Then, once I've had the dubious pleasure of hearing that beautiful but static speech read out, I cut it. Beautiful words are usually the first darlings to get culled. Start by asking what characters want, and what they have to do to get what they want. Who opposes them?

Script is simple when it comes to structure. Scriptwriters freely ask the crude, basic questions that embarrass novelists: for example, is it a happy or sad ending? Are the audience supposed to like this character? Who's the hero, who's the villain? Script is all about choices, challenges, questions. One character wants something, and then tries to get it in a series of situations from a series of other people. The hero will probably ask the wrong person first. If your play is strong, there'll be a good reason why they have to ask the wrong person first. If your script is weak, then they ask the wrong person because if they asked the right person it would all end too quickly.

An illustration from the world of literature. In the Conan Doyle story 'The Lion's Mane',[15] a body is washed up on a beach with strange wounds. Sherlock Holmes happens along, suspects are identified, motives postulated, timescales investigated, only for Holmes (eventually) to reveal that the culprit was in fact an eponymous jellyfish. Case closed. The story then could be reduced thus:

Holmes and Watson walk along a beach.

WATSON: Look at this body with strange wounds. Let's search for the killer.

HOLMES: No need to search, I recognize these wounds; the culprit was certainly the variety of jellyfish known as the Lion's Mane.

If you can analyse your script down to this, then it may be as lacking in legs as a jellyfish. A good exercise is to ask students to take this story and find a way to give it real (rather than padded) substance. How? By trying to link the death to some human intention or agency.[16]

Every scene represents a choice, a decision to be made, and every scene should have 'impulse', that is, it points somewhere else. As a scriptwriter in any medium your job is to raise expectations, and then either satisfy or disappoint those expectations. Script is binary; however complex the motivations of your characters, they either do something or they don't. Take Hamlet: what's the basic underlying structure? The hero is either going to kill his uncle/stepfather, or not. It may take him four hours and much poetry and heart-searching to resolve this dilemma, but that is the key underlying engine, towards which everything should contribute.

So, if you can understand what the key choices are, and build scenes round them, then you are beginning to feel towards good structure.

Let's apply these principles to a typical beginner's radio play opening:

A car pulls up. The engine is switched off. The door opens. MRS DUVALIER steps out of the car and breathes in the fresh country air. We hear her feet scrunch up the twenty-seven yards of gravel path to the front door. She rings the door bell. She clicks open her compact and checks her make-up. The door opens.

BUTLER: Good afternoon Mrs Duvalier, do come in.

Lesson one: think of the microphone as the camera. As with a camera, there are a lot of clever things you can do with a microphone, and it is usually the beginner who wants to do these things (tracking, close ups, sunsets in the distance framed by blasted trees, etc.): but when you're learning I recommend that you imagine you only have one microphone, and it is fixed. If you have to move the microphone, then you must switch off your recorder, move the microphone, and then start recording again. Therefore, each location of the microphone will constitute a new scene.[17] If you then apply the rule that any scene in which nothing happens must be cut, you'll be somewhere on the way to only writing the bits that need to be written.

Therefore, going back to the arrival of Mrs Duvalier at the mansion, we see that the microphone performs an illegal act: it follows her from the car to the front door. We must avoid this movement, and decide where to put the microphone. By the car? Very well. But does anything happen by the car? Mrs Duvalier switches the engine off, and gets out; she breathes the air. Are any of these actions significant? It's possible (we can't tell without the full context) but unlikely. Therefore cut that section.

Shall we put the microphone by the front door of the mansion? If we do, then the pulling up of the car and all the business there will be too far away to register. However, a short 'approach' to the microphone might give a sense of perspective. But what happens at the door? Mrs D. powders her nose, and the Butler invites her in. Significant? It's possible, but unlikely. Most likely the best place to put the microphone (and hence start the play) is in the room with the person she's come to visit: hence car gone, gravel gone, door gone – and no need to agonize over whether the butler should say 'Do come in Mrs Duvalier', or 'Mrs Duvalier, do come in'.

Analysing your material in this way will cut out a lot of dead time, and help you start where you need to start.

Why now?

Characters in beginners' plays often say things like, 'we've argued this out a thousand times before'. The immediate response from the tutor/editor should be: why is today different? What is the trigger? Or put another way, in Aeschylus' *Agamemnon*, the Watchman's been watching out for the fires that announce the fall of Troy for ten years. On which night does the dramatist choose to start his play? Pretty obviously, the night that the fires are lit;[18] but metaphorically, many of us as beginners start the play on the first, second or third night, and our watchman manfully mounts the steps, spends an uneventful watch, and descends again in the morning with nothing accomplished, and nothing to report.

Of course, if you're writing a soap opera, then the rule is different. Depending on the story level – you may well want all 3,650 nights to string the thing out – raising expectation ('Is that a fire? I'm not sure. I don't know what I feel any more. We've got to talk, yes, but not now') and then deferring it. But if you're writing single drama, beware of phrases such as, 'I need to set the scene', or 'I need to establish the context', or 'there's a lot of exposition to go in the first scene'.

When I wrote the first three pilot episodes for a Radio 3 soap opera, the first was never used or broadcast. Why not? Because I'd written it for myself, so that I knew the characters and what was going on. Nothing actually happened in it.

Hearing the play in your head

Perhaps more than any other form of drama, a radio play needs rhythm. In this respect it is closer to music. As you write a radio script, you must constantly hear it running in your head. There will almost certainly be a tension between what you may regard as NECESSARY INFORMATION, and the internal rhythm of the sound (independent of meaning).

'Necessary' information is very often in fact unnecessary. In *The Governor*,[19] a play based exclusively on historical research, I imagined (in my first draft) that I needed to apprise the listener of the precise dates of each diary entry or memoir excerpt. My producer rightly pointed out that no listener could (a) take in the complex timescale I was trying to set up, (b) remember it in any meaningful way during the course of the play, or (c) have enough interest so to do. The listener will latch on to events, problems, characters, but not abstract information. There's a positive corollary here: characters don't have to be anywhere. They can speak, their speeches can be juxtaposed, and the listener doesn't have to know where or when they're speaking. Radio drama can stop time, and step out of time.

Similarly, listeners respond first and foremost to the emotional states of character. So, don't feel you have to spell everything out. One of the best pieces of advice I've had from a director was that a certain portion of my script was 'too much about what it was about'. In other words, the characters conversed something on the lines of:

A: I'm not sure if I love you enough to commit to you. You have a lovely laugh but also you have a tendency to be miserly and are something of a control freak.

B: Yes, I would agree about the miserliness, but this also reveals in me a certain carefulness about other people as well as myself, which could be beneficial in a long-term partner.

Much better to let your characters discuss something mundane and apparently insignificant: if there is a problem/story between them, it will come out whatever they talk about.

Take your characters out of the play. Trick them, tell them you just want them to talk, to think, to express themselves; promise them you won't use a single word of what they say in the script. This can loosen them up no end, if they don't feel they have to carry the plot and convey necessary information. That's how I found this play, and this opening, where I used virtually every word they said. If the characters had known they were in a play, I think they might have clammed up:

MARGARET:	I saw a man with a fox, this afternoon. He was carrying it, like a baby. It was asleep. Well, it wasn't moving. A little girl came up and stroked it, and it didn't move.
SELWYN:	(*Noiselessly reading credit card catalogue*) Probably a dog.
MARGARET:	No, it was a fox. I know what foxes look like. The little girl had to stand on tiptoe, but she stroked it, and it didn't move.
SELWYN:	They look like Corgis from a distance.
MARGARET:	They went by right outside the window. I was sitting there, where you are now. That's not a 'distance', is it?
SELWYN:	Otherwise, you've been OK?[20]

This happens to be one of the few plays I've written straight through from first words to end without any conscious planning. I never did find out what it was about.

Perspective

A common misconception is that radio drama must be 'flat' in terms of perspective and space. Nothing could be further from the truth. A standard and extremely effective exercise to demonstrate this is the 'chase' scene. One actor is close to mike, delivering a quickly concocted monologue expressing fear, regret, sense of threat. Three or four other actors go off to a distance (how far depends on the acoustic) and call out quickly invented threats (equals, we're going to get you, we're coming, etc.). 'Live', no one can hear what the hunted actor is saying, and there is no sense of perspective, even if you're near him or her. Play back the recording, and feel the intensity of the 'inner voice', and the vast canvas created between that voice and the remote hunters.

A note on presentation and drafting

In any kind of scriptwriting, there is the logistical question of format and presentation, not just which format to use, but at what stage of your drafting to start using it. One disgruntled student confronted me after several weeks of a course and demanded to know 'when you're going to tell us how to write a script'. It turned out he wasn't looking for deep insights into structure, character, or even dialogue, but for the format for presenting script. The implication also was that, once I'd given him this format, he would be able to write a play, and there is a serious danger here of confusing format with content.

Some writers (especially those who work on the American screenwriting system of total structural analysis before any 'wording in') write in format from draft one. They say they can't visualize what they're writing if it isn't correctly formatted. Others (especially writers like myself who find it difficult to say exactly when they are starting 'draft one') will only introduce standard format at a late stage. Why? I find if something looks 'official' it takes on a rigidity, is resistant to change. This is even more the case with student writers, to whom (as we have seen) the idea of revision can be repugnant. When I am experimenting with characters and dialogue, I get it down on paper as fast as possible. I don't even use speech prefixes. The common wisdom is, if you can't tell who's speaking without reference to the prefixes, then there's something wrong with the dialogue.

When it comes to final presentation, there is a BBC standard[21]. Trouble is, not all BBC practitioners know it or use it, and there have been contradictory statements in the BBC's own *Guidelines* for writers. Take, for example, the knotty subject of 'scenes'. On one page the would-be dramatist is told:

> Radio has no 'scenes' in the way that a stage play has. A sequence in a radio play might be one line long, or last for 20 pages.

Two pages later the reader is advised:

> Here is an example of how a radio script is laid out. Remember to always number your pages and your scenes.

Even more confusingly, in the example that follows, the scenes are not numbered.[22]

In practice, except in the most unusual of circumstances, the production will involve serial rehearse/recording of sections of the script, and almost certainly not in order. For logistical reasons, and simple convenience for communication with technical staff and actors, these sections must be divided up and labelled. Why not call them 'scenes'?

CONCLUSION

So, these are the paradoxes of radio writing, and teaching radio writing: one has a medium of potentially infinite breadth, subtlety and power, but actually chained to its current somewhat lame and limited cultural niche. Further, though, it has a large audience, most of whom are middle aged, getting older, and doing something else while listening. And though it is one of the best places for a writer to start their career, most young writers regard it with suspicion. Perhaps the growth of university-based creative writing courses, teaching radio writing as both a respectable and an exciting medium, may go some little way towards spreading the gospel, and increasing general appetite for this wonderful, underrated medium.

Chapter 8

Writing for Film and Television

Jack Epps, Jr
University of Southern California

1. THE IMPORTANCE OF ORIGINAL VOICE

> The reason one writes isn't the fact he wants to say something. He writes because he has something to say. (F. Scott Fitzgerald, *The Great Gatsby*)

Screenwriting has the unique distinction of being the only form of creative writing not intended to be read directly by the public. Poets and novelists publish, but there are no screenplays published without first having been produced as a motion picture. Yet, a screenplay must be a 'good read'. Like a novel, a screenplay must also be well written, demonstrate depth of character, have dynamic relationships, be compelling and inventive, and provoke powerful images in the mind of the reader. If the writer is lucky, the screenplay will be purchased and slated for production. At that point, the screenplay will be interpreted by the director, translated to film and essentially 'published' before an audience.

Today many students arrive at film school for the wrong reasons. Instead of looking to examine themselves and their world through their writing, they are looking to hit the jackpot. They arrive expecting the Holy Grail in the form of a secret 'formula' that will enable them to plug in a few characters, with a few plot turns, and become overnight sensations. They are more focused on trying to figure out their first big sale instead of trying to answer the essential questions of 'Who am I?' and 'Why are we here?' This kind of end result thinking creates 'formulaic' screenplays students mistakenly think will appeal to producers, network executives and studio heads. Time after time, students choose ideas that are geared to the commercial market instead of writing something true, honest and meaningful. So time after time, producers and studios are not interested in an imitation of a previously successful movie.

It is the nature of writing students to play it safe. They seem to have the misconception that writing 'familiar' will show producers and studio executives they can write a screenplay just like the last hit movie. This is flawed reasoning. The familiar does not stand out from the pack. Writing students must learn to take chances, to push their writing beyond their comfort zone. Good writing is original, provocative, takes a position, and challenges the reader to take a fresh look at life and the world around them.

Movies are not about happy people in wonderful situations. Movies are about lives in crisis – people whose lives have been shattered and who are desperately trying to piece them back together. This is true for both comedy and drama whether it is *Groundhog Day* or *American Beauty*.

All forms of creative writing are an examination of the greater human condition. Therefore, the single most important element an aspiring writer must bring to a creative work is an 'original voice'. First and foremost, the writer must tell a story with the ring of universal truth. Students should be encouraged to write 'naked' on the page, to have the courage to reveal their own faults and flaws. Students must learn to tap into their own unique experiences, their hopes, dreams, fears and failures as the source of their inspiration.

The process of screenwriting involves a certain amount of personal archaeology. One must be willing to dig up secrets buried in the past. Writers need to open locked doors, travel down dark corridors, and look within themselves to find the hidden treasures of life that reveal uniqueness and originality. By writing out of personal experiences, by creating characters based upon hopes, dreams, fears and failures, writers can create characters and situations that have the ring of truth to them. The end results are excellent screenplays based on real emotions with authentic stories.

Original voice also plays a critical role in the field of television. When a television producer asks to see a writing sample from a new writer, they want to see three things: an original screenplay, an original plot, and a writing sample of an existing show in a similar genre. They want to find a writer who can bring something special to their programme. They do not want 'imitations' of their show; they want insights about life and the human condition. Because dramatic and comedic television is based around a continuing cast of characters with established locations, the structure and format of episodic television has a repetitious pattern. Each week a cast of characters must solve a series of problems confronting them. While the episodic characters may have flaws and weaknesses, they usually do not dramatically grow or change from week to week. So, even in the world of television where there is a high degree of formulaic writing, the writer's original voice rises from the uniqueness of the characters, their problems and the clever ways they find solutions. The importance of the original voice cannot be understated.

Beyond the necessity of originality, screenwriting is at its very roots a craft. Study the craft long enough and a student can create a well-written screenplay. Yet, what cannot be crafted is the talent, the soul of a writer. For the most part, young talent tends to be fragile and highly insecure. If not treated delicately, with respect, talent can be easily destroyed. While we cannot teach talent, we can nurture it and provide an atmosphere to help it grow and flourish. We do this by creating a learning environment that is free, safe and devoid of excessive criticism.

All creative people have a constant battle with the two sides of their minds – the creative and the critic. The creative is the playful, adventurous side that wants to create stories, characters and situations. It's the freewheeling side that inspires students to write. The critic is the voice that says, 'This is not good enough, I can do better than that!' Too much of the critical voice can stifle the creative voice of the writer. If we let the critical side take over early in the process, the writer's creative side is handcuffed, unable to be adventurous and discover where the story and characters are going.

One of the first instructions I give students is to acknowledge their inner critic, then set it aside. I encourage them to be playful, take chances and allow themselves to write badly. Yes, write badly. The pressure of making every word perfect and every line brilliant is impossible and stifling. I also caution students against trying to be 'perfect'. Instead, I give them permission to be simply 'good'. Being loose and adventurous frees the young writers to explore the potential of their creativity. Rigid theories and rules that constrain young writers can be detrimental to their creative process.

Writers need to allow their characters to breathe, and at some point in a story determine their own fates. It's best when a character looks the writer directly in the eye and emphatically states, 'No, I won't do that. It doesn't make sense. This is who I am and this is who you must write – like it or not!' While this challenge can be disconcerting, and the novice writer may wish to turn off the computer to show the character who is the boss, clearly the character is now determining the course of his/her own story. Encouraging students to follow this process encourages original voice. The creative process is complete – what began as an artificial device now becomes organic and alive.

The mission of a writing instructor is to give students the freedom to make mistakes and fail. Failure is the best teacher. Those students who spring back from their mistakes are stronger, better writers. Once a student writer has a firm grasp on screenwriting techniques, it is time to begin to focus with a more critical eye. Yet, too much criticism even at this point can shatter the fragile confidence of an original voice. Only after a student completes the first or 'discovery draft' is it time to bring the critical voice back into the picture. Now the student can take a look at the story from a new, different perspective. If the student has had fun and been playful with the discovery draft, it is time to begin the hard work of rewriting. This is where the real work of writing is done – combining creativity with the practical application of screenwriting craft.

This is not a suggestion to distribute courtesy passes to our aspiring writing students, or to handle them with kid gloves. Any knowledgeable writer wants constructive criticism. It is up to the instructor to find the right time, when it is in the student's best interest, for hard criticism. Growth happens in incremental steps. Giving a student one area to focus on can yield much better results than giving a top-to-bottom criticism that may overwhelm and paralyse the student's creative efforts.

When approaching student work, it is important to celebrate their successes. It is much easier to point out what went wrong in a screenplay, rather than compliment what went right. When my students give notes to each other, I encourage them to first comment on what was good about the work. It's essential for a writer to have a positive feeling for what works, as well as knowing what areas need to be strengthened. Secondly, look to support the student's original voice. It may be faint, just beginning to emerge, but present nonetheless. Practise restraint when suggesting ideas for the student's script. Focus on trying to discover what your students want to write and help them develop *their* original ideas. The teacher's primary role is to support the students, to help them gain confidence in their vision and in developing their original voice.

Professional screenwriting has the additional burden of merging both commerce and art. As writing instructors, our job is to teach our students the art of screenwriting, and let commerce fall where it may. Stress process over product. If your students enjoy what they are writing, if they are involved in the lives of their characters, if the story talks to them in some personal way, then they have succeeded. Success in screenwriting needs to be measured in small victories over time that add up to winning the bigger battle.

Today's creative artist must have dedication, perseverance and original artistic vision to succeed in any of the arts, but especially when writing for motion pictures and television. Original thought, a unique point of view and creative honesty are necessary attributes for the aspiring screenwriter. As teachers, it is essential to inspire our students to reach deep within themselves to uncover and confront those qualities that make them unique and then to encourage them to express this in their writing. With our encouragement, we can help them to find their original voices and equip them with their most powerful creative tool – their own individuality. Creative writing celebrates honesty and personal self-discovery.

2. ESSENTIAL SCREENWRITING FUNDAMENTALS

> A screenplay is about distilling the essence of a story and its characters. You really have to find the heart and soul of your story and hew to it. The difference between books and movies is that books are about what happens within people, and movies are about what happens *between* people. (Ron Bass, *Rain Man*)

Screenplays are blueprints for motion pictures and television shows. Unlike prose or poetry, screenplays are not the end result. The most important elements writers must aspire to communicate are intent and story. The best way screenwriters can ensure that their work is produced as written on the page is to write intriguing characters and a story so compelling, no one in their right mind would change a single word.

When writing a screenplay, the power of the narrative is essential to grab the audience. The writer must use the narrative to involve the audience in the story. Well-written screenplays possess a strong relationship between the action, or 'what' happens, and the characters, or 'who' is involved in the action. Plot and character share interdependent roles in both motion picture and television writing. It is not only important to have a narrative that holds the audience's attention, but we also need characters to whom the audience can relate, and with whom they can become emotionally involved.

A screenplay is meant to be sparse on description. Economy of words is important. One must never allow the writing to get in the way of the story. Skilled screenwriters often create settings and locations with quick brush strokes, using a single image such as a broken window blind, to represent a room in disrepair. Although setting and location are important in creating the world of a screenplay, it is the art director's job to detail the set, and the director's job to set the camera angles. The job of the screenwriter is to concentrate on telling the story.

Motion pictures and television shows rely on intimacy and immediacy. A screen narrative should be told dramatically, and characters revealed through their actions. Dialogue can also be used to reveal character. What characters say – the issues they are concerned about, their personal philosophies, attitudes towards the people around them and the world they live in – ultimately reveal their true identities. Simple props can also reveal character. The character Caroline Burnham in *American Beauty* prizes a $4,000 sofa more than intimacy with her estranged husband.

The following craft components may be used with the exercises to help students master the fundamentals of writing for screen and television.

Ideation

The concept of ideation poses the age-old 'chicken or egg' question: 'Which comes first? The story or the character?' Screenplays can begin with a character in search of an idea, or with an idea in search of a character. Ideas can be found everywhere, in the electronic or print media, through conversations with friends, from personal observations of life, or even just updating old stories – like turning H. G. Wells's *The Time Machine* into *Back to the Future*.

Character

Once a student settles on an idea, the next question becomes 'Whose story is it?' The writer's challenge is to create meaningful and dynamic characters. Students tend to begin with imitation, borrowing from characters they have seen in movies. This kind of writing results in cardboard characters who lack unique voices and clear goals within the story.

Writing character entails much more than describing 'a man who wears an eye patch', or 'a woman who is nervous and smokes too much'. These are character traits that do little to reveal the true essence of the character. Strong characters come from scripting a unique 'inner story' that drives each character to make certain decisions throughout the course of the screenplay.

Each character must possess an individual story that may result from the emotional or physical scars of past experiences, deeply buried secrets and/or lies they are hiding, a certain lack of confidence, or the failed quest of a long-sought-after dream. Character might also rise out of a strong need for redemption or personal recognition. Great characters are often based upon a combination of these forces causing such an inner pain that it must remain well hidden from the audience, or from the characters themselves. Although the audience may not know what is going on inside the character, the writer needs to clearly understand what is 'driving' the character. The writer needs to know exactly what the characters are trying to achieve in each sequence and scene. Therefore, the best advice to give your writing students is 'to write from the inside out'.

Film and television stories are about 'lives in crisis'. By the middle of the script, the main characters should find themselves at a crossroads and be forced to make a difficult decision. Usually the decision is life changing and the characters struggle to get back to normal over the rest of the screenplay. But what is 'normal' has been lost; it is something that doesn't exist anymore. In the end, the characters must come face to face with themselves, admitting their faults, weaknesses and flaws. Then they will grow and change to become better people, or stay as they are and allow life to pass them by.

Because movies are immediate, screen characters must have immediate goals. This is referred to as the character's 'want'. In *Casablanca*, Rick wants Ilsa back. What a character 'wants' is the external goal that motivates the character's actions. A character's 'inner need' is the internal goal that must be satisfied by the end of the movie. Rick wants Ilsa, but he needs to get over his cynicism to rejoin the world of the living. In *Casablanca*, these two conflicting forces mean giving up Ilsa for the greater good. In the end, cynical Rick becomes hopeful.

Character growth is an essential element of great screen and television writing. Due to the dramatic experiences of the character throughout the story, the main character is changed in some way to become a new and different person – usually a better person. A story featuring a character that doesn't change is either a tragedy, or simply weak writing. Redemption and rebirth are strong themes driving character change in Western story-telling traditions. This is true for both film and television.

Strong characters create strong plots. The main character must pursue a clearly delineated goal in order to solve a problem. The physical pursuit of that goal creates the action or narrative of the story. Each story must be tailored to the individual character's wants and needs. The problems and obstacles the character encounters creates the plot which tests character will and mettle. The higher the stakes and the more difficult the obstacles, the stronger the character becomes and the more the audience yearns for the character to succeed. In the end the main character must grow and change to accomplish his/her goal.

Conflict

Conflict is the lifeblood of the dramatic arts. The entire screenplay revolves around the main character resolving the major conflict of the story. Conflict must exist in some small way in every scene, act, line of dialogue, and character. Conflict is also used to reveal character. Conflict forces the main character into the 'fight or flight' mode, where the character can no longer stand on the sidelines and watch life pass them by. The main character must take sides and act. To survive, the main character must step out of the comfort zone, take chances and face the consequences. Failure to act means certain defeat.

It is important to create conflicts larger than the main characters so they are forced to fight against overwhelming odds, with the outcome always in doubt. Whether it is an action film like *Star Wars* where Luke Skywalker battles the powerful Darth Vader or a small character-drama like *Erin Brockovich* where an unemployed divorced mother of three takes on a multi-billion-dollar utility, the main characters must struggle against a stronger opponent. In the end, they ultimately succeed by using their guile, wits and ingenuity. Without solid conflict running like a raw nerve through each and every scene, the writing is merely words upon paper. There is no screenplay.

Opposition forces

Today's world is more grey than black and white – and nothing reflects this blurring of conflicts better than the movies. The terms 'protagonist' and 'antagonist' are anarchistic by today's terms. In good screenplays, main characters now face many 'opposition forces' that directly conflict with their efforts to reach their desired goals.

Multiple opposition forces provide a layer of complexity by challenging the main character at every turn. In *Casablanca*, Rick faces the multiple opposition forces of General Strasser, Ilsa, Victor Laszlo, Captain Renault and most importantly himself. Rick is in opposition to himself. He is his own worst enemy. Each character has something they want from Rick. In turn, Rick is forced to deal with each of them to reach his goal. With each twist and turn, Rick confronts further complications and opposition forces that stand in his way. On the surface, the main opposition force is General Strasser, but underneath, Rick's personal world is much more complex. This is an excellent example of the writer creating multiple conflicts that continually confront the main character at every turn. The end result is a much more exciting plot and narrative storyline. Multiple opposition forces add another level of tension that is necessary to sustain audience interest in the screenplay. They also provide the writer with more options to develop and explore.

Theme

Ultimately, theme is the glue that holds a screenplay together. Theme embodies the larger-than-life philosophies or ideas that the screenplay sets out to examine and define. The theme of *One Flew over the Cuckoo's Nest* examines how individual spirit will always prevail against tyranny. Like a symphonic orchestral theme, the thematic idea in a screenplay must be repeated again and again until the audience clearly understands the questions being examined. Without a clear theme, the screenplay will wander and feel unfocused. With a clear theme, the characters, scenes and overall writing will feel more cohesive.

Theme transcends the individual character's story by posing larger questions about the common issues of the human condition. Theme is not necessarily something that should be stated in words, but often something that is better presented dramatically. This can be done by creating scenes with well-defined characters interacting with the world around them.

Time

In a sense, movie time is a compressed time. Events happen with a sense of immediacy. Scripts unfold in terms of days and hours. It is important for the student to know how to tell the story within a confined time frame. To use the term 'a ticking clock' describes the immediacy of the problem or obstacle facing the main character within such a time frame. In *Casablanca*, the plane to Lisbon is set to leave on a certain day, at a certain time. The constant underlying question of the screenplay is just who will be on that plane. Time becomes a driving force that motivates the characters to act quickly. Television shows such as *24* are based on a specific time frame to define weekly plots, create character conflicts and heighten dramatic tension.

Narrative structure

The easiest element to teach in screen and television writing is narrative structure. Character development is clearly the most difficult element to master. As a result, many instructors make the mistake of starting with structure. By exposing the novice writing student to narrative structure too early, students become attached to structure at the expense of character development. Stories are about people, and people are defined by their relationships. By focusing on structure first, the instructor sends out the wrong message. The most important element is not 'how' the story is constructed, but 'who' are the people within the story and how are they defined by their relationships. Only then are the students ready to focus on structure.

The three-act design is the basic narrative structure of screenwriting. George M. Cohan, the great Broadway playwright of the 1920s, defined the three-act structure very simply. The first act you get your character up a tree. The second act you throw rocks at him. The third act you get him down from the tree. While deceptively simple, Mr Cohan's definition cuts to the heart of screenwriting. The first act exists to set up the problem, the second act develops complications of the problem, and the third act brings a resolution of the problem. This basic three-act structure remains true for both film and television writing today.

Narrative structure is the spine that holds the individual character stories together; it is the underlying framework for the screenplay. Just as effective stories must serve the needs of the character, narrative structure must also serve those same needs. Plot elements are far easier for a student to grasp than the difficult problem of finding the 'inner story' that motivates the character and drives the dramatic tension. The more a student depends on structure, the less humanistic their story will be, and the more formulaic the screenplay.

Sub-plots

Sub-plots are those small inner stories, usually told in three to four scenes that run concurrently within the main plotline. Sub-plots should involve the main character and examine or reflect the theme of the screenplay. Each minor character should have a sub-plot with a little problem to solve. Concurrently, each minor character should also have a personal story they are seeking to resolve. Sub-plots commonly resolve before the end of the second act or at the beginning of the third. Sub-plots must be resolved prior to the resolution of the main story. As a craft device, sub-plots are further ways to add complications and conflicts to a story. *Tootsie* is a movie that demonstrates the effective use of sub-plots. Sub-plots are also used extensively in television, especially in situation comedy.

Dialogue

Students love to write dialogue – tons of it. With screenwriting, usually the less dialogue, the better. Why use two lines when the writer can say it in one? Why use any dialogue at all if the writer can show character intent through action? The axioms of 'less is more' and 'action speaks louder than words' are particularly applicable to screenwriting. A character's actions reveal who they are. Dialogue should be used to indirectly reveal personal life philosophies, attitudes towards other people, hopes, dreams, secrets and fears. Well-crafted dialogue becomes a window into a character's soul.

There are basically two types of dialogue used in a screenplay. Either the dialogue is very direct, specific to a subject, or the dialogue is subtextual, i.e. indirect, with implied, symbolic meaning. If students' characters are always talking about the plot, then their screenplays are in trouble. Plot and character should primarily be revealed through action. Dialogue should be used sparingly for exposition.

In *Casablanca* we learn about Rick in two ways. First, he *acts* cold, cynical and distant. When Ugarte (Peter Lorre) comes to Rick in a panic and asks for his help, Rick is heartless and refuses. We learn a lot about Rick by his actions. Later, Rick reveals more about himself when he says, 'I stick my neck out for nobody'. Never does Rick say he is a cynical man with a broken heart. We observe his behaviour, then draw our own conclusions, based on what we have seen and heard.

Writing the screenplay

Once students know their main character's story, the plotline and the theme, then they are ready to break the story down into a treatment or an outline. Each scene should be focused to highlight the main character's struggle, with the various sub-plots, opposition forces and conflicts along the journey.

Writing is rewriting. When creating screenplays, students must expect to revise their treatments or outlines many times. It's easier to revise a four-page treatment than to revise a 110-page screenplay. Once the students have a good sense of their stories and their characters' journeys, then it is time to begin writing the screenplay. Again, it is important to remember not to allow the writing to get in the way of the story. Advise the students to write short, concise treatments, rather than long, detailed story outlines. They should save their best writing for when they sit down to write the screenplay.

Four-by-six-inch index cards work well when writing the treatment. They can be laid out on a table, adding the dimension of visual design to the story. Since there are approximately 45 to 55 scenes in a feature-length screenplay, the student may expect to write a similar number of index cards when outlining the screenplay. Each card highlights one major scene point – the essence of what the scene is about – and a few details on what might happen in the scene. Once satisfied with the card outline, the student may set each card on their computer and write the scene as indicated from the card. There should be enough key points on the cards to give them a solid sense of where the story is going, but not too much detail. The card is the catalyst for the creative mind, rather than reiterating a scene the student feels they have written already.

In my classes, students must make an index card presentation of their screenplays before they begin writing. They pitch their stories off their cards to the class, and then their peers give them notes for improving their screenplays. These notes are invaluable, usually extensive, and help to flesh out the first draft. The students then revise their cards and turn in a two-page outline prior to starting the actual screenplay. This saves them considerable revision time and results in focused first drafts.

The first draft is always a draft of discovery. My students have a free hand at this point to write the story as outlined. Comments and criticisms must be held to a minimum until the students reach 'The End' of their first drafts. Once they have a completed screenplay, the class works together to further refine and focus characters, plots and themes.

In conclusion

The simple goal of teaching motion picture and television writing is to encourage the students to think in simple terms. Whose story is this? What does the character want? What does he/she need? What is the most important relationship in the character's life? What is stopping the character from realizing his/her goal? What will happen if the character does not achieve his/her goal?

All students try to run before they can walk. Forcing them to focus their characters, to understand the importance of character growth and development early in the writing process, helps them to focus more on the human aspects and less on the plot events when it comes to actually writing the screenplay. Their screenplays will be more meaningful, their characters more emotional and sympathetic, and their resolutions more unique and original. Steering students away from structure until they have developed a solid understanding of character allows them to mature as writers. When they are finally introduced to narrative structure, they will have the experience to see clearly how great characters write great stories.

3. (4) EXERCISES FOR FILM AND TELEVISION WRITING

If you're not failing every now and again, it's a sign you're not doing anything very innovative. (Woody Allen, *Annie Hall*)

One of the more enjoyable aspects of teaching screenwriting is the use of creative exercises to help students improve their writing skills. The following examples illustrate various exercises from my classes in screenwriting fundamentals.

Ideation – ways to inspire original ideas

Current Events
This exercise requires the students to develop a newspaper article into a feature-length movie idea or television show. The instructor divides the class into multiple teams of two students. Each team randomly picks an article from my extensive collection of dated, and current, human-interest newspaper articles. The teams have 45 minutes to develop their articles into movie or TV ideas. They then take turns pitching their stories to their peers in class, who question and critique each team's approach. Since none of the students are emotionally tied to their stories, they tend to do an excellent job of defining strong characters and building good stories. The learning experience is further enhanced by peer demand for viable, entertaining stories.

Quotes, Questions and Philosophies
Ask the students to bring in a quote, a question or a statement of philosophy to build into a story, and then write a three- or four-page treatment based upon their choice. For example: 'Can ex-lovers still be friends?' is the central question that inspired the movie *When Harry Met Sally*. 'No man is an island' could be the quote that best encapsulates *Casablanca*. The movie *Forrest Gump* revolves around a simple life philosophy: 'My momma always said, "Life is like a box of chocolates. You never know what you're gonna get." '

Use What You Know Best
Much of creative writing is semi-autobiographical. Ask your students to choose an event from their lives, or from another person's life, preferably someone who is close to them, and use it as a defining moment around which to build a screen story. The students should not feel tied to the 'true' event, but see it simply as a device, a launch pad to inspire a larger movie concept. Students should allow themselves the freedom to create characters and unique situations that reach beyond the original event. The focus of this exercise is to build a story that answers the important question of 'Whose story is this?' The finished product should be a three- to four-page treatment.

Essential Story Questions
The following list may also help students focus on defining the main character, the love story, and the opposition force.

1. Who is your main character and what is important for your audience to know about him or her?

2. Describe your main character's inner story. What inner truth is he/she hiding from, and what psychological wounds does he/she need to heal?

3. Use one word, such as 'ambitious', 'defeated', or 'frustrated', to best describe your main character.

4. What is your main character's personal goal or quest? What is he/she trying to achieve by the end of the story?

5. Describe your main character's greatest flaw or weakness.

6. What is your main character's secret wish? If he/she could wave a magic wand, what would his/her new life look like?

7. What stands in the way of your main character achieving his/her deepest wish?

8. If your main character could escape to anywhere in the world, where would he/she travel, why, and with whom?

9. Describe your main opposition character. What is important for your audience to know about him or her?

10. What is your main opposition character's goal? What is he/she trying to achieve by the conclusion of the story?

11. What is your main opposition force's greatest weakness or flaw?

12. Use one word to best describe your main opposition force's character.

13. Who is your main love interest in the story and what is important for your audience to know about him or her?

14. What is your main love interest's inner story? What is he/she hiding from, and what does he/she need to heal?

15. What is your main love interest's secret wish? If he/she could wave a magic wand, what would his/her new life look like?

16. What stands in the way of your main love interest achieving that wish?

17. Use one word to describe your main love interest's character.

18. What is the problem that keeps your main character and your main love interest apart?

19. Who are your important supporting characters and what are their inner stories?

20. Use one word to describe each supporting character.

21. What is the event that sets in motion the irreversible chain of events that throws your main character's life into crisis?

22. What is the major story problem that must be solved by your main character so that his/her life can return to normal?

This is simply a partial list. Expand the list to include character, relationship, sub-plot, structure, act breaks, sequence breaks and character arcs, as well as theme, tone and genre. Specify that questions cannot be simply answered with a 'yes' or 'no' response. The questions can then be used to frame three separate assignments that correspond to the three separate acts of a screenplay. Act One concerns the set-up and introduction of character and story; Act Two concerns the complication of story, plus the development of character and relationship; and Act Three focuses on the resolution of both the plot problem and the characters' goals and desires.

Character exercises

Discover the Defining Event
Assign the students to write a newspaper article about an important event in their main characters' lives, as if it had just happened. Students should interview their main characters and quote them in their stories.

Reveal Secrets
The main character keeps a special box hidden under his/her bed. Ask the students to describe the contents of that box and explain what each item tells us about their main character. Ask the students to limit the number of items in the box to five items.

Write a Letter to the Main Opposition Force
In all good screenplays, one person in the main character's life must stand in the way of achieving their goal. Assign the students to draft a letter from the main character to the main opposing character explaining why he/she is a problem. Students should include just how the main character plans on solving this problem. Then, flip the assignment. Ask the students to draft a second letter from the main opposing character to the main character describing how they are a problem in his/her life.

The Talk Show Host
Encourage your students to stage an impromptu national television talk show. One student takes on the role of the main character, while another assumes the persona of the talk show psychologist. The psychologist analyses the main character and the fun begins. Where does he/she 'hurt' and where do they need to 'heal'? This is a dynamic exercise that can help students discover more about their own characters, and explore their hidden issues or secrets. Encourage the students to be highly creative, perhaps staging a surprise family 'intervention', or introducing a second 'surprise guest' to confront the main character.

The Confessional Scene
Suggest the students create a scene where their main character reveals a secret about him/herself. Then, ask them to motivate the confession by setting the scene after a recent traumatic or emotional event, such as breaking up with a lover or experiencing a bad car accident. This forces the students to be clear with their main characters on the page, as well as with themselves.

The Biography Show
This exercise is similar to the talk show concept. The students write a mock TV biography show which includes interviews with the main character's friends and family members. Encourage dissenting points of view – those who think highly of the main character as well as those who find him/her less than desirable. Each interviewee should have different stories to tell about the main character, and different points of view concerning the main character's current life and future goals. Finish the interview by including an interview with the main character.

Discover Supporting Characters
Pick a universal holiday – perhap a family gathering like Christmas, Thanksgiving, or a

special celebration – where the in-laws, relatives and out-of-town guests arrive to visit the main character. Allow the students to explore the family dynamics between characters, establish past histories, conflicts, buried broken hearts and dreams for the future. Ask what, as a class, do we learn about this family. Siblings, spouses, relatives and friends all have issues. This exercise provides the opportunity to explore character development in depth, balancing lightness with a more serious overview.

Directed writing

Revealing character through action and props
This exercise is dubbed 'The Job Interview – Part I'. Students write a non-verbal scene that describes their main character preparing to go to a job interview. They must reveal their character using only the preparation process and the various props required to accomplish this goal. 'The Job Interview – Part II' builds upon this first assignment, yet we never see the actual interview. Instead, the main character has just returned from the job interview. Students must use the mannerisms, gestures and actions of their character, along with the earlier props, to show the reader the results of the job interview.

Creating tension and conflict in a scene
Dubbed 'The Unpleasant Task', this exercise helps students develop the craft skills of tension and conflict without exaggeration or a false scenario. From the students' own growing cast of characters, they choose one to write as if preparing for an unpleasant task, while another character tries to persuade him/her not to get involved. The actual task is not important and should not be mentioned directly, but only alluded to throughout the exercise. Leave it up to the writer's choice as to whether the opposing character is successful in deterring the main character. Here again, this exercise develops the craft skills necessary to create character and relationships.

Revealing secrets and confessing mistakes
For 'The Plane Ride', the students are assigned to write about two previously acquainted characters (again, of their own choosing) seated next to each other on an aeroplane. The depth of their past relationship may vary, but from the onset, it must be clear that the two characters have issues between them that they would rather not resolve. The plane takes a sudden nosedive and appears as if it is going to crash. What do these characters say to each other now that death is imminent? Suddenly, the engine restarts and the plane pulls up, out of danger. Now how do the characters react to the truths that have been revealed? What might they have learned about each other? How has their relationship changed as a consequence of the intimacy of a terror-filled moment? An example of this exercise may be found in the movie *Almost Famous*.

Confronting the main opposition force
To help students comprehend the importance of establishing a strong relationship between their main character and the main opposing character, you might use 'The Show Down'. In this exercise, students are assigned to write a short version of a confrontation between their two main characters. The scene should open with one of the characters having the upper hand, but throughout the course of the action, he/she loses it to the other character. The power shifts, and the upper hand changes. The first 30 minutes of *In the Heat of the*

Night illustrates this craft device by swinging the power back and forth between a white Southern policeman and an African-American New York police detective.

Movie breakdowns

Understanding how to break down a successful movie into its many individual parts is an excellent exercise for teaching students character development, structure and sequencing.

- Assign the students to write a scene-by-scene breakdown of a produced motion picture. They should begin by describing the scene in one sentence, and then focus on the writer's intent, rather than just repeating the plot.
- The First, Second and Third Acts should be clearly marked.
- The overall screenplay should be broken down into the components of the eight-sequence structure. Each sequence should ask a question of the main character.
- Students should highlight the scenes tracing the progression of the emotional arc of the main character.
- In addition, have the students outline sub-plots, delineate motivations, highlight character goals and state major complications in the screenplay.

Writing dialogue

Writing text and subtext
Text assignments can be fun. Start with a scene where two characters blame one another for their relationship problems. First, encourage the students to write the scene and its dialogue very directly, or 'on the nose'. Then ask the students to rewrite the same scene in subtext, or 'off the nose'. This helps the students find creative ways to have their characters express feelings indirectly, either though implication or action.

Finding individual character voices
One of the hardest aspects of writing dialogue is the creation of multiple characters with individual voices that do not all sound the same. Ask the students to write a specific scene between two characters, perhaps a battling married couple getting ready for an anniversary party. The students must assign each character a specific attitude, such as optimistic, pessimistic, overbearing, self-deprecating, apologetic, sarcastic, timid, and so forth. As they compose their scene, the students are required to use each character's specific attitude in every line of dialogue throughout the scene. Then have each student read their scene aloud to the class. The other students should try to define the attitudes of the two opposing characters. If the attitudes are not clear, the student needs to rewrite the exercise.

The result of this writing exercise is the ability to craft two distinct voices, attitudes and points of view. The pessimist is always going to have a negative and dark view on all subjects. Someone who is self-deprecating will always be apologizing for what they say and do. An angry character will always be angry, no matter what circumstances may ensue, and so on. But the reader will be able to clearly delineate the varied voices and points of view.

115

In conclusion

There is no end to the inventive and challenging exercises that can be created to help students develop screenwriting skills. Each exercise takes them one step closer to the mastery of the craft. Your support and encouragement as their instructor goes a long way to help students gain the confidence to take chances and further explore their creativity. Pushing your students to challenge themselves to do better through focused rewriting is an important lesson for the aspiring screenwriter.

4. (3) FILM AND TELEVISION READINGS

> Whether a person becomes an artist or a master of the form will take a lifetime of effort to discover, but first, every artist or master learned the craft. (David Howard, *How to Build a Great Screenplay*)

There has been an explosion of screenwriting books published recently. Many of them are repetitious or too dogmatic. Screenwriting is an art form – not a science. The following titles include both classic screenwriting books and newer titles students find most helpful.

Screenwriting books

The Art of Dramatic Writing by Lajos Egri (1960) is still one of the best books written about dramatic writing. While many of the examples are dated, the creative philosophy and craft skills are timeless. Mr Egri emphasizes strong characters with immediate, clear problems that drive the narrative.

The Art of Creative Writing by Lajos Egri (1993) contains invaluable tips and craft information such as 'Emotion: Source of Reader Identification', 'The Shaping of Character' and 'Introduction to Motivation'. This book is a companion piece to Mr Egri's earlier work, and together they form an excellent starting point for any serious young writer.

The Tools of Screenwriting by David Howard and Edward Mabley (1993) offers an analysis of classic motion picture screenplays by outlining the key elements used to create them. Mr Howard is a professor at the University of Southern California's School of Cinema-Television, in the Writing Division. The text is an excellent discussion guide when used in conjunction with screenings of the referenced films. These include *Citizen Kane, Chinatown, North By Northwest, Witness* and *One Flew over the Cuckoo's Nest*. The authors cover the basics such as premise and opening, conflict, obstacles, theme, unity and characterization. Currently, the book is in its twelfth printing.

How to Build a Great Screenplay by David Howard (2004) is a primer on all aspects of screen and television writing. This book is highly recommended as a core course guide, as Mr Howard speaks to all levels of screenwriting: from basic to advanced. He takes a complex subject and makes it easy to understand through the creative use of both contemporary and classic film screenplays.

Teach Yourself Screenwriting by Raymond G. Frensham (1996) is an excellent book that explores all aspects of screenwriting in a precise primer that is easy to read and uses numerous clear diagrams. Mr Frensham uses contemporary motion picture references. The book is a concise reference guide which is useful when planning curriculum, as brevity is one of its strong points.

Advanced Screenwriting by Dr Linda Seger (2003) is better suited to the advanced screenwriter who has mastered the basic elements of screenwriting. Her work on theme, visual metaphor and advanced scene construction provide the opportunity for writing students to work on a more challenging level.

Screenwriting: The Sequence Approach by Paul Joseph Gulino (2004) explains the theory of sequencing as a tool for constructing a feature-length screenplay from eight separate sections. Mr Gulino cites examples from contemporary films such as *Toy Story, North by Northwest, One Flew over the Cuckoo's Nest* and *Being John Malkovich.*

How to Sell Your Screenplay by Lydia Wilen and Joan Wilen (2001) explores the challenging terrain of marketing screenplays. In addition to many practical tips on how to sell a screenplay, the book contains informative sidebars and interviews with successful screenwriters. The authors cover basic script form, collaborator agreements, the pitch, and writing query letters. It is highly relevant in the classroom, because it is more than just about sales. This book emphasizes how important it is for aspiring screenwriters to present their work to the industry in a professional manner.

Interview books

Interview books are extremely useful in helping the aspiring writer understand the realities of the business, as well as how successful screenwriters approach their craft. Students gain insights into the professional writer's commitment from firsthand 'war stories'. Interview books also serve as excellent discussion topics.

Oscar-winning Screenwriters on Screenwriting by Joel Engel (2002) shares interviews with many notable screenwriters such as William Goldman, Ron Bass, John Irving, Frank Pierson and Alan Ball. Students learn firsthand how successful screenwriters approach their work, as well as the enormous effort and persistence that builds a successful screenwriting career.

The New Screenwriter Looks at the New Screenwriter by William Froug (1992) includes interviews with successful writers such as Joe Eszterhas, Jeffrey Boam, Anna Hamilton Phelan, and the writing team of Jim Cash and Jack Epps, Jr.

Feature films

There are few artistic mediums beyond feature films that lend themselves so readily to the simultaneous study of both the visual and the written forms. Each of these films offers specific examples of many craft aspects that can be referenced in the classroom.

Character development:	*On the Waterfront, American Beauty, Erin Brockovich, Glory, Stand by Me, The Celebration*
Character arc:	*Atlantic City, As Good As It Gets, Groundhog Day, Sex, Lies and Videotape, Casablanca, Toy Story, Midnight Cowboy*

Dramatization:	*Unforgiven, Friday Night Lights, On the Waterfront, Punch-Drunk Love*
Relationships:	*When Harry Met Sally, Rain Man, Diner, Casablanca, Good Will Hunting, Midnight Cowboy, Annie Hall*
Narrative structure:	*On the Waterfront, One Flew over the Cuckoo's Nest, Schindler's List, Citizen Kane, The Godfather, Casablanca, The Third Man, Rocky*
Alternative narrative:	*Memento, Traffic, Sliding Doors, He Loves Me, He Loves Me Not, Rashomon, All About My Mother, Eternal Sunshine of the Spotless Mind*
Multiple stories:	*Tootsie, Traffic, As Good As It Gets, American Graffiti, Talk to Her*
Effective use of time:	*High Noon, Back to the Future, Run Lola Run, Dog Day Afternoon*
Dialogue:	*As Good As It Gets, Erin Brockovich, American Beauty, His Girl Friday, You Can Count on Me*

Chapter 9

New Media Writing

Thomas Swiss and Cynthia Lewis
University of Iowa/University of Minnesota

1. INTRODUCTION

Bad writers borrow; good writers steal. We've all heard this maxim. But who said it? A look at a few documents on the Web that borrow this line suggests the following writers might have said it: T. S. Eliot, Oscar Wilde and Mark Twain.

We want to make two points here, one rooted in the implications of the quote itself; the other on its unverified and diverse attributions. Our first point is that writing that 'steals' has a long and interesting (though not well-known) history and includes work by the French poet Blaise Cendrars, the American novelist William Burroughs, the Scottish poet Hugh MacDiarmid, and many other writers. Later in this chapter we'll offer strategies for teaching new media writing that encourage borrowing, appropriation, replication, piracy, sampling and plundering as compositional methods for writing. In short, we'll make a case for 'stealing'.

We call this writing – after Kenneth Goldsmith, who coined the term – 'uncreative writing'. Our perspective on writing is in tension with the prevalent focus in the teaching of creative writing, evident in some chapters in this book, that places an emphasis on authenticity, voice and unity at the centre of the writing curriculum.

Our second point is that the unstable attribution of the Eliot/Wilde/Twain 'quote' is a good example of how information and knowledge 'floats', especially in the age of the Web. That is, a lot of writing (like a lot of music), produced or re-produced in digital formats, has been stripped of those particular signifiers that can give a piece a certain kind of authenticity and authority. Without branding, often without a named author, and emanating from sources that themselves have no particular credibility, media files can become free-floating works, uploaded to peer-to-peer distribution systems and travelling in circles that they would not normally reach in the pre-Web world. On balance, we believe this is a good thing.

We have agreed to write this chapter on New Media, knowing full well that the term 'New Media' is hard to define. As Adalaide Morris (forthcoming) writes in her essay, 'New Media Poetics: As We May Think/How to Write':

> The rapid evolution of software and hardware, the variety of uses they can be put to, and

their roles in the constant flow of morphed and sampled data through global networks make it all but impossible to give the term 'new media literature' a stable definition.

When Morris and one of the authors of this chapter, Thom Swiss, were recently editing a book on new media poetics, they were often confronted with problems of taxonomy as these literary compositions are variously known as 'new media literature', 'e-lit', 'digital literature', 'computer-literature', 'net.art', 'codework', and other, more specific names such as 'interactive fiction'.

The first generation of these electronic literary texts were 'hyper-textual', primarily or exclusively language-based, generally employing temporal or spatial organizational styles that fell outside the conventions of most print texts. The best-known, most widely circulated literary works were published (disk-based and then later CD-based) by a small company in the US called Eastgate Systems. Eastgate produced hypertexts such as the widely reviewed *afternoon: a story* (1990) by Michael Joyce, *Victory Garden* (1991) by Stuart Moulthrop, and *Patchwork Girl* (1995) by Shelly Jackson.

The second generation of electronic literature, post-1995, has been composed for the most part in JavaScript, QuickTime, DHTML, Macromedia Flash, Shockwave, and other programs that combine verbal elements with graphics, images, animation, sound and other multimedia effects. Second-generation electronic texts, such as *V: Vniverse* by Stephanie Strickland with Cynthia Lawson (2002), *Dakota* by Young-hae Chang Heavy Industries (2001; a collaborative team), and *[N]+Semble* by Talan Memmott (2005), tend to be time-driven and multilayered. And as Morris (forthcoming) notes, they tend to reconfigure the familiar field of literature by bringing back into view vital but marginalized lineages of print, sound and image poetics, as well as procedural writing and conceptual art.

As a poet, one of the writers of this chapter, Thom Swiss, began his own collaborative, Web-based work with visual and sound artists several years ago, working mostly in Macromedia Flash. Flash, a vector-based animation software, was used by programmer/ artist Motomichi Nakamura to create *Hey Now* (Swiss and Nakamura, 2002), for example, a collaboration that had its roots in conceptual art. Swiss and Nakamura began by experimenting with the idea of 'wrapping' language. Following the work of Christo and Jeanne-Claude, contemporary artists well known for wrapping artefacts, buildings and landmarks with fabric, Swiss and Nakamura were interested in what 'wrapped language' might look and sound like. Christo's 'The Pont Neuf Wrapped, Paris 1975–85', for example, draped the famous French bridge in fabric, and was widely regarded as a fascinating experience for its viewers – wrapping and unwrapping objects hides and then re-reveals the familiar, allowing us to see objects in a new light.

In the case of the Swiss/Nakamura composition, as Megan Sapnar (2003) writes in her explication of the poem, the language is hidden and revealed by animated characters, who whisper jibberish before speaking verses of a cut-up poem. Just as we're taken aback by a 24-mile fence of fabric (in the case of the Christo's 'Running Fence, Sonoma and Marin Counties, California 1972–76'), the agency of a pacing man on the screen of *Hey Now*, who, when clicked, kicks the head of a cartoon figure who whispers like an alien before launching into the next sounded and imaged section of the poem, we're surprised and curious. What is a 24-mile-long curtain doing crossing hills and running along the coastline in Christo's piece? What is a boing-boing sound effect doing in a meditative, lyrical poem? 'Readers' of new media poems are often challenged to make sense of synthesis, but it's an opportunity to broaden our own interpretations and to look critically at how language is shaped by new media.

In her essay, Morris asks:

What can new media literature tell us about thinking and writing in a world increasingly reliant on databanks, algorithms, collaborative problem-solving and composing, instant retrieval and manipulation of information, the play of cutting, pasting, morphing, and sampling, and the ambient and nomadic aesthetics of a networked and programmable culture? (forthcoming)

Plenty, we believe. But for the purpose of the teaching strategies we discuss below, we'll focus on collaboration and appropriation.

To hear the critics tell it, as we've argued elsewhere, one problem with emergent digital literary and art forms is that they don't yet have established stars. Where's our Shakespeare of the Screen? Our Pixel Picasso? How long before we have a Digital DeMille? The assumption is that we'll have them eventually – undisputed geniuses working in what is now generally called 'New Media'. But behind this assumption is another assumption, one with a long, sometimes thorny history – that the 'best' or 'most important' art is created by an individual, a single pair of hands in the study or studio. When Thom Swiss first began to collaborate with visual and sound artists several years ago, he had a sense that the opportunities and demands of Web-based poetry, like many other New Media practices, have their roots in the shared notion of community that was integral to the development of the Internet. He was also increasingly interested in what Hal Foster calls 'the twin obsessions of the neo-avant-garde': temporality and textuality (1996: 40). Web-based poems – especially those involving links, animation, and attention to the pictorial elements of writing – suggest novel approaches to thinking about time and the text.

Collaborative work redefines artistic labour in what is for Swiss and others new and complicated ways: what is the relationship, for example, between Swiss's language and the images and sounds others create, even if under his 'direction'? How do the images and sounds 'change' the meaning of the language (and vice versa) and in what ways can the piece be said to still be a 'poem'? Collaboration allows writers and artists – like Swiss and those he composes with – to reconsider both their work and their identities, to literally see them anew as they move from individual to composite subjectivity. Yet while the art world has sometimes been open to collaborative work – in the long shadow of Duchamp's experiments with Man Ray, the shared labour of producing art in Warhol's Factory, the many hands needed to make a film – the literature world has always had a hard time accepting collaborative work, even in these networked times.

As we've been suggesting, then, new media have led to new social practices related to producing, representing and consuming literature, writing and knowledge in general. Colin Lankshear and Michele Knobel, whose work focuses on new media in education, describe these changing epistemologies as:

more performance- and procedure-oriented than propositional, more collaborative than individualistic, and more concerned with making an impact on attention, imagination, curiosity, innovation, and so on, than with fostering truth, engendering rational belief, or demonstrating their justifiability. (2003: 176)

Like Lankshear and Knobel, other scholars of new media point to the differences between print and digital technologies, the resulting epistemological shifts, and the need for educators to rethink what it means to teach and learn in light of these shifts. Meanwhile, some point to important continuities as well, arguing, for instance, that features typically attributed to digital texts – that they are more interactive, lateral, multimodal – can also be attributed to print literacies. Both the discontinuities and the continuities inform our discussion of teaching new media. That is, we are interested in how new media texts afford encoding (writing) and decoding (reading/viewing/listening) practices unlike those ordinarily engaged in off-line and off-screen. However, we are also interested in the ways that practices surrounding new media texts have been shaped by print practices, thus providing students oriented towards print a familiar starting point.

2. KEY POINTS FOR TEACHERS: THEORIES ABOUT NEW MEDIA WRITING AND READING

Although writing has always been multimodal (relying at the very least on visual and aural cues), contemporary writing practices rely on an increasingly complex range of modalities. The visual mode is particularly salient, with writing displayed alongside image (or with writing displayed graphically as image), demanding a set of semiotic skills that is not commonly part of the classroom repertoire. The linguistic elements of texts are becoming less complex (e.g. fewer embedded clauses) while the visual elements are becoming more so, shifting the focus from linguistic features to elements of design.

These changes in textual form and function come with a change in literacy practices. Readers and writers regularly make meaning across modes, laterally. They sample the multimodal resources available to them (often on the screen), creating coherence from the panoply of surface features and the juxtapositions of texts and genres and modes.

As Lankshear and Knobel (2003) argue, most writing instruction emphasizes texts over practices, but beyond the classroom, texts take a second seat to practices. That is, texts outside the classroom are most often used in the service of accomplishing particular practices and social interactions, thus increasing the role of the reader/writer in the reader/text transaction, and in shaping the nature of the text through interaction. Process, rather than product, plays a central role in forms of representation on the Internet. This change in the nature of literacy practices in New Media and, especially, electronic networks, has implications for teaching and learning. As educators, we need to understand the changing nature of literacy – changing practices and epistemologies – in order to effectively teach writing in digital times. The interactive nature of New Media has led to dimensions of practice specific to New Media writing. These practices – performativity, hybrid textuality, and circulation – have implications for teaching New Media writing.

Performativity

Kress, Jewitt and Tsatsarelis (2000) argue that contemporary conditions such as the global, fast-capital economy, communicative webs and multiple modes of representation demand performativity, flexibility and adaptability on the part of readers and writers. Writers, they suggest, are 'remakers, constantly of the materials with which they engage' (p. 28). As already mentioned, this perspective on writing is out of sync with one that places an emphasis on authenticity, voice and unity.

Envisioning voice as 'authentic' privileges stability across texts rather than the dynamic, fluid concept of voice exhibited by writers of New Media as they enact identities that depend upon a running analysis of complicated on-line and off-line contexts. Everyday uses of digital writing – text messaging, for instance – require that users present themselves differently as they shift from window to window, taking on different identities and tones almost simultaneously. The technology (multiple windows, synchronicity, graphical possibilities) and, also, what Mizuko Ito (2005) refers to as the 'hypersociality' of digital media, makes for a performative practice.

Textuality

As N. Katherine Hayles (forthcoming) notes in her piece, 'The Time of Digital Poetry: From Object to Event':

> The materiality of digital text increases the writer's sense that writing is not merely the fashioning of a verbal abstraction but a concrete act of making, a production that involves manual manipulation, proprioceptive projection, kinesthetic involvement, and other physical senses.

Consider the print poet who types a line of poetry, revises it and then sits back, satisfied. As far as that line is concerned, she considers her work done. As Marjorie Luesebrink writes:

> Compare this to the same line typed by an author working in new media. In addition to considering the effects of the words, this author must also decide the background on which the words will appear, the behaviors that will attach to it, the color, size, and type of font in which it will appear, whether it will have links anchored to it or not, and a host of other factors that the digital medium makes possible. (Quoted in Hayles, forthcoming)

In other cases of digital writing, such as Instant Messaging (IM), the hybrid nature of textuality in Internet communication also contributes to performative enactments of identity. The textuality of writing is used to perform the textual qualities of speech. This blending of spoken and written textuality results in hybrid language forms to represent the casual, insider exchanges of informal speech through written textual features.

To achieve a speech-like quality, electronic writers use syntax, vocabulary and usage more common in speech as well as abbreviations to make for quick speech-like exchanges and to communicate paralinguistic features of face-to-face communication contexts. Using examples from a study of IM carried out by one of the authors of this chapter, Cynthia Lewis (Lewis and Fabos, 2005), IM users' vocabulary included words with dropped endings, 'just chattin'' and abbreviations made for speedy responses, 'Im' for (I am) and 'u' for (you). Abbreviations such as 'LOL' (laugh out loud) or 'POS' (parents over shoulder) were used to communicate what interlocutors would have seen had they been communicating face to face. The textual shape that IM takes, then, is an innovative blending of speech and writing. As Guy Merchant points out:

> traditional distinctions between speech as synchronous face-to-face communication in a shared location and writing as a means of communicating through time and space are challenged by new technology. (2001: 299)

The textual shape of Internet communication is significant as it relates to the kinds of social identities afforded through its use. Again, performativity is central to this discussion. Angela Thomas, whose research focuses on young people's uses of digital writing, pointed out: 'In the online context ... to write is to exist ... writing is an essential component for performing identity' (2004: 366).

One of the participants in Thomas's study explained in an interview the strategies she used to create interaction through textuality (e.g. exclamation marks, references to actions and facial expressions). Thomas made the link to identity performance:

> ... what is rarely reported is that the linguistic variations of cybertalk are directly related to identity performance. Violetta revealed that her words had to look just so, and that she would vary her style of speech according to the persona she was performing. (p. 366)

Writers who write on-line often enact identities through language that sounds and looks like speech, but is accomplished through writing. One of Lewis's participants in her study of IM (Lewis and Fabor, 2005), a 13-year-old, wrote her way into the textual worlds of a new group to which she wanted to belong, hearing the cadences of their inside jokes and trying to 'sound' right in writing.

The visual and aural elements of digital writing are prominent. The role of the visual is most often evident in the purposeful use of emoticons, colour, and font types. Digital writers often use variations on these devices to produce the sound of speech, using very large font to represent anger or shouting, for instance, or a cool colour to embody a sense of calm. Enacting identities, then, involves performing multivocal textual repertoires with speed and flexibility, using texts in new ways, reconfiguring messages, cutting and pasting, parodying, creating textual forms to fit one's social needs.

Circulation

As Kevin Leander and Kelly McKim (2003) suggest, examining how digital texts travel or circulate can lead to insights about the kinds of practices and relationships a particular technology affords. Digital writers often cut and paste, rearrange and reconfigure elements of their texts and others to be offered up in the digital landscape.

Being an agentic participant in these patterns of circulation requires quick, in-process thinking. It requires that users swiftly assess the nature of the circulating text, the purpose or agenda that led to its circulation, the audiences involved, the allegiances it may foster or damage, and so forth. Participants perform selves – enact identities – in relation to these circulating texts. These patterns of circulation function to reinforce social connections, creating bonds between particular users, sometimes at the expense of others.

Sonia Livingstone (2002) points out that Internet spaces are more often 'based on bricolage or juxtaposition'. This representational style is keyed not only to new epistemologies and new ways of being and thinking, but also, we believe, new practices of circulation. These new practices depend on the cut-and-paste style of bricolage and juxtaposition for production and exchange.

In her book *Young People and New Media*, Livingstone asks a question pertinent to this chapter.

> To the extent that we are indeed witnessing a transformation in the notion of the text, one must ask whether there are parallel changes in the user (or reader). And if so, are such changes in young people's ways of knowing to be encouraged? (2002: 229)

Like Livingstone, we believe that those of us interested in pedagogy must focus our attention on the user (reader/writer) of digital texts, not because the texts themselves are not important but because the user plays a more prominent role in digital media practices. A prominent feature of IC is interactivity, with reader, writer and text merging in a fast-paced exchange of words in print, words to be encoded, decoded, interpreted, invented, revised, inflected, and so on, moment to moment. Add to this drama, the incorporation of graphical elements such as photo and video-streaming, emoticons, colour, and font variations, and we can begin to imagine the active involvement of the user, and therefore the need for educators to understand the user's role in the reading and writing practices on-line. Scholars of new media literacies (Kress, 2003; Luke, 2003) point to the need for flexible reading and writing practices that include reading laterally across surfaces, genres and modes. Students with flexible reading and writing repertoires are more likely to be adept producers and consumers of multimodal, quick-access texts.

3. NOTABLE RESOURCES FOR CREATIVE WRITING TEACHERS

New media literature: organizations and resources

Born Magazine: www.bornmagazine.org
Directory of new media literature: http://directory.eliterature.org
The Electronic Literature Organization: www.eliterature.org
FictionBlogs: http://fictionblogs2.blogspot.com
The Iowa Review Web: http://www.uiowa.edu/~iareview/mainpages/tirwebhome.htm
Trace Online Writing Center: http://trace.ntu.ac.uk/
Ubu Web: http://ubu.com

New media literary projects

aND, mIEKAL, 'Seedsigns for Philadelpho': http://cla.umn.edu/joglars/SEEDSIGN
Beiguelman, G., 'Egoscópio': www.desvirtual.com/egoscopio
Chevrel, S. and Kean, G., 'You and We', *Born Magazine:* www.bornmagazine.org/youandwe
Joyce, M., 'Reach': www.uiowa.edu/~iareview/tirweb/hypermedia/michael_joyce/ReachTitle.html
Memmott, T., 'Lexia to Perplexia': http://trace.ntu.ac.uk/newmedia/lexia/index.htm
Niss, M. and Deed, M., 'Oulipoems': www.uiowa.edu/~iareview/tirweb/feature/sept04/
Stefans, B. K., 'the dreamlife of letters': www.ubu.com/contemp/stefans/dream
Swiss, T., 'Genius': www.thomasswiss.com

Notable readings in print and on websites on new media literature and literacy

Alvermann, D. E., *Adolescents and Literacies in a Digital World* (New York: Peter Lang), 2002.
Beiguelman, G., 'Egoscope' (www.desvirtual.com/egoscopio/english/about_more.htm).
Bolter, J. and Grusin, R., *Remediation: Understanding New Media* (Cambridge, MA: The MIT Press), 2000.
Goldsmith, K., 'Uncreativity as a Creative Practice', *Drunken Boat 5* (Winter 2002–03). (http://drunkenboat.com/db5/goldsmith/uncreativity.html).
Jewitt, C. and Kress, G. (eds), *Multimodal Literacy: New Literacies and Digital Epistemologies* (Vol. 4) (New York: Peter Lang), 2003, pp. 1–18.
Kellner, D., 'New Media and New Literacies: Reconstructing Education for the New Millennium', in L. A. Lievrouw and S. Livingstone (eds), *Handbook of New Media: Social Shaping and Consequences of ICTs* (Thousand Oaks, CA: Sage Publications), 2002, pp. 90–104.
Kress, G., *Literacy in the New Media Age* (New York: Routledge), 2003.

Lankshear, C. and Knobel, M. *New Literacies: Changing Knowledge and Classroom Learning* (Philadelphia, PA: Open University Press), 2003.

Lankshear, C. and Knobel, M., ' "New" Literacies: Research and Social Practice'. Opening plenary address presented at the Annual Meeting of the National Reading Conference, San Antonio, TX (available at: www.geocities.com/Athens/Academy/1160/nrc.html), 2004.

Montfort, N., *Twisty Little Passages: An Approach to Interactive Fiction* (Cambridge, MA: The MIT Press), 2003.

Morris, A. and Swiss, T. (eds) *New Media Poetics: Contexts/Technotexts/Theories* (Cambridge, MA: The MIT Press), 2006.

Sapnar, M., ' "The Letters Themselves": An Interview with Ana Maria Uribe', *The Iowa Review Web* (www.uiowa.edu/~iareview/tirweb/feature/uribe/uribe.html), 2002.

Strickland, S., 'Poetry in the Electronic Environment', *electronic book review* (www.electronic bookreview.com/v3/servlet/ebr?command=view_essay&essay_id=stricklandtwoele), 1997.

Wardrip-Fruin, N. and Harrigan, P. (eds), *First Person: New Media as Story, Performance, and Game* (Cambridge, MA: The MIT Press), 2004.

Wardrip-Fruin, N. and Montfort, N. (eds), *The New Media Reader* (Cambridge, MA: The MIT Press), 2003.

4. TEACHING/LEARNING/UNDERSTANDING NEW MEDIA WRITING

To demonstrate some of the key points from the previous section in action, we offer a description of a course titled 'Uncreative Writing'. The class combined new media writing with the aesthetics of appropriation, and was designed to help students develop adaptable reading and writing practices across genres and modes. Offered at the university level, the class enrolled undergraduate and graduate students, some of whom were high school teachers of creative writing.

Students understood that the class would offer possibilities for creative writing while examining traditional notions of 'authorship', 'the artist', and so on – all notions that are increasingly complicated by contemporary practices such as file-sharing, sampling and digital replication. During the term we traced the rich history of forgery, frauds, hoaxes, avatars and impersonations across writing and the arts; examined how Modernist notions of chance, procedure and repetition influence a variety of current writing and art practices; and gave students experience employing strategies of appropriation as a compositional method for writing in new media.

Students were asked to read, write and 'create' each week. The Web, spam, file-sharing, chat rooms, and so on were employed as objects of study and as sources for writing material. Readings, listenings and viewings included, among others, writing and sound pieces by John Cage; John Oswald's *Plunderphonics*; Yoko Ono's work; various writers on the concepts of 'originality' and 'authorship', including 'Gathered, Not Made: A Brief History of Appropriative Writing' by Raphael Rubinstein (1999), Michel Foucault's 'What is an Author?' (1977), 'Reconfiguring the Author' by George P. Landow (1997), and *Writing Machines* by N. Katherine Hayles (2003); art by those who appropriate materials for their own work; *A Book of Surrealist Games* (Brotchie and Gooding, 1995); and materials developed out of the Oulipo, Fluxus and Conceptual movements. These readings were chosen to open students' eyes to various conceptual frameworks that do not follow the orthodoxy of the traditional writing workshop and to offer conceptual possibilities and ideas for creative writing projects the students might undertake during the term.

On the aesthetic end, students learned about appropriation, its history, its contexts and its possibilities for writing in new media. On the writing end, students learned how to take possession of another's material and reuse it in a context that differs from its original context in order to examine issues concerning originality or to reveal meaning not previously seen in the original. Along the way, we waded into related concepts (literary, artistic and legal) such as analogy, copyright, facsimile, homage, replica, representation, reproduction, simile, simulacrum and simulation.

While it is impossible to reproduce what the students wrote during the term (their products, of course, were not print-bound, but digitally based or physical objects/ installations), we'll offer three brief assignments that led to successful student pieces, all of them requiring, at most, only basic Web skills, although students were encouraged, later in the term, to develop projects using Flash, Photoshop, Apple's iMovie, and other multimedia software.

1. Let's start low-tech and think about appropriation as collage. Taking a magazine of your choice, cut out as many images as you like. Using the same magazine, cut out as many words, phrases and sentences as you like. Now build something with them: a physical object that employs at least some of the images and language you chose. You only have a week, so you won't be building anything too elaborate, but whatever you make should somehow 'work' with the language and images you chose. Finally, write a few paragraphs about what you did and why.

2. Design a web page (or a number of linked pages) that incorporates the following: lines from poems, professional or amateur, that you find on the Web, images you find on the Web, links you find on the Web, and sounds you find on the Web. The design of the page, however, should be your own. Write a few paragraphs about what you did and why.

3. Locate, in digital form, an official document that has social power over some aspect of your life: a state law, a marriage contract, a work or school policy, etc. Take any written part or parts of the document and connect them, in any manner you choose, with other 'found' digital language – language from a different genre of writing. Create a web page. By 're-purposing' the language and possibly adding images or sound, you are creating new contexts for the contents of both originals. Can you help us 'see' meanings not previously seen in the originals?

In these assignments, it is process, rather than product, that plays a central role in what we wanted students to learn about new media writing. More importantly, however, the assignments work with and foster the dimensions of practice that are key to digital writing. Students are invited to experiment with appropriated language, sounds and images to remake and recirculate these semiotic resources. In one student's project, for instance, canonized poetry lyrics were juxtaposed with magazine copy for make-up ads and then the project was made to look like a brochure, thus allowing the student to cross modes and genres to create new meaning.

The assignments encourage students to mesh sound and print, adding new dimensions to the traditionally language-based textuality of writing. Varied font styles, colours and sizes were used to represent multiple voices that were held in productive tension with the residual voice of the 'original'. In one student's project, for instance, the doctrinaire language and misguided assumptions about teaching and learning behind the President Bush-sponsored 'No Child Left Behind' legislation in the US was exposed as nonsense by situating the official language of the document among the language of fairy tales as well as 'instructional' books from the 1950s on subjects such as childhood, social mobility, and so on.

The practices we are spotlighting in this piece – appropriation and circulation, collaboration, hybrid textuality, performativity, multivocality – are fundamental to producing, consuming and exchanging new media. Students who have grown up in digital times understand these practices in ways that teachers often do not. They are accustomed – not just from the digital, but from film, television and music, as well – to making intertextual connections in order to 'get it'. All the jokes are 'in jokes' that combine appropriated language, images and sounds for satiric, comedic, or dramatic effects. As teachers of creative writing, we need to understand how new media works and provide opportunities for our students to analyse new media across genres so that they, too, can begin to articulate the nature of the practices and features they may know only intuitively from direct experience. Assignments such as those we shared engage students both in production of new media and in analysis, allowing them to articulate the intertextuality at the heart of the enterprise. As teachers of creative writing, we need to understand the shifts in practices and epistemologies that have taken place and consider how these shifts should inform our teaching of reading and writing in digital times.

WORKS CITED

Brotchie, A. (complier) and Gooding, M. (ed.), *The Book of Surrealist Games* (Berkeley, CA: Shambhala Publications), 1995.

Foucault, M., 'What is an Author?', trans. D. F. Bouchard and S. Simon, in D. F. Bouchard (ed.), *Language, Counter-Memory, Practice* (Ithaca, NY: Cornell University Press), 1977, pp. 124–7.

Hayles, N. K., *Writing Machines* (Chicago, IL: University of Chicago Press), 2003.

Hayles, N. K., 'The Time of Digital Poetry: From Object to Event', in A. Morris and T. Swiss (eds), *New Media Poetics: Contexts/Technotexts/Themes* (Cambridge, MA: The MIT Press), forthcoming.

Ito, M., 'Technologies of childhood imagination: Yugioh, media mixes, and everyday cultural production' (available at www.itofisher.com/mito/archives/000074.html), 2005.

Kress, G., *Literacy in the New Media Age* (New York: Routledge), 2003.

Kress, G., Jewett, C. and Tsatsarelis, C., 'Knowledge, identity, pedagogy: pedagogic discourse and the representational environment of education in late modernity', *Linguistics and Education*, Vol. 11, No. 1 (March 2000), 7–30.

Landow, G. P., *Hypertext 2.0: The Convergence of Contemporary Critical Theory and Technology* (Baltimore, MD: The Johns Hopkins University Press), 1997.

Lankshear, C. and Knobel, M., *New Literacies: Changing Knowledge and Classroom Learning* (Philadelphia, PA: Open University Press), 2003.

Leander, K. M. and McKim, K., 'Tracing the everyday "sitings" of adolescents on the Internet: a strategic adaptation of ethnography across online and offline spaces', *Education, Communication, & Information*, Vol. 3, No. 2 (2003), 211–40.

Lewis, C. and Fabos, B., 'Instant Messaging, literacies, and social identities', *Reading Research Quarterly*, Vol. 40, No. 4 (2005), 470–501.

Livingstone, S., *Young People and New Media* (London: Sage), 2002.

Memmott, T., *[N]+Semble* (available at http://memmott.org/talan/rtp27/), 2005.

Merchant, G., 'Teenagers in cyberspace: an investigation of language use and language change in Internet chatrooms', *Journal of Research in Reading*, Vol. 24, No. 3 (2001), 293–306.

Morris, A., 'New Media Poetics: As We May Think/How to Write', in A. Morris and T. Swiss (eds),

New Media Poetics: Contexts/Technotexts/Themes (Cambridge, MA: The MIT Press), forthcoming.

Rubenstein, R., 'Gathered, Not Made: A Brief History of Appropriative Writing', *The American Poetry Review* (March/April 1999) (also available at www.ubu.com/papers/rubenstein.html).

Strickland, S. with Lawson, C., *V: Vniverse* (available at www.vniverse.com), 2002.

Swiss, T. and Nakamura, M., *Hey Now* (available at http://bailiwick.lib.uiowa.edu/swiss/web/heynow.html), 2002.

Thomas, A., 'Digital literacies of the cybergirl', *E-Learning*, Vol. 1, No. 3 (2004), 358–82.

Young-hae Chang Heavy Industries, *Dakota* (available at www.yhchang.com/DAKOTA.html), 2001.

Chapter 10

Critical-Creative Rewriting

Rob Pope
Oxford Brookes University

> Look before you leap is criticism's motto. Leap before you look is creativity's.
> E. M. Forster, *Two Cheers for Democracy*, 1951

1.

I would not say that I teach creative writing. If asked, I simply say that I get my students to *'play around with texts seriously'*. And then, if pushed, I add: *'they do critical-creative rewriting'*. At that point the subject is changed or we get into an interesting discussion: about what we mean by 'creative' and 'critical', and why 'rewriting'. *Playing around* sounds right because I strongly believe that education is first and foremost a *play-space*, and only secondarily and sometimes a training-ground: more of a dance than a route-march. Above all it is a space in which people get to experiment and stretch and bend as well as observe the 'rules of the game' (in our case, language and culture, texts and genres). And to do that, I insist, everyone must realize that they have a crucial part to play in how all the various 'games' change and evolve. They do this palpably in the present case by changing other people's texts and generating their own out of them. It should be stressed that these are acts of *intervention* – not imitation or simulation, and still less dissimulation (more on this shortly). I'd also emphasize that they do this *seriously* – though not necessarily solemnly. Getting in on the intertextual act is demanding as well as rewarding work. That brings us to the two key terms already introduced, which I prefer to tie with a hyphen and treat as a compound.

Why *critical-creative*? The answer is simple: because in education, especially self-consciously 'higher education', evidence of critical understanding is as important as a demonstration of creative capacity. Whatever you may do with writing 'outside the academy', within it you have to *show that you know* what you're doing, or at least make some informed and plausible gestures. It's like doing maths: you have to show the workings not just the results. In short, you have to be *critical* as well as *creative*. Of course, all mature courses in Creative Writing require some evidence of 'process', too. But unless this is supported by a work-log and a full record of research and reading as well as reflection (as in a comprehensive portfolio), the critical element is often perfunctory: a dutiful bolt-on attached after the event.

With critical-creative rewriting the emphasis is different from the start. Research into and comparison with the text you are rewriting (what I call the 'base text') are foundational and integral – not optional or secondary – elements of the process. Further, it is called the 'base text' – rather than, say, 'the original' or 'the source' – for several significant reasons that help clarify the nature of the project. Firstly, many texts exist in more than one version and virtually all went through more than one draft (think of the various drafts and edited versions of *Hamlet* or an Emily Dickinson poem or a Virginia Woolf novel – or of a critical essay); so the notion of 'the original' (definite and singular) is at best a convenient illusion. Secondly, no text is 'original' in an absolute sense; all texts at the very least draw on the resources of language and culture at large and many have identifiable sources, influences or precursors. Indeed, up to the eighteenth century 'original' tended to mean 'ancient, going back to the origin, the beginning', and had a sense diametrically opposed to its predominantly post-Romantic and modern sense of 'new, novel, never been done before' (see *OED* senses 2 and 3). Thirdly, 'base text' is a reminder to keep building on or from someone else's text while rewriting, and to 'return to base' explicitly in the commentary.

Rewriting is therefore central to the present approach. We always start with a text that already exists, preferably in more than one version, and then we rewrite it: adapt it, critique it, intervene in it. (So in that sense it involves plenty of 'rereading', too.) Rewriting has such a crucial role to play, I suggest, because of its capacity to connect practices of critical reading to those of creative writing. Institutionally, meanwhile, it offers a way of connecting the analytical and historical study of 'Literature' and 'Language' to the practices of both 'Composition and Rhetoric' and 'Creative Writing'. Rewriting – along with its corollary process of Rereading – can therefore be conceived as the 'missing link' between Reading and Writing, just as a recognition of the Critical-Creative dimensions of both confirms the connection and continuity between Criticism and Creativity as notionally distinct entities. In fact, all these processes are so *inter*linked that they are worth trying to represent in a single diagram (Figure 10.1).

REREADING / REWRITING

(CRITICAL-CREATIVE)

CRITICAL READING   CREATIVE WRITING

Figure 10.1 *The missing link between critical reading and creative writing*

This should be read dynamically and cyclically, not just linearly and left to right. And in the present case the emphasis is on the highlighted terms at the apex. These draw attention to the continuous and iterative nature of the processes of 'rereading / rewriting': readings that become writings that are themselves reread and rewritten, and so on. These are also the points of 'critical-creative' convergence and cross-over. They confirm the fact that reading is not just 'critical' but also 'creative' (we imagine worlds in responses to words); and that, conversely, writing is not just 'creative' but that there is always a 'critical' dimension to it too (we weigh the words we choose). The terms at the apex are a reminder not to miss these 'links' but keep on forging and refashioning them. For how often do we hear the complaint that many Creative Writing students 'don't read', or overlook the equally curious fact that many Literature students 'don't write'! Well, this is a simple but I hope memorable attempt to help mend as well as mind the gap. It is also the general framework in which the various 'play-spaces' of this approach to textual practice operate. Such a model of Critical-Creative Rewriting may not be a cure-all, personally or institutionally; but it does offer a kind of hold-all.

But there is a more specific side to this approach that I want to introduce, something with more edge to it. It is what I elsewhere call 'textual intervention' (see Pope, 1995, 2002, 2003). *Textual intervention* is the more or less deliberate challenging and changing of a text so as to put it off balance: to point it in a fresh direction or develop it in an alternative dimension – to de- and re-centre, de- and re-construct it. This might involve anything from tinkering with a few words to full-scale textual transformation. Playing with the opening line of Hamlet's most famous soliloquy so as to produce 'To buy or not to buy, that is the question nowadays' is a slight, small-scale example. Bringing some background characters centre-stage and recasting the whole play accordingly, as does Tom Stoppard in *Rosencrantz and Guildenstern Are Dead*, is a famous example of complete overhaul and radical reorientation. Another, equally classic instance is Jean Rhys's *Wide Sargasso Sea*, which 'writes back' to Charlotte Brontë's *Jane Eyre* and gives us a kind of prequel in which the early life story of the otherwise invisible and now famous 'madwoman in the attic' (Bertha Mason) is told through the words and world of a Creole woman on Dominica. Countless other examples could be cited, and some more are later.

The important thing is that students can and do rewrite in these ways, too. What's more, if it's set up properly (and not just offered as a passing gesture), they tend to do it with real commitment and resource, and produce some remarkable work. One of them recently referred to it as 'adaptation with attitude'. But before we consider student examples of the practice in detail, I want to cue the theoretical issues – and the intellectual challenges – more clearly. Provocatively, too. So I shall flag them up in the form of a manifesto.

2.

Manifesto for rewriting – 10 proposals in search of a response

1. In reading texts we rewrite them.
2. Interpretation *of* texts always involves interaction *with* texts.
3. Interaction *with* texts always involves intervention *in* texts.
4. Translation fully grasped is a form of transformation, never mere transference. All writing and reading is a form of 'translation'.
5. One text leads to another and another and another – so we had better grasp texts intertextually, through their similarities and differences.
6. Our own words are always implicated in those of others – so we had better grasp our selves interpersonally through dialogue: voicing dissent as well as assent, and thereby joining in the ongoing 'conversations' we variously call Culture, History, Life.
7. Because textual *changes* always involve social *exchanges*. You can't have the one

without the other – and one another. Perhaps we should think therefore in terms of *ex/changes*.

8. Responding fully and being responsive are responsible acts. Perhaps we should talk about '*response-ability / responsibility*', too.

9. *De*-construction is best realized through *re*-construction, just as thoroughgoing *critique* comes out as radical *re-creation* – taking apart to put together differently. Then we really notice the bits that are missing ... or added ... or modified.

10. For 'interpretation' can be done through acts of critical-creative performance (as in dance and music) as well as in commentary and analysis. And we are all in various ways or at different moments both performers *and* commentators, critics *and* creators. (The knack is to know when and how and how much.)

There's obviously a catch with this manifesto. And you must decide for yourself whether it's a productive paradox or a fatal flaw. There's also a kind of cumulative logic that you may find compelling or bullying. For the curious fact is that if you agree with the above propositions completely – and wouldn't want to change a single word or link – then both you and they are wrong! But if you care to challenge and change some or perhaps all of those words – either because you disagree with them or want to put them in your own way – then both they and you are right! For my part, it's the spirit rather than the letter that counts. In fact, if you and your students felt moved to rip up this manifesto and write one of your own in response, it would have succeeded more than I could hope.

We now look at some specific rewriting activities and some samples of actual student work. For convenience, I shall distinguish these as *object lessons, one-liners* and *extended activities*, as that is how I tend to think of them. One-liners are handy as preludes to get people warmed up and tuned in, or to reinforce a particular point and vary the pace during a session. Extended activities are the work at the core, the main play-space, and can take anything from half an hour to half a day, depending on how long you've got. But before considering these I would briefly like to mention what I call ...

3. (4)

Object lessons

Like many people who teach Creative Practices of one kind or another, I will sometimes start or punctuate a session with an object: an artefact, an image, a sound, anything. My favourite one involves some pieces of hessian sacking which I distribute, get people to smell, feel, pull apart, and wonder and talk about (what precisely is it made of? where is it from? what stories might it tell? what histories might it be implicated in?). Meanwhile, we also use the sacking as a focus for an exploration of the nature of 'text'. For it is pointed out (on an overhead transparency) that the word comes from the Latin *texere*, 'to weave', and *textum*, 'a woven thing, web' – whence English 'textile' and 'texture'. Students are also told that all the pieces in fact belong to the same sack, which happens to be for cocoa beans from Ghana. By these means we get into discussion not only of 'intertextuality', language as a 'web of words' and 'the World Wide Web' but also the intricate interrelations of world trade, colonial history, cash crops, monoculture and the continuing legacies of post- and neo-colonialism. (Cocoa was brought to Africa from South America by Europeans in the seventeenth century; it is still produced in the 'poor South' chiefly for consumption in the 'rich North', particularly in chocolate.)

More generally, again like many colleagues, I draw attention to the fact that stories and histories readily attach to and spin out from just about any object (the contents of pockets, purses, wallets and bags are virtual treasure troves, of course – and bunches of keys unlock whole universes). It all depends on how you look at and handle them. My favourite references here are to the actual Ring and Book that helped prompt and inform Robert Browning's epic verse narrative of that name (1868, described in its opening lines); and to the actual Scarlet Letter ('A') that acted as catalyst and fixing point for Nathaniel Hawthorne's novel, as worked up in 'The Custom House' section (1850). (Both these 'object lessons' are featured in Pope 2005: 224–6.) In the present context, what I would emphasize is that all these bits of the world, natural and/or otherwise, in effect get *rewritten* (or *respoken*) simply by the acts of being selected, attended to and talked about. In other words – for one of the main points is that there are always 'other words' – we tell and constantly retell stories and histories in our own and others' terms and times; and they in turn, in the (re)telling, tell us a lot about ourselves and one another. It's as simple – and complex – as that.

My favourite 'object lessons' with images tend to involve cartoons and news photos with the words removed, sometimes paintings without their titles. Students 'just add words', either as captions and titles or speech and thought bubbles. We then go on to talk about which aspects of the image have thereby been drawn attention to ('centred'); also how captions and titles tend to develop a 'narrative' mode while speech and thought bubbles develop a 'dramatic' mode. This is a good way into critical-creative rewriting as it confirms the fact that words are one of the main ways we 'anchor' and 'articulate' worlds. They help resolve potentially infinite differences into particular preferences; theoretically limitless interpretative possibilities become just a few, actual, performed 'interpretations'.

Finally, just for the hell of it, I must mention 'Bibi'. Bibi is a wild orange glove puppet with a wheezy squeaker. She or he or it – Bibi's gender and sexuality have never been fixed and the name may be 'Beebee' or even 'Beepbeep!' as it's never been written down before – is great for passing round in class. Students take it in turn to insert their hand and then speak/squeak/squawk/whisper and generally 'ventriloquize' their way through tricky or potentially dull parts of a task. In fact, 'interpreting' and 'translating' Bibi's response to just about anything that's going on in class encourages some remarkably forthright (often very funny) checks on the current state of play. The only thing you've got to be careful of is calling Bibi a 'transactional' or 'transitional' object to her/his/its face. Though that's precisely what makes puppets and suchlike so invaluable as facilitators and go-betweens. Child's play? Certainly. Adults play? Seriously, I hope so.

One-liners

Here we pick up single sentences and very short texts that can be used for brief yet intensive rewriting activities. Snatches of pop songs, adverts and public pronouncements are all good for this; so are well-known quotes from the arts and sciences, also conversational clichés. The main thing is that the texts should be pithy and provocative or, conversely, over-familiar and apparently inert. But wherever it's from, the instruction to students, who as usual are best working in groups of two or three initially, is simple and the same: *Change this line a little or a lot. Then analyse the differences and weigh the preferences.* Here are some examples with the base texts in upper case and the student rewrites below. There isn't space here for the analyses, which can be remarkably complex (for extensive analyses of some related but different examples, see Pope 1995: 31–9). So please feel free to supply some yourself, and think which aspects of the rewrites you would help draw students' attention to:

I THINK, THEREFORE I AM (*Cogito, ergo sum*, René Descartes)

I FEEL, THEREFORE I AM (*Je sens donc je suis*, Jean-Jacques Rousseau)

I shop, therefore I am.

I shop (drink, screw, believe …), therefore I am poor (happy, shagged out, a believer …).

It thinks therefore we are thoughtless.

Because I feel sleepy I don't think too well.

'I wonder how he feels,' thinks woman.

'I wonder what she thinks,' feels man.

Get you. You're thinking logically: 'Therefore!'

[Often there is a suggestive slide towards a hybrid allusion or a straight counter-reference]

BRIAN: 'You're all individuals. Think for yourselves!' CHORUS: 'We're all individuals. Think for us!' (adapted from Monty Python's *Life of Brian*)

'Thou art that' / 'It is you' ('*Tat twam asi*', Upanishads)

'I am that I am' (*Genesis*)

'Iyamwhatlyam – I'm Popeye the Sailor Man!'

'What if am a butterfly dreaming I am a man dreaming I am a butterfly …?' (Lao Tzu – or his pet butterfly)

Obviously texts that feature personal pronouns (such as the Descartes and Rousseau) offer abundant opportunities for sporting with constructions of identity, subject position and perspective – and thereby critique of dominant rationalist or emotionalist constructions of the individual. They can also, as the above examples attest, provide focuses for experiments in kinds of narrative and dramatic reframing, as well as prompts for explorations of intertextuality. Much the same can be said of and done with the next example – but differently. For there the base text is contemporary and more overtly socially engaged.

Smoking cigarettes can seriously damage your health
Some years ago I showed how students went about exploring and exploding this, the main, then-current UK Government Health Warning (Pope, 1995: 39–43). At that time, rewrites ranged from relatively slight yet still significant variations such as 'Smoking Cigarettes may slightly (will totally) damage (affect, destroy) your health (wall-paper, lungs)' to more radical transformations and travesties based on further reading, research and reflection. Examples of the latter included: 'Tobacco is a cash crop you cannot eat and it makes those who grow it economically dependent. Are you dependent on tobacco too?'; 'Taxing Question: Why isn't this Government Health Warning in huge black letters on every side of an empty pack?'; and 'It is your God-given, democratic and commercial right in a free society with a free market and freedom of expression to smoke wherever

and whenever you damn well like'. Since then, of course, the official warnings have got more direct ('Smoking kills', 'Smoking causes cancer') and explored a variety of alternative angles and targets: 'Smoking during pregnancy may harm your baby'; 'Protect children: don't make them breathe your smoke' and, latterly (2005), 'Smoking screws your sex life'; 'If you smoke, you stink'. Significantly, if unsurprisingly, none of these later 'official' versions comes anywhere near identifying or challenging the main economic drivers behind tobacco production and cigarette consumption: multi-million-dollar profits for tobacco companies and massive tax rake-offs for governments. They keep the onus on personal choice and the focus on the lifestyle of the consumer. As a result, questions posed by seriously funny student rewrites at the end of the last century have still not been addressed in public health – or should it be private wealth? – warnings. In this respect, to rip off a well-worn and long-running advertising slogan (for Heineken Lager), we might say that: 'Critical-Creative Rewriting refreshes the Parts other Approaches cannot Reach' – or that '... official discourses dare not touch'!

Since then, I should add, students have been invited to use these same Smoking Warnings as prompts and templates for one-liners on all manner of topics. For the 'smoking' slot can obviously be filled by all sorts of broadly similar, strikingly different or utterly daft alternatives: 'Drink' and 'Drugs', of course, but also 'Global Warming', 'G8 summits', 'Student Fees', 'Working while at University', 'Weapons of Mass Destruction (Lies about)', 'Al Qaeda (Threat of)' ... 'Politicians', 'Unprotected sex' ... 'Fast Food' ... 'Love', 'Rock "n" Roll' ... 'Two essays due in at the same time' ... English ... Creative Writing ... Critical-Creative Writing ... (The list is endless; though by the time we get to the latter, we're probably hoping for witty inversions and covert approval.)

There are two broader issues that I would like to signal here. One is that while such parodic rewriting practices chime with a tendency in popular culture at large, they may represent a radically leading – not just a commercially trailing – edge: counter-culture not just consumer culture. 'Postmodern playfulness' need not be a creature of the market – even though it often is. The other point has to do with a useful but not absolute distinction between text-based activities for 'Creative Writing' and for 'Critical-Creative Rewriting'. Whereas the former uses texts as prompts or templates to make something fresh and will generally leave the cue text behind, the latter uses them to make something fresh and will return to the base text for explicit comparison and contrast. In Forster's terms (offered in the opening epigraph), these are different kinds of 'leap' as well as different ways of 'looking'. To be sure, these are *not* mutually exclusive approaches: the one may turn into (or return to) the other. But it is still handy to distinguish the overall trajectories, if only to get the initial aims and expectations clear in our own and our students' minds. Creative Writing takes off and goes elsewhere. Critical-Creative Rewriting takes off but eventually comes back.

There are obviously many ways in which one-liners can, if you wish, be extended into more elaborate and demanding activities. One is to get students to put together a joint text based upon a selection of their individual rewrites and thus produce a 'many-liner'. This can be left relatively raw and be realized simply by reading round in class or by listing on the same sheet of paper. (In that sense the above list of responses to Descartes and Rousseau forms a kind of ramshackle many-liner.) But more considered and polished collaborations are possible, too. These often entail small groups of two or three students going off and doing some sustained crafting, as well as perhaps some research. Here, for example, is a highly finished collaborative text that began as a group rewrite of GOD DOES NOT PLAY DICE (various versions attributed to Albert Einstein) together with, finally, a rewriting of Nietzsche's 'GOD IS DEAD'. (This one was put together by members of the 'Language, Literature, Discourse II' group at Oxford Brookes in 2000.)

God!
God does?
God does not.
God does not play?!
God does not play dice –

She plays poker.

And yet
the Devil
the Devil played fast and loose
at Los Alamoooose (Boom!)
then Hiroshima and Nagasaki
and Long Island and Chernobyl ...
and still
has not presented the bill,

Perhaps God plays loaded dice

Or is dead
drunk.

A further related activity, also involving information search, is to get students to track down their one-line text *in context*. And when they do, they invariably find that it is far more complex and vexed than they imagined. They discover, for example: that Descartes' famous dictum turns out to be a passing elaboration in parentheses in his *Discourse on Method* (Ch. 4) and that an earlier, rather different version crops up in his *Meditation*; that there is considerable argument over what precisely Einstein said and meant about 'God' and 'dice', and how precisely to translate his German, for he said similar things differently, in different languages, at various times; and that Nietzsche in his *The Gay Science* added a significant rider to what, again, turns out not to have been a free-standing statement at all: 'God is dead, but considering the state the species Man is in there will perhaps be caves for ages yet in which his shadow will be shown'. The wonder of working and playing with such tiny texts is that, as with Blake's 'grain of sand', students can come to grasp that they 'hold infinity in the palm of *their* hands'. And with particularly lively sessions they may even get an intimation of 'eternity in an hour' (which is very different from a dull session that just feels like eternity!).

Extended activities (life-rewriting)

While one-liners quickly turn into many, and with rewriting any text is as long as you make it, there are some more complex texts that require extended attention and more elaborate treatment from the outset. Here I shall outline three such extended activities, to do with various kinds of life-writing. To be precise, they all involve life-*re*writing. For the point of these activities is to explore the issue of who is rewriting whose life, how, for whom and why. And this applies whether the 'biography' in question is 'auto-' or otherwise. Needless to say, students are in on the act too.

Emily D. and 'I'

The first activity I shall simply outline, as versions have been published and reviewed elsewhere and an interactive version is being prepared for Web access at the English Subject Centre (www.rhul.ac.uk/ltsn/english). What is important pedagogically about this activity is that it uses what I call a 'split text/task' format. This entails choosing a text that exists in markedly different drafts or edited versions and exploring it through two distinct yet related activities. In class, these two texts/tasks are done by two halves of the class separately to begin with; then they come together to pool their various makings and findings. A similar 'split text/task' followed by 'pooling' can be handled outside class or on the Web. The main thing is that one half of the group initially doesn't know then gets to know what the other half has been up to. (Something similar happens with the 'Re-Joyce!' activity later.)

Here, then, is what happens with 'Emily D. and "I"'. Each half of the group (working in sub-groups of two or three) is given a differently edited and in places substantially distinct text of an eight-line poem by Emily Dickinson. One is the text beginning 'I'm nobody! Who are you? / Are you nobody, too?' as edited and deliberately 'tidied up' by Todd and Higginson in 1890 (Todd and Higginson, 1990). The other is the text as edited by Johnson for his scholarly edition of 1970, and begins 'I'm Nobody! Who are you? / Are you – Nobody – Too?' There are differences other than of punctuation between the two versions: the first has the lines '... don't tell! / They'd banish us, you know' and 'To tell your name the livelong day'; whereas the second has the lines 'Don't tell! They'd advertise – you know!' and 'To tell one's name – the livelong June'.

The tasks for each half of the class are rather different too. The first group (with just the earlier, 'tidied up' version) is asked to 'Rewrite this text so as to produce an alternative version that is distinct yet recognizably related. Keep quite close to the text's genre and structure.' Meanwhile, the second group are getting to grips not only with the later, scholarly text but also with an additional text that supplies some information on Emily Dickinson's life and work. This thumbnail sketch is drawn from a variety of referenced sources. As well as giving what is evidently a highly 'selective' – even 'slanted' – biography (it begins 'Emily Dickinson (1830–86) lived all her life in Amherst, Massachusetts. By the age of 30 she had become an almost total recluse ...'), it includes information on the state of her manuscripts, their subsequent textual transmission (including reference to both the editions featured) and her modern critical reception and reputation. The task for this second group is therefore markedly different. They are asked to 'Combine these two texts [the poem and the biographical and critical information] so as to produce a third text that is distinct yet in some way recognizably related. You are free to use whatever genre or structure you choose.'

That, in a nutshell, is how this particular 'split text/task' is set up. Obviously it is readily adaptable to all sorts of authors whose texts and lives and critical reception have a complex history that is in a more or less fragmentary state. (And whose haven't and aren't!) Needless to say, by design, the texts generated by the two halves of the group are markedly different. In the present case, for instance, responses to Text/Task A (the early text rewritten on its own) have begun with such lines as 'I was some body! But who were you? / Couldn't you have been somebody too?' and 'I've no body! What you too! / Or have you a body – two?' Meanwhile, responses to Text/Task B (later text plus critical biography) – which are often much longer and complex and even more inadequately represented by sampling – have been cast in everything from a concrete, snail-shaped poem to a bundle of letters tied with string and an email. One of the letters, for instance, begins 'Dear Nobody / I'm Emily – Who are you? / I know you are – not Emily – too. /

(She said putting on her white dress.) / There's only one of me. You as well. / (She said, not answering the door.) / Don't tell – or pull the bell ...' This version was all the more striking in class, as the group responsible performed it in two voices: one, female, clear and composed for the 'I'; the other, male, quiet and insistent for the bracketed 'She saids'.

A crucial and in every sense 'critical' point is reached when the two halves of the group come together; for then they get to see what each has been working on and playing at. This is the point at which the 'split' is in a sense 'mended'; but it is also the point when the nature of the 'gap' that had been opened up becomes fully visible. For the critical and theoretical issues exposed by this textual and pedagogic procedure are both obvious and profound: fundamentally divergent and yet palpably shareable. While the one group has been tackling the poem in an exclusively Formal, narrowly Textualist way (concentrating upon what Practical or (old) New Critics would call 'the words on the page', 'the 'poem in itself'), the other has been grappling with Texts-in-Contexts in a more inclusively Functional way (and in ways that might be termed New Historicist or Cultural Materialist, depending upon political emphasis). Put another way, while one is trying to grasp 'Writing as Literature', the other is grappling with 'Writing and/in/as Life'. There are profound implications in all this for ourselves as actively involved subjects as well as the reconfiguration of the educational subjects in which we operate, whether these be called 'Literature', 'Writing' or something else entirely.

Re-Joyce!

This is another life-rewriting activity that involves a 'split text/task'. This time the focus is on prose and the two base texts in play are: (A) the opening of James Joyce's *A Portrait of the Artist as a Young Man* (1916) (from 'Once upon a time and a very good time it was there was a moocow coming down along the road ...' to 'His mother had a nicer smell than his father'); and (B) the opening of the biographical blurb about Joyce that prefaces Harry Levin's influential collection first published in 1963 in the UK as 'Penguin Books 2009 – *The Essential James Joyce*' and later in the US as: 'Viking Books – *The Portable James Joyce*' (from 'James Joyce was born in Dublin on 2 February 1882 ...' to 'to the continent, where he planned to teach English'). Each text is presented on one side of a single sheet of paper (as it was for the Dickinson activity), so the two can be read separately by the two halves of the group. Not only is this economical, it also means that when they come to 'turn over the page' there is a palpable sense of grasping 'two sides' of notionally 'the same life'.

The first step is really by way of a 'warm-up' and is essentially a one-liner. Like all the instructions in this particular activity, it is the same for both halves of the group. Each simply applies it to a different text. *(1) Rewrite the title of your text [i.e. Text A or Text B] in some way that you consider interesting (provocative, playful). Go on to weigh how and why.* Here are some examples of what students have come up with in response to Text A (with an indication of their comments), and a couple of the alternatives to Text B.

A1.1   *a portrait of an artist as a young man*

(Making all the articles indefinite confirms how 'definite' and discriminating Joyce is in the distribution of his. Putting all the words in lower case also levels the otherwise grand-sounding common nouns.)

A1.2   *A Picture of Me as a Kid Writing*

(The colloquial, chatty feel of this points up the formal nature of Joyce's title and the – perhaps ironic? – 'arty' aspirations of its subject.)

A1.3   Some Self-obsessed Confessions by the Irish Piss-artist as a Guilt-ridden Adolescent Catholic

(No beating about the bush here! A gloriously rude, deliberately 'ideologically unsound' airing of prejudices about Joyce and the book. But with some 'home-truths', too, it was insisted.)

A1.4   Wot – no Pictures of Artisans as Old Women?!

(Another apparently simple inversion and change of register, this time on gender lines and turned into a question. But again the effect can be complex. It partly depends whether you connect this to the protagonist's mother or the old whore that he goes with.)

B1.1   An Inessential James Joyce or The Insupportable Joyce

All of him that's not worth reading or just too bloody difficult – including most of *Finnegans Wake.*

B1.2   'Which' Publishers, Which James Joyce?

A Consumer Guide to English Literature
One of a series including *What the Dickens?* and *Which Woolf?*

The second step requires some preparation, or a quick trip to the library or an Internet terminal during the session. Alternatively, there can be preliminary experiments and discussion in the session, or a follow-up afterwards so as to produce some more fully informed and polished versions. The latter is how the examples below were produced, and brought along the following week. The instruction was again the same for the whole group but applied to the two texts by different sub-groups: *(2) Recast the first sentence of your text so as to draw attention to other, relatable persons, places, times and points of view.* For reasons of space, I shall concentrate here on rewrites of the first sentence or two of Text B, the biographical blurb: 'James Joyce was born in Dublin on 2 February 1882. He was the oldest of ten children ...' We pick up rewrites of the opening of the novel, Text A, at the next stage. (Again, an indication of the proposed rationale and the ensuing discussion is added in brackets.)

B2.1   Mrs Mary Jane ('May') Joyce (née Murray, b. 1859) gave birth to her first son when she was 23 years old.

(This concerted refocusing of the moment of birth on the bearer's life rather than that of the born, the mother rather than the son, struck some as banal ('But surely we're interested in *his* life?!') and others like a bombshell ('Yes, but when did it begin?!').)

B2.2   In Dublin's fair city, where the maids are so pretty, the world set its eyes on sweet Jai-aimie Joyce.

(Foregrounding a mythic version of the city instead of the persons, and sporting with the melody while inverting the gender of the song's traditional subject – 'Sweet Molly Malone' – this was also defended as a reference to the encounters with the street-women in *A Portrait* and *Ulysses.*)

B2.3   February 1882. Fog on the Liffey. Famine not long before in Ireland. What was one birth among so many deaths? Who notices or cares when a 'star' is born?

(Rich in literary and popular cultural allusions – to the opening words of Dickens's *Bleak House* and a Judy Garland musical – as well as a historical reference to the recent potato blight and the ensuing (avoidable) famine, this aimed to pose questions about the assumed naturalness of beginning a 'life' with the famous named individual. And again, by contrast with the lively hybridity of the rewrite, the seemingly natural first line of the base text stands revealed as the standard and routine formula for the genre of biographical blurb.)

The third step is the final one reviewed in detail here. It, too, explores generic multiplicity and results in a textual hybrid. But now this is achieved by bringing the two base texts themselves together. Instead of occupying spatially and generically distinct positions some pages apart within the same *larger* text (*The Essential/Portable James Joyce*), they are compressed right down until they collide or coalesce within the same *smaller* text. A single sentence, in fact. The verbal energy generated and released by this process is both strange and colossal. Though whether it is best conceived as a process of textual 'fission' or of textual 'fusion' depends upon the particular reaction in hand – as well as the precise responses in the minds of rewriters and readers. Here are just two dynamic and highly condensed examples. I leave it to you, the present reader, to gauge whether my broadly 'nuclear' analogy is over- or under-blown. I also invite you to blend – extend, transcend – the two base texts as *you* wish. Here goes: *(3) Combine the openings of Text A and Text B so as to produce the beginnings of a third text. Go on to analyse the precise differences and similarities of all three texts, and to weigh the implications of what has taken place.*

A/B 3.1   Once upon a time James Joyce was born in Dublin on 2 February 1882 – and a very good time it was.

A/B 3.2   Joyce James. Cow moo. Born along down upon the good road time. 2.2.82. Very Dublin was. February was. In, in, in. A. a. It. When?

The suggested rationales for and ensuing discussions of these (and other) responses were variously bemused, amused and amazed. They ranged over such issues as: the tensions between 'sense' and 'nonsense'; the vexed and shifting relations among 'story' and 'history' and 'fiction' and 'fact' (with students declaring energetically both for and against such coinages as 'faction' and 'hi/story'); the impossibility of writing anything without at least some acceptance of conventional generic distinctions, and the impossibility of writing anything interesting without shaking them up; the claim that this was a travesty of Joyce and he would be appalled, and the counter-claim that he constantly did such things himself and would have approved this; and so on. There were also insistent questions about the (im)precise status of *A Portrait* as a kind of autobiographical fiction or *Bildungsroman* in the first place; and the value of a publisher's biographical blurb in the last.

There are another five steps of the activity that set out to address these issues. But again you will have got the idea; and will doubtless have more and different ideas of your own. So I shall just run through the other steps quickly, and leave you to fill them out or in – or add some others of your own – as you see fit. (This is, as I said, meant to be a dance everybody can join in with or change to suit themselves – not a route-march.)

(4) With all the resources at your disposal (the library, Internet, critical and creative intelligence, rhetorical skill), make a case for Text A (A Portrait) being 'truer' than Text B (the biographical sketch). Define your criteria and produce your evidence.

(5) Add some sights, smells, a sense of touch and a touch of music to Text B. Take them away from Text A and replace them with sensible but relatively 'sense-less' alternatives.

(6) See what happens to Text A and Text B if you try to turn them into (i) first-person narration (singular or plural, 'I' or 'we'); and (ii) second-person narration (again singular or plural, 'you'). Put whoever you choose in the 'I' or 'we' or 'you' positions: James Joyce, his mother or father or wife, Harry Levin, a version of yourself, anyone.

(7) Draw up lists of the three main kinds of noun in Text A and in Text B: common nouns (e.g. time, children); proper nouns/names (e.g. baby tuckoo, James Joyce); and personal pronouns (e.g. He, it). (You should therefore have three lists for each text.) What do these lists show you about the way the 'wor(l)d' is constructed in each text?

(8) Get hold of a copy of Joyce's Stephen Hero *(an earlier version of A Portrait) and of one of the 'classic' biographies of Joyce (by Ellman or O'Brien, for example). Read them for what they tell or show you about the issues involved in writing a life, whether nominally 'fictional' or 'factual', of 'oneself' or 'another'. Then consider how you might 'rewrite' them – separately or together – so as to explore life and/or/as writing for yourself and with others.*

Who's 'Dora'? Whose Dora!

This last activity is an instance of life-rewriting that involves not only a recasting of narrative but also an exploration of academic discourse through performance. There are some 'translation' issues, too. The text featured is Freud's *Fragment of an Analysis of a Case of Hysteria*, commonly known as 'Dora', after the pseudonym Freud gave his patient. But the same performance strategy, leading to the identification and construction of alternative subject positions, can be applied to virtually any text of a palpably multilayered and potentially many-voiced kind. For Freud's *Dora* is certainly multi-layered. It represents Freud in three quite distinct roles corresponding to at least three moments or levels of textual reproduction of the 'case history': Freud as interviewer (dramatic); Freud as reporter (narrative); and Freud as annotator (scholarly). 'Dora', meanwhile, is represented in just one role and mode of discourse: that of interviewee (dramatic). As a result, we are shown Freud *talking with* and *writing about* Dora and *adding annotations* on her case; but we are only shown her talking. What follows is the (slightly cut) opening of a longer passage from the case history that is used to set up this activity. But it gives the flavour of it, and some sense of the textual strategies that characterize the case study as a whole. We come in about half-way through. Freud is telling how he pressed Dora about her second dream, in which she dreamt her father had saved the family from a fire but her mother wanted to return to save her 'jewel-case':

> Much of the dream, however, still remained to be interpreted, and I proceeded with my question: 'What is this about the jewel-case that your mother wanted to save?'
> 'Mother is very fond of jewellery and had had a lot given her by Father.'
> 'And you?'
> 'I used to be very fond of jewellery too, once; but I have not worn any since my illness. Once four years ago' (a year before the dream), 'Father and Mother had a great dispute about a piece of Jewellery. [...]
> 'I dare say you thought to yourself you would accept it with pleasure.'
> 'I don't know. (1) I don't in the least know how Mother comes into the dream; she was not with us as L— at the time.' (2)
> 'I will explain that to you presently. Does nothing else occur to you in connection with the jewel-case? So far you have only talked about jewellery and have said nothing about a case.'
> 'Yes, Herr K. had made me a present of an expensive jewel-case a little time before.'
> 'Then a return present would have been very appropriate. Perhaps you do not know that "jewel-case" [Schmuckkästchen] is a favourite expression for the same thing that you alluded to not long ago by means of the reticule you were wearing (3) – for the female genitals, I mean.'
> 'I knew *you* would say that.' (4)
> 'That is to say, *you* knew that it *was* so. – The meaning of the dream is now becoming even clearer. You said to yourself: "This man is persecuting me; he wants to force his way into my room. My "jewel-case" is in danger, and if anything happens it will be Father's fault. For that

reason in the dream you chose a situation which expresses the opposite – a danger from which your father is saving you.'

(1) The regular formula with which she confessed to anything that had been repressed.

(2) This remark gave evidence of a complete misunderstanding of the rules of dream interpretation, though on other occasions Dora was perfectly familiar with them. This fact, coupled with the hesitancy and meagreness of the associations with the jewel-case, showed me that we were here dealing with material which had been very intensely repressed.

(3) This reference to the reticule will be explained further.

(4) A very common way of putting aside a piece of knowledge that emerges from the repressed.

(The passage appears on pages 104–5 of Freud's *Case Histories I: 'Dora' and 'Little Hans'* [1905] (1977), and can also be found with further comment in Pope (1998: 322–3).)

The first part of the activity is both simple and deeply revealing. Four students read the text out loud: three for Freud in his various roles as interviewer, narrator and annotator; and one for Dora as interviewee. This serves to demonstrate, palpably and audibly, a number of crucial dynamics of the discourses in play: (i) Dora is outnumbered three to one; (ii) she nonetheless has plenty to say for herself; (iii) there are places where yet another 'voice' may be needed (when the English editor and translator inserts '[Schmuckkästchen]') and where you have to decide whether two voices are needed simultaneously or just one (when Freud projects what 'You said to yourself'); and (iv) there is a lot of 'interpreting' going on at various levels (Dora and Freud about the dream; the students in their performance of it). There is therefore considerable room for manoeuvre and, in every sense, 'play' within the performed interpretation of the passage as a whole.

The second part of the activity is of a more deliberately *interventive* nature. The task now is to *rewrite the text* so as to explore possibilities that have either been implicit in the foregoing 'interpretation' (including the performance as well as the discussion) or have actually been precluded by Freud's text as it is written. That is, you can basically tinker with '*Dora*' or transform it completely. Both have things going for them, and students may need to be reminded that judicious tinkering can sometimes be more subtle and searching than total transformation (just see what happens if you systematically invert the personal pronouns, beginning with Dora's 'I knew *you* would say that', turning it into '*You* knew *I* would say that'!). Below are a few of the titles of (and rationales for) versions of Freud's *Fragment of an Analysis of a Case of Hysteria* ('*Dora*') that students have actually come up with. Some of these were sketched after experimenting with just a couple of passages. Others went much further and were fully worked up after extensive reading of and about the 'whole' case, including Freud's repeated revisions of it and what subsequently happened to the actual '*Dora*'. (Invaluable in this respect is *In Dora's Case: Freud, Hysteria, Feminism*, ed. Charles Bernheimer and Claire Kahane (1985), which includes essays by Jacques Lacan, Jacqueline Rose and Jane Gallop.)

Dora as Annotator and Translator: Dr Freud's 'Explanation' Complex
(Where the roles and levels of textuality are more evenly distributed, and the overall patient–doctor role is reversed.)

Educating Dora
(In which Dora, like the eponymous heroine of Willy Russell's *Educating Rita*, is not so much educated by her mentor as eventually instrumental in educating him.)

Ida Bauer: The real 'Dora' who stood up
(Based on a reconstruction of how she broke off the treatment and an account of her later life, counterpointed with Freud's continuing broodings over – and efforts to revise and recuperate – this 'fragment'.)

Not So Happy Families – the Group Therapy Version
(Treats the problem as one of the family and friends – especially the Father and Mother and Herr K. – not of the individual, 'Dora'. This was also a Gestalt Psychology approach that emphasized present choices and future possibilities rather than past conditions and child-hood.)

Sherlock Freud as Sigmund Holmes: The Case of the Missing Genitals – sorry – Jewel-case
(Playing on the more-than-coincidental contemporaneity of Conan Doyle's super-sleuth and Freud's role as a tireless investigator of the unconscious and childhood sexuality: both being celebrations of the Western (male) myths of positivist rationalism and comprehensive empiricism.)

'Fragmentary' or 'unfinished' texts are obviously especially appealing for the rewriter, and *'Dora'* has prompted more rewrites than most (versions by Cixous and D. M. Thomas and others referred to in *In Dora's Case*, for example). Yet it is interesting to consider how far most texts, in Valéry's words, are in the event not so much absolutely 'finished' as arbitrarily put a stop to, that is to say, 'accidentally abandoned'. For even – perhaps especially – the most apparently finished and polished text only achieves an illusion of 'wholeness' by dint of the 'holes' (gaps, silences, exclusions) it manages to cover up, get round or fall into completely. (Barthes explores this paradox in *S/Z* by systematically exploding Balzac's classic realist novella *Sarrasine*.) As far as rewriting is concerned, *all* texts offer kinds of fascinating or frustrating 'w/hole'. And as with the assumed 'gaps' or 'bridges' between creativity and criticism, the challenge – to recall the opening epigraph – is both to 'look' *and* to 'leap' – if not at the same moment or in the same movement then at various times differently and in terms that suit yourself. Change the text and add a commentary. Read and rewrite, and research and reflect. Re-create and criticize. However you put it, Critical-Creative Rewriting is a 'link' that perhaps only appears to be 'missing'. Grasped afresh, it is crucial to what we already do all the time.

4. (3) FURTHER READING AND REWRITING

Depending on the course, the students and the occasion, these are examples of the kinds of reading that I most frequently suggest and turn to myself. More extensive reading with further comment and plenty of other examples can be found in my *Textual Intervention: Critical and Creative Strategies for Literary Studies* (1995), especially pp. 183–91, and *Creativity: Theory, History, Practice* (2005), especially pp. 271–93.

For a more PRACTICAL emphasis upon innovative PEDAGOGY, embracing language and literature in openly cross-cultural contexts, see Jane Spiro's *Creative Poetry Writing* (2004) and the companion volume *Creative Story Telling* (forthcoming); Susan Bassnett and Peter Grundy's *Language through Literature: Creative Language Teaching* (1993) and John McRae's *Literature with a small 'l'* (1991). Shaun O'Toole's *Transforming*

Texts (2003) is well designed for use in schools. Rather more advanced theoretically and also full of resourceful reading and (re)writing strategies are *Text Book: Writing through Literature* (2002) by Robert Scholes, Nancy Comley and Greg Ulmer, and David Bartholomae and Anton Petrosky's *Ways of Reading: An Anthology for Writers* (2005).

For some inspiring examples of CRITICAL-CREATIVE REWRITING *avant la lettre*, see Deirdre Burton's 'Through A Glass Darkly – Through Dark Glasses: Sylvia Plath's *The Bell Jar*', in *Language and Literature: A Reader in Stylistics*, ed. R. Carter (1982), pp. 195–216, and many of the pieces in Walter Nash's *An Uncommon Tongue: The Uses and Resources of English* (1992). Lucid introductions to the theory and practice of texts that openly rewrite other texts or sport with their own textuality are Patricia Waugh's *Metafiction* (1984), Brenda Marshall's *Teaching the Postmodern: Fiction and Theory* (1992), and *Metafiction: A Critical Reader*, ed. Mark Currie (1995). Examples of modern rewrites of earlier classics are now legion and multiply by the year; but remember the obvious ones, too: Jean Rhys's *Wide Sargasso Sea* (1972, of *Jane Eyre*); Tom Stoppard's *Rosencrantz and Guildenstern Are Dead* (1967, of *Hamlet*); J. M. Coetzee's *Foe* (1986, of *Robinson Crusoe*); and Derek Walcott's *Omeros* (1990, of *The Odyssey*); etc. These may be over-familiar to some teachers, but to many students they are 'new to me!' – and still inspiring as well as instructive. So are encounters with older texts framed so as to come at them through their sources and subsequent reception, translation, imitation and adaptation: from Ovid, Chaucer, Cervantes and Shakespeare to Joyce, Brecht, Borges, Calvino and Carter. Meanwhile, text-to-film adaptation has become one of the most pervasive and potent ways in which all of us now regularly experience and understand rewriting (reviewing, revisioning); for which, see *Adaptations: From Text to Screen, Screen to Text*, ed. Deborah Cartmell and Imelda Whelehan (1999) and Robert Stam's *Literature through Film: Realism, Magic, and the Art of Adaptation* (2005).

The CRITICAL THEORIES and THEORISTS (and other writers) who may be invoked to inform, interrogate and enrich the practice of critical-creative rewriting are also legion. A beginning list includes: Bakhtin for 'dialogism' and 'another's words in one's own language'; Barthes for 'the birth of the reader' at the expense of 'the death of the [individualist conception of the] author'; Derrida for 'writing under erasure', 'counter-signing' and a whole host of other 'marginal' techniques of glossing and critique; a wide range of (German) 'Reception Aesthetic' and (American) 'Reader Response' critics – from Iser and Jauss to Bleich and Bloom; a still wider and more contentious range of Marxists, Cultural Materialists and New Historicists dedicated to 'brushing history/culture against the grain' and 'making the silences speak' – after Benjamin, Macherey, Foucault, Belsey, Eagleton and Jameson; also Woolf, Cixous, Rich and Ward Jouve, as well as Dollimore and Sinfield, and Butler (for various kinds of feminist 're-visioning' and gay/queer 'dissident reading' and 'performative' sexuality); Fanon and Bhabha for various kinds of post/ colonial 'mimicry' and 'mockery', and Spivak and hooks for promoting various kinds of 'subaltern speech' and 'transgression'. Deleuze and Guattari, and Haraway and Braidotti I also value for their vigorously iconoclastic and endlessly inventive way with theoretical discourse, and their emphasis upon kinds of ceaseless 'becoming' and 'metamorphosis'. To engage with many of the above theories and theorists, in the first instance I especially recommend *Modern Literary Theory: A Reader*, ed. Philip Rice and Patricia Waugh (2001) and *Modern Criticism and Theory: A Reader*, ed. David Lodge and Nigel Wood (2006). For some sharp and provocative essays on approaches and applications – rather than a dutiful plod through the '-isms' – see the two volumes edited by Julian Wolfreys: *Introducing Literary Theory* (2001), which includes Mark Currie's 'Criticism and

Creativity: Poststructuralist Theories' on pp. 152–68, and *Introducing Criticism at the 21st Century* (2002).

Relevant INSTITUTIONAL CONTEXTS for this kind of work are supplied by Robert Scholes, *The Rise and Fall of English: Reconstructing English as a Discipline* (1998), especially Chapters 4 and 5; Andrew Bennett and Nicholas Royle, 'Creative Writing', in their *An Introduction to Literature, Criticism and Theory* (2004), pp. 85–92; Michelene Wandor, 'Creative Writing and Pedagogy 1: Self Expression? Whose Self and What Expression', *New Writing: The International Journal for the Practice and Theory of Creative Writing*, Vol. 1, No. 2 (2004), pp. 112–23; Jon Cook, 'Creative Writing as a Research Method', in *Research Methods for English Studies*, ed. G. Griffin (2005), pp. 195–212; and the two volumes of *The Art of English* (forthcoming): *Literary Creativity*, ed. Sharon Goodman and Kieran O'Halloran, and *Everyday Creativity*, ed. Janet Maybin and Joan Swann. My own take on these institutional and pedagogic issues can be found in *The English Studies Book* (2002), especially pp. 9–11, 196–9, 276–80, and in 'Rewriting Texts, Reconstructing the Subject', in *Teaching Literature: A Companion*, ed. Tanya Agathocleous and Ann Dean (2003), pp. 105–24. Finally, looking to the celebration of kinds of workshop and play-space that are always to come and yet in some respects already prepared, I recommend seeing what Queneau, Perec, Calvino and others got up to in the 'Workshop of Potential Literature' (*Ouvroir de Littérature Potentielle – Oulipo*, for short); for which see *Oulipo: A Primer of Potential Literature*, trans. and ed. Warren F. Motte (1998).

This chapter is dedicated to the memory and in celebration of Colin Evans. Inspiring teacher and supportive friend.

Chapter 11

Workshopping

Stephanie Vanderslice
University of Central Arkansas

1. WHAT WE KNOW BY HEART: WORKSHOPPING DEFINED

In my 20 years in higher education I have participated in at least 37 writing workshops, either as a student or a teacher – an approximate number, of course. I am, after all, a writing, not a mathematics, professor. Like many of my colleagues in creative writing, then, writing workshops were a constant throughout my maturation in academia. In accordance with their prominence in the landscape of my life (yes, I even met my husband at my first graduate workshop), I have given them and their pedagogy(ies) a great deal of reflection over the years and have come to not a few conclusions about the benefits, drawbacks, indeed, the purposes as well as the best practices of this twentieth-century phenomena, conclusions that are at once far too complex to begin to address in a single essay and simple enough to contain in a four-word sentence:

Writer, meet your Reader.

Or Readers, as the case may be. Literary salons of Europe aside, which were unavailable to American writers except those in large cities, the craft of writing is an inherently solitary pursuit, and yet essential to learning that craft is the transformative understanding that one writes not only for self-expression but also to communicate to a *reader*. In fact, preliminary studies of developing writers have long described the epiphany that one writes to transcend oneself and reach out to others as the catalyst that spurs most novice writers from a canter to a gallop. The 'Workshop' emerged – first at Harvard and then later in its most ubiquitous form at the University of Iowa – as an incubator full of readers designed to hurry this process along.

A century later, most of us recognize these various definitions of the writing workshop: a place where a 'master writer or mentor discusses drafts of student writing in near-finished state' (Bishop, 1998: 10); fellow classmates 'respond orally and often in writing, suggesting changes, offering interpretations and responses to the piece' (p. 10); a place where, in Wallace Stegner's words, a manuscript is put into a 'posture of dignity, demanding' the kind of critical attention that will 'help it be what it wants to be' (1988: 62).

Yet, we also recognize the writing workshop as so much more than that. Most of us have experienced the workshop as a *variation* on this theme throughout our writing lives.

Workshops that consisted of a professor sitting at the head of a long seminar table with a stack of books from which she read passages or stories held up as examples for us to follow – this usually in the weeks before any of the students were ready to bring in their own material and thus she was somewhat at a loss for what to teach.[1] Workshops where students had barely read the work under consideration but felt competent to talk about it anyway (this was the aha moment early in my career when I began to require some kind of written response to work under consideration – a purely practical decision that grew to have enormous pedagogical implications). Workshops where students were asked to provide not only written response to their peers' work but also substantive critical introductions to their own work. Workshops where, in addition to leading class discussions about student work, professors also assigned weekly exercises in forms designed to help students understand the components of the genres in which they were attempting to write. Workshops in which students signed up to bring cookies and punch for consumption during the break, when it was understood that the teacher would be delivered a cookie and a Dixie cup of punch afterwards but would not participate in the actual socializing; and workshops after which everyone, instructor included, retreated to the local watering hole (after one particular post-workshop sing along, I would never hear the Eagles 'Best of My Love' in quite the same way again); and workshops that were all business, confined more by the limitations of class time (a 50-minute period in the middle of the day) than anything else. I have my own ideas about the effectiveness of these variations on the theme, some of which have to do with my own personal needs as a writer at the time and most having to do with the actual effort the professor had put into teaching the class. Nonetheless, this range of difference has little to do with other essential elements of the writing workshop, those that make it a unique, sometimes hotly contested and, in tandem, little understood – and often under-explained – site on the academic landscape.

Intensity and rigour

Often, in part due to its mysterious nature (and the unwillingness of many of its practitioners to demystify it – something I will touch on briefly later), those outside the creative writing community (who may or often may not have experienced a writing workshop themselves or have not, perhaps, experienced the form at its best) have been quick to accuse it of lacking in rigour and academic integrity, a rich academic province where A's are as plentiful as zucchini in midsummer. Courses considered more 'academic', such as those in literary analysis, for example, are thought to require more advanced critical and textual thinking skills. Yet, as many of us who have been immersed in this form of teaching for many years know, this could hardly be further from the truth. For example, students routinely evaluate my introductory workshop as *far* more work than they expected, their expectations usually a reflection of the myth of the 'ease' of creative writing workshop.

In fact, in the very best workshops, we recognize that there is often *'more* at stake than in the [traditional] academic classroom' (Garber and Ramjerdi, 1994: 14). As Garber and Ramjerdi point out, for example, in the writing workshop there is no 'object of study that filters, directs, constrains and distances response as there is in other (academic) classes' (p. 14), thus the 'energy of the workshop is unmediated by a discipline' (p. 15), or, as Lynn Domina agrees, 'in writing classes, students lack the defense a disengaged-receptor-mode allows' (1994: 27). Thus, the dynamics of putting one's own work at the centre of the classroom for deconstruction and analysis considerably turns up the heat in the writing workshop. I agree, along with Francois Camoin (1994) and others, however, that these unique circumstances of the writing workshop are to be celebrated; writing workshop participants and leaders are present at the precise moment in which a text 'become(s) something else' (p. 7). Literary scholars work with the *products* of these efforts; they may see archival drafts, but these are 'texts already frozen, traces of a process always already completed' (p. 7). Workshop participants are fortunate midwives commonly attendant at the miracle of birth and no less exhilarated by the regularity of the experience.

Or a PR problem?

The network of factors that have inspired the workshop's detractors over the years, especially those who claim this form of teaching lacks rigour, is a densely complex one. Nonetheless, it is the belief of many practitioners, myself included, that the workshop's somewhat tarnished reputation outside the immediate writing community stems from an unwillingness on the part of that very same community to make the inner workings of this relatively unorthodox form of teaching apparent to the uninitiated. Early attempts to protect the 'secrets' of the workshop may be traced back to the Romantic ideal of the artist for whom any description or discussion of the artistic process would most surely corrupt that process beyond recognition. Indeed, a cursory glance at the media today reveals that the images of the writer as an incurable, incorrigible Romantic with a capital R remain abundant. What's more, this is not an image society seems ready to part with any time soon. Yet, it is this very image that shrouds the writing workshop in mystery and excuses some workshop leaders who, as Hans Ostrom puts it, 'retreat from theory and pedagogy' in order to 'fall back on the workshop in its simplest form: going over poems and stories in a big circle, holding forth from time to time, pretending to have read the material carefully … marking time' (1994: xiv).

Ostrom further suggests that this unfortunate line of reasoning owes much to George Bernard Shaw's famous maxim: 'Those who can, do; those who cannot, teach.' Likewise, so the implication goes, 'Those who can write, do; those who can't, theorize' (p. xiv) often about teaching. Such rationales give 'the writer-teacher great authority but in another way, provide an avenue for exerting minimal effort in teaching' (p. xiv) or defending that teaching against detractors with the specificity and credibility it so richly deserves, offering an 'out' that dovetails nicely with the Romantic implication that the inner workings of the workshop must remain, at all costs, under wraps. In other words, as D. W. Fenza reminds us in 'Creative Writing and Its Discontents' (2000), 'few writers in the academy know the long history of their own profession as teachers of writing. As a result they sometimes find it hard to defend their work against the scholars, theorists and commentators who trivialize it.'

Oh, and by the way, can this *really* be taught?

I first encountered this question at the age of 18, in the stands of a college basketball game, when, in answer to the questions of a well-meaning friend's mother about my collegiate intentions, I said that I might like to study writing. Little did I know at the time that 'Oh, but can that kind of thing really be taught?' was going to be such a constant refrain over the course of my career that I would soon be able to predict when it would rise from someone's lips or in the next sentence of an article simply from a certain slight lift of the eyebrows or foreboding shift in the tone of a phrase. This predictive ability has done little, however, to mitigate the internal wince that commences each time I hear this timeworn phrase *again*.

Personal experience aside, the mythological 'unteachability' of creative writing has done much to undermine the reputation of the creative writing workshop, a teaching site which has nonetheless produced some of finest writers in the past century that the English-speaking world has seen,[2] a list that, when combined with the writing workshops that produced them, is far too long to enumerate here. Again, the PR problem rears its head – even the writing faculty at the University of Iowa have been found to hem and haw when the age-old question arises (as if they weren't expecting it!) and mutter something about giving the talented fertile soil by way of time and space to write and grow and an audience to provide the occasional direction (a narrative in which anyone who has parented a preschooler and/or been one herself recognizes more than one Fairy Tale trope – magic beans anyone?). Yet as a student and teacher of creative writing who observed not only the development of my own craft but also that of my colleagues and *then* my students in the rich, varied soil of the writing workshop, I knew that there was much more going on than the care and feeding of a handful of seeds. I saw, over and over, that some methods *within* the workshop pedagogy seemed to produce better uniform results than others. In fact, in the footsteps of Marilyn Sternglass's *Time to Know Them* (1997) and Anne Herrington and Marcia Curtis's *Persons in Progress* (2000), respectively two exhaustive studies of the development of college writers, I envisioned a similar study of my own students, until I discovered Greg Light's seminal research on 'how students understand and learn creative writing in higher education' (www.nawe.co.uk) and found that the task had already been completed. Here, in Light's painstaking elaboration of the 'stages of knowing in creative writing', based on exhaustive interviews with over 40 students at various stages in writing programmes all over the UK, was proof positive of what I knew by heart. It was gratifying, to be sure, to finally have something outside the realm of the anecdotal to say in defence of the workshop that had featured so prominently in the story of my life, a set of criteria to apply to the work I was doing in the hopes of continually doing it better – almost too good to be true! Yet, why was I only one of a few of my US colleagues who knew of such a landmark study? Ah yes, that is another article, for another day – one my colleagues and I have already written in a myriad of forms but which we will keep writing until the need no longer exists . . . but not here, where we have other fish to fry. I have already established that the workshop, as many of us have come to know it, is effective because writing *can* be taught, that the workshop is not always perfect and could benefit from a pragmatic PR campaign. Now its time to look at what makes the workshop, well, *work*, at the height of its considerable potential. I'm ready to pull open the curtain on the mysterious workings of this well-shrouded machine, if you're ready to peer inside.

Writer meet your reader, redux

In order to communicate the unique qualities of workshopping, the merits of the intensity that may initially frighten some novice writers and the unorthodox methods themselves that, when described by the traditional-age college student (surfer dude, sorority girl, Goth – insert your stereotype here), might appear deceptively simple and lacking in rigour, it may be well to start with the students themselves. Without committing death by inflated seriousness, teachers need to raise student awareness of the sacred space which they are entering, where they will find readers for the first time, what's more, readers who care as much about the written word as they do, a rare find today, as we all know. In beginning workshop courses especially (more about that in just a bit), moreover, they need to make visible the rationale behind all the course components, rarely passing up the opportunity to explain why elements of the course have been deployed to help them become better writers. A complete show of one's hand might even be in order here: assigning students a few of the more accessible pedagogy essays that describe a rationale for workshopping. This is one case where it never hurts to let the marionette wires show.

Beyond letting students in on the unique mechanisms that make the workshop effective, teachers need to keep their eyes on the prize themselves, continually inscribing and revising the essential elements that contribute to the success of the workshop, just as we ask our students to do with their own work. Based on my experience and continual research and reflection, these elements include: Demographic Awareness, Cultivating the Writerly Reader, Developing the Writerly Critic, and Encouraging Revision as a Habit of Mind.

Demographic Awareness: Just as we teach our students that different situations and audiences require different writerly responses, we must recognize that graduate and undergraduate creative writing populations (the last further subdividing into beginning and advanced undergraduates) are inherently unique and require more tailoring than the one-size-fits-all workshop to which both have traditionally been subject. Undergraduate creative writing populations, especially those at lower levels, tend to not only be more diverse (the serious writer who has been toiling since kindergarten, the cheery utter beginner exploring her options, the lacrosse player who couldn't get in to Introduction to Geology) but also naturally far less experienced. In fact, in America, few but the largest high schools have creative writing courses, a condition recently illustrated in my introductory workshop when I asked for a show of hands of those who had already experienced 'workshopping'. In an eager, sharp group of students, a single hand went up. In Britain, moreover, as Michelene Wandor has pointed out, there are no GCSEs or A levels in creative writing (2003: 13). Throwing students like this into the traditional workshop cold is like holding a 'minnows' swimming lesson in the deep end of the pool. Instead, they are most likely to benefit from a range of teaching techniques. In addition to 'workshopping', which should be introduced with considerable preparation and explanation, students in these classes will also benefit from invention exercises – while most are eager writers, they haven't learned yet how to overcome writer's block and sometimes the mere idea that someone else will be reading their work (often for the first time) can cause the ink to drain from their pens. They will also benefit from continual reference to and emphasis on the true realities of the writing life as opposed to the Romantic myths they have been exposed to throughout their lives: that few writers get it 'right' on the first go round; that, initially at least, they must often 'fit' writing into their busy schedules as opposed to toiling away at leisure in an attic or a pavement café.

Graduate workshops, on the other hand, naturally tend to be populated with more experienced writers who are better suited to the traditional workshop since they are the audience for whom the teaching method originated. Workshopping here can occur at a higher level and can afford to be somewhat more product- (as opposed to process-) oriented. While these differences may seem obvious to many, the problem remains that because graduates of writing programmes (who often lack training in creative writing pedagogy[3]) usually seek to recreate the circumstances in which they themselves were most recently taught, their fallback position in the undergraduate classroom may still be the loose, unfitted trappings of the traditional, unrevised workshop.

Cultivating the Writerly Reader: In a culture dense with alternative media, we are accustomed to pundits who regularly bemoan the decline of reading and, sadly, we know that they are not far off in their proclamations. As a result, in tandem with workshopping student texts, we must also cultivate the student as literary reader, acquainting them as well with the responsibilities of the writing life. If we are lucky, students in the workshop may have read eagerly and widely, as I did as a young student, but more often than not, they have read more deeply in the realms of popular and genre fiction than anything else. These students need to be introduced to the universe of literary reading and encouraged, perhaps directed, to develop extensive reading lists of authors who might enlarge their sense of the world and their own work. While these lists might have their share of classics, they might also include more contemporary literary works of which even English majors might not yet be aware, as they reside at the outer limits of the canon. They need to be exposed to the rich store of memoirs about the writing life (and by this I truly mean memoir, not, as some students might misunderstand, *How to Write a Novel on Your Christmas Break*), and they need to be introduced to the lively world of literary journals – both in print and on-line – that lies just at their fingertips. Finally, they need to be taught to read as writers and not as literary scholars, to not only appreciate texts for pleasure but to continually ask 'why', to try to get inside the head of the author and 'workshop' what they are reading in the same way they might do with a student text.

Developing the Writerly Critic: Nurturing a critical sensibility in students may well be as important as teaching the particulars of good writing, for this is the sensibility students will bring to their work during the rest of their lives, long after the workshop has become a dim memory (along with distant refrains of 'Ohhh, sweet darlin', you've got the best of my looove'). What the student author learns in continuously responding to and discussing the work of other students, then, is, in addition to meeting the reader face to face, perhaps the greatest collateral benefit of workshopping as a method of instruction. For this reason, a considered introduction to the etiquette and elements of workshopping, or an annual review of these processes for even the most advanced workshops, is vital to each course before the manuscript review begins (see Appendix A, p. 156, for an example). Also vital to the development of this critical sensibility is the modelling of the instructor, who shows respect for the work by having read it thoroughly beforehand and responding in writing as well as verbally in class. While this last might sound like a no-brainer, even the best of us may get a little too comfortable (translation: lazy) as the years go by.

Encouraging Revision as a Habit of Mind: For various reasons – not the least of which is the *legend* of so-and-so who is supposed to have altered none of the initial results of the famous meeting of his pen with paper or fingers to keyboard – revision remains something which many students are reluctant to undertake. Even those who are more willing still harbour a limited concept of the process (as in 'Whew! I must have written, like, *three* drafts of that poem'). Sometimes, when we workshop texts more as finished products than as drafts in progress, we re-inscribe students' misperceptions. As a result, it is important to emphasize the unfinished nature of the work under consideration, to cele-brate its mutability (while still granting the writer the final call, of course). When Michael comes to me holding his head, then, and saying, 'but the ending is terrible. I don't know how to end it', I can easily respond, 'Perhaps we can offer some suggestions.' Moreover, revision ought to be incorporated into the grading scheme of any workshop class. In my courses, while students are not required to incorporate all or even most of the classes' suggestions into their work, their portfolios *must* show evidence of their own thoughtful revision, either through a written introduction, highlighting or italicizing altered material, or both. Some students will inevitably try to finesse this, taking me aside after class and whispering conspiratorially, 'Do we *really* have to revise for our portfolio?' While I may be tempted to reply 'Well, everyone but you, of course', 'If you want a decent grade, you do' usually suffices.

3. LISTENING IN ON THE CONVERSATIONS: ESSENTIAL WRITING ABOUT WORKSHOPPING

Much of what has been written in the realm of creative writing pedagogy is relevant to workshopping; however, there are a handful of resources that can save anyone beginning to teach creative writing or re-vamping her pedagogy from re-inventing the wheel. For the most comprehensive view of the workshop itself – where it fits in the academy, how and why it can be best taught, and how its pedagogy may be defended against the naysayers who would nip at its heels – look no further than D. W. Fenza's 'Creative Writing and Its Discontents', first published in the US in the March/April 2000 issue of the Association of Writer's and Writing Programs (AWP) Journal and later made available in the exhaustive database of articles on the UK's National Association of Writers in Education (NAWE) website. This is not to be confused with Francois Camoin's 'The Workshop and Its Discontents' (1994), which delves a bit deeper into some of the subjects over which Fenza necessarily sweeps, specifically the approach–avoidance interplay of the workshop with critical theory and the rationale behind perceptions of the workshop in the wider academic community. Finally, Eavan Boland eloquently extends the conversation by examining the political and social exigencies of a society in which the workshop is necessary in order to grant writers 'permission' to pursue their vocation in 'In Defence of Workshops', also available on the NAWE website.

Eugene Garber and Jan Ramjerdi's epistolary essay 'Reflections on the Teaching of Creative Writing: A Correspondence' (1994) and Wendy Bishop's 'On Learning to Like Teaching Creative Writing' both provide ample overviews to the kinds of issues likely to be encountered in the workshop course as well particular features of the course (such as intensity, etc.) and how to deal with them. Greg Light's 'How Students Understand and Learn Creative Writing in Higher Education' and 'Conceiving Creative Writing in Higher Education' (2000) offer an exhaustive analysis of the effects of workshopping as a pedagogy on the learning outcomes of students that sheds considerable light on the optimal elements of course design. Moreover, Graeme Harper's 'Creative Writing in Higher Education: Introducing Gramography' (1997) works well in tandem with Light's research. Together all three articles are likely to leave any creative writing teacher looking for overarching principles for course and curriculum design with more ideas than he can use.

For practical guidance and moral support for the first-timer, few books (present company excepted) can beat Wendy Bishop's *Released Into Language: Options for Teaching Creative Writing* (1998). The Dr Spock of the teaching of creative writing, Bishop's *Released* is chock full of resources, from comprehensive chapters on student response and peer review to appendices that provide not only a mini-bibliography for creative writing teachers but also extensive practical materials such as portfolio rubrics and peer response worksheets. For the short form, one would do well to turn to Siobhán

Holland and the English Subject Centre's *Creative Writing: A Good Practice Guide* (Holland, 2003), which includes a brief chapter on workshopping as well as articles by Michelene Wandor and Graeme Harper that also touch on the subject. For good measure, David Starkey's edited collections, *Teaching Writing Creatively* (1998) and *Genre by Example* (2001), are full of articles – by noted writers in the field – on creative approaches to the writing workshop. Finally, though aimed more at beginning teachers of the composition 'workshop', Donald Murray's *A Writer Teaches Writing* (2003) has, according to my own advanced creative writing pedagogy students, much to offer the beginning creative writing teacher in workshopping, optimizing student conferences, and effectively teaching a wide range of students.

4. STRATEGIES FOR TEACHING: WORKSHOPPING TRICKS OF THE TRADE

Before the first workshop

There are a number of approaches teachers can take in order to properly set the stage for optimum workshopping. First of all, encouraging a sense of trust among students and a willingness to share will provide a stable foundation for future efforts to consider work seriously. I find that sharing my own work with the class goes a long way towards establishing this environment and often workshop an informal piece of my own writing with the class first. Sometimes, I even bring in copies of my rejection slips, both the form rejections and those that discuss my work extensively, in order to show students the value of the latter response. It helps students to know that the process of submitting writing to an outside reader for evaluation never ends for a writer and that they are being initiated into the lifelong process of seeking and finding an audience.

Before the workshop, especially in an undergraduate course where learning about the meta-cognitive processes of writing is of key importance, I usually require that students write me a cover letter (fashioned after Bishop's *executive summary*) narrating the genesis of their work, describing its perceived strengths and weaknesses and noting any specific questions with which I might be able to assist them. In addition to developing their own sense of the mechanisms of their particular writing process, such a cover letter assists me in honing in and focusing my response on any specific concerns a student might have.

Finally, on another practical note, it is important to require students to read and respond to one another's work thoughtfully and *in writing*. Besides enforcing accountability, writing offers students the opportunity to think more deeply about their classmate's work and to formulate their ideas in a coherent form. The process of such formulation will have a cumulative effect on the students' development of critical reading skills. I ask students to provide two copies of these responses on workshop days, one which they hand in to the author whose work is being considered and one which they hand in to me, for a grade. Requiring these written responses also gives students something to refer to during workshop discussion and prevents the bandwagon effect whereby a few students may hastily decide during class that they like or dislike a work and dominate the discussion in that way. These written responses also give students whose work is being considered a paper trail of suggestions to consider at a later date.

During the workshop

Instructors need to be mindful of their power as models of workshop technique and behave consciously and accordingly. For example, it is important to point out the strengths as well as the weaknesses of any work – students are often just as confused about what they are doing well as by what is not working. Further, by *beginning* with what is effective in a piece, students are better prepared to hear what they need to work on. Instructors must also make students aware that workshopping offers numerous opportunities for all students to learn about creative writing *in context*, thus they must continually remind students to listen for opportunities to learn more about their own writing during the discussion of a classmate's piece. I try to do this by availing myself of phrases such as 'I'm going to back up here and make a point that it's important for all of us to consider when writing poetry', to signal to students that the discussion is relevant to writing technique in general and not just the particular work under consideration.

After the workshop

In an atmosphere as intense as the writing workshop can be, it never hurts to end on a high note that inspires students to return to the solitude and arduous work of their writing desks. This can often be best achieved through a class publication or presentation that celebrates each student's best work. Such a celebration can occur in several forms of varying degrees of complexity. For example, students might give a group reading of their work for families and friends. Or, they might end the course with a 'portfolio party', a class period where students gather and peruse each other's final portfolios, writing responses on post-it notes and sticking them to various parts of the work that moved them. Or, the more adventurous instructor might aim for a class anthology on-line or in hardcopy, asking each student to submit one piece of work of which he or she is most proud. In each case, such 'publication' not only celebrates class work, but gives students a final product to work towards.

Troubleshooting: FEWPs (Frequently Encountered Workshop Problems)

1. *I have an especially timid class. All they want to do is damn everything with faint, non-specific praise.* Ask the class specific questions about the work. 'Was anyone else confused about where this story was set?' Chances are, this is merely a matter of students afraid to speak out.
2. *The same students dominate the workshop discussion each time.* Quite often, the most critically astute students are also rather quiet. They don't mind being called on but they may not volunteer comments. You've read their comments; you know they have something to say. Give them permission to say it. Ask them.
3. *A few students are excessively, unconstructively critical of most work (except, usually, their own).* Exhaustive preparation for the first workshop often mitigates this problem. But if it persists, it may be useful to remind an excessively critical student that, since they've spent a good deal of time on their critique, they want it to be heard.

The author under discussion will 'hear' criticism better if it is made in a constructive fashion that also provides some insight as to what is working in a piece.

4. *Related to 3. There are students in the class who feel certain classmates should be gently told they have no talent as writers and should hang it up. They have made it clear that if I don't have the nerve to do it, they will ...* This is an easy call in an undergraduate workshop, where I emphasize that I am in the business of teaching students to be better writers, not casting out the chaff. It is also a good time to explain that I am not in the business of teaching one or two students in a course, which, if I followed their advice and only taught the most talented *at that moment*, I would be doing. It is stickier in a graduate workshop, however; in either case I always have several stories I can relate about the uneven pace at which writers develop. The most experienced creative writing teachers I have ever known tell me they would never tell a student to 'hang it up'; too many students that they had written off actually, through hard work, sacrifice and not a few epiphanies, achieved well-deserved literary success later in life. Learning to write is a (life)long distance marathon, not a 10k run.

Workshopping: when it's good, it's very, very good ...

The creative writing workshop classroom holds a dozen or so (in an ideal world) students eager to devote considerable psychic energy to learning the craft of writing by *doing* and *discussing*. As such, it is a sacred space, something we must never forget no matter how many times we walk through that classroom door, no matter how many years intervene between that moment and the time when we first took our seats in the workshop classroom. Each time we step into the workshop classroom, then, we have the opportunity – the obligation – to serve our students as the novice writers we once were and to continually invent and re-invent the workshop with them in mind.

Appendix A: Workshopping basics

Responding to your classmate's work

- Critique does not necessarily mean be *critical*. It means talking about what you like and why you like it, and what you see as problematic and why. Beginning with praise is a good idea. This is about constructive critique, with the emphasis on constructive.

- Be specific. Whether discussing what you admire, what you think might be changed, questions you have about a piece, BE SPECIFIC.

  Vague: I love this poem. I can relate to it.

  Specific: The last line, 'discarded like day old bread', is so evocative. We know how that feels.

  Vague: I don't understand this story. What is going on?

  Specific: This piece is confusing. Are we to think the narrator is reliable or is he just as crazy as the rest of the characters.

- Ask questions. Even if the writer can't answer at the moment, a question indicates respect, as well as raising legitimate concern about the piece.

- The golden rule rules. Be respectful, honest and sensitive. Imagine how you want people to respond to your work in the full-class workshop and respond to other people's work *that way*. Being honest doesn't mean attacking, and being sensitive doesn't mean massaging the truth.

- Alienating through insult or personal attack (i.e. 'You might as well give it up right now. You'll never be a writer' or 'I feel like I just wasted the last hour of my life reading this') is self-defeating anyway. The writer won't hear the critique you're trying to give; they'll just shut down and stop listening.

Receiving critique

- Keep in mind that you are *learning* about creative writing. Getting feedback on your work will help you to improve; not getting any will leave you to stagnate. Remind yourself that you *want* critique.

- Take notes. It will be hard to remember what was said later.

- Take it all in but know that you can pick and choose the comments you receive, focusing on what is most helpful to you. Give yourself some time to think over all the ideas you've received. In fact, you may not want to read the written responses right away but let them sit for a few days while you digest the workshop itself.

- If you're unsure what to choose for a full-class workshop, one idea is to select something you are open to suggestions about. Sometimes we have pieces we've been working on for years, pieces we've revised extensively and maybe even, in some small way, published. These are not usually good choices for critique because they feel 'finished' to us and we don't really want to hear if they're not working.

- Try not to explain or defend your piece too much while the critique is going on, but an occasional 'thanks' or 'ouch' is fine.

Chapter 12

Research in Creative Writing

Graeme Harper
University of Portsmouth

1. TYPE

A.

What type of research is Creative Writing research? The research, naturally, required to write a creative work – but bear with me a moment.

Creative writers travel to exotic places, seek out unusual people, find incredible stories, and write about them. No wonder everyone wants to be us. What a life! What a great research method!

It was, of course, a creative writer who reported the location of El Dorado; shame she forgot it. And, naturally, it was a creative writer who discovered the undersea city of Atlantis – guy, name of Hector Tremmel.

All this guy was, to tell the truth, was a dough-headed short-story jockey from the little town of Hogsmaw in Montana. Wrote stories about fishing and the Flathead Valley Cornfield, mostly. But, what do you know: he goes off doing his creative writing research and discovers the ancient city of the Atlanteans. Man, what a guy!

Or not.

Truth is, I guess, you're more likely to know Hec Tremmel as the bozo who runs the Drop-n-Buy shop 'round on Smyuk Street. As his ex points out:

'Hec ain't no creative writer.'

And that's a fact. The guy would offer to take your kid sister off your hands for a five spot a whole lot quicker than he'd talk about the writing arts.

'course he is a good negotiator. What he got himself out of his first marriage would make some of those high-flying literary agents seem like freckle-faced kids with lemonade stands. He's one sharp operator. And his ex would attest to that too. She'd say:

'Hec's sure got his clever ways.'

Then again, his ex would tell you Hec never once cared who, or what, he had to jam to make his a packet. And that his living habits are no Presbyterian picnic, generally, either. She quotes his swift peddling of old Mrs Lambert's entire shebang as evidence of that. But I know Mrs Lambert's son, Merle, didn't want any of that stuff: he was happy to see her place cleared out. It made his heart ache just to see the old house like that, with his mother no longer around to fill it, and him not even living in town anymore, but out near the Smithers' place, instead, on account of having an interest in duck hunting, among other things. Sometimes the truth lies in the uncovered record of real life, real people, or something like that.

But let's cut the hooey: we all know research in Creative Writing doesn't involve exotic travel.

Rather, research in creative writing involves books. Lots of books, actually, if I'm being totally honest. A lot more than Hec, or his ex, or Merle Lambert ever seen in their meagre fictitious lifetimes.

In fact, most creative writers have bought up so many books those big insurance companies you read about in the papers all the time won't insure them any more. All that paper, you see.

Those companies aren't stupid: they figure creative writers are too formidable a fire risk, for one thing. They look at your garden variety contemporary poet and the first thing they think is:

'Never mind your sestinas, lady, you're goin' to go up in smoke.'

The biggest companies rate creative writers somewhere between cops and downtown dentists on their Pay-Out-O-Meters. Anyone who's got relatives in those fields will know how hard it is to get good insurance.

The trouble for cops, for instance, is that what it costs to get underwritten depends on how many people you up and plecked the year before. You pleck a bunch of losers doing hard toffee in the neighbourhood park, sometime around Easter and in between little kids playing pixies on the vertical play maze, and the next thing you know you're paying twenty cents more in the dollar on your health plan. It sure sucks; especially as cops are the backbone of a civilized society, right? I mean, you got honest, clean-living blues and you got your town's social problems half solved. As to dentists – well, no one need flesh out what happens when some buck-toothed mechanic from West Lavelle, or from one of those dark, pit bull places out on Upper Fifth, comes in demanding you fix his lip monkey, and all you can do is tell him it's going to cost half a month's salary just to put his two front fangs back in, never mind to take the pouch tobacco off his canines. So now he thinks you're a shyster and that because you drive a Beemer, which you fully earned by his way, and wear those crocodile sports shirts, you're probably too well stocked for your own good. Word gets around. Soon you're getting horseshoes chucked through your front window. Patients hear about it. Your business gets rocky. A rocky dentist's business is nobody's hunk of cheese. Who wants some guy in their mouth who is seven months late on his rent and just did a deal with Vic Marcuso to cover his back while putting Vic's nightclub chits through marked up as 'twenty-four new electro-mechanical patient chairs'?

You can find all this out in books.

And that's what creative writing research is all about: books. Frankly, for creative writers, books are a bit of a social disease. Creative writers buy books like they're alcoholics – for books, I mean: book drinkers. You don't want to go reading with a writer, they'll leave you right under the table. Maybe someone should build some rehab centres for creative writers and put in them nothing but satellite and on-line games and some of those great ring-tones you can listen to over and over again. Many creative writers at the moment are pretty much ruining their lives. Some can hardly even buy their own ink. All their money goes to Hell in a handcart on boxes of cheap hard covers and six packs of paperbacks. It's awful.

'Hey, but hold up a minute,' you call, 'much of this doesn't make sense! You mean creative writers do all their research either by travelling around or by reading books? That can't be right. Hoot, I've heard tell of writers who haven't left their own bedrooms for wellnigh two decades! The last thing those folks read was two notices in the *Yodeltown Times* about their first novel, saying, in not so many words, that it made Aldo Minkie's mongrel duckhound look like the Mona Lisa. You mean those folks ain't writers?'

Fair comment.

It's true: there are some creative writers who just sit around in their rooms and write. Research for them is thinking about what their dear old dad once said about the lives of lumberjacks in Minnesota, or how their mom was from Manchester and used to play snooker for money with a kid who became a real live soccer champion. There's a whole bunch of those kinds of writers for whom research in creative writing is all about drilling down as smooth as a tungsten bit into the hard soil of their own lives. These are the writers you see standing on the Gimbur Street Bridge sniffing the stink of the water rushing below. They drive themselves crazy, these writers. Gimbur Creek's full up with them, sunken bony and brute onto its green and rusty bottom.

The other half just plug away at their research, day in and day out, dragging up who knows how many horrible memories poor old Aunt Madge didn't want anyone to repeat, or that cousin Jim, who's married to a really nice Germanic girl he met while backpacking somewhere unpronounceable, can't adequately deny.

So Jim, who might or might not really be a fan of silk shorts and chenille slippers, is fictionally outed and Katharina takes it badly and goes home, to Flugerheilgart or somewhere, where she maybe becomes some chemical company receptionist for the rest of her sad life. Such is Flugerheilgart: it's no picture postcard of the Danube.

While Aunt Madge, who works two days a week in a charity shop in Upper Chidley, a nice little village in nice little rural Essex, starts getting strange looks from the other ladies and, before she can say 'O my goodness gracious me!', she isn't being invited to the cream tea and jewellery parties any more.

Turns out, of course, that Phyllis read in *Beauty in Repose*, Madge's nephew's latest novel, that a character called Wilda, whom Phyllis knows for sure is actually Madge, hates the 'twit twit twitting sound that those old biddies from next door make when they're dissing their friends', to quote from Chapter Twenty-Three or, to quote from Chapter Forty-Four, that the narrator 'would rather eat dirt than join some kind of card club'.

That's the kind of research creative writers do. They dig up the souls of the living and denigrate the hearts of the dead. You'll find them peering around buses. You might be looking at one now – the girl in the big green cable-knit jumper, her chewing the ends of the cuffs, feet on the seat, knees in the air, staring up front at that poor innocent guy reading the back of shampoo he just bought. She may look cute, but this girl's a freaking vampire; she's sucking the story right out of that big feller. He'll be Bald Barry Winchester in about two years' time, vain, sullen, an inept lover, and a minor character in the short story 'One Too Many'. You're best not to relax in that girl's company; project you're chosen image; make sure you appear how you'd want to appear. Though, actually, she isn't nothing compared to the guy on train, two seats up from where you're sitting, dressed in khaki dungarees.

That guy's a poet. You may have read his latest collection *The Suburban Urn*. He'd won six national prizes before he was twenty-six. Now he's more recommended for anthologizing than Walt Whitman's 'O Captain! My Captain!' at a meeting of the Society of Retired Merchant Seamen. But, you think all this exposure makes him innocent? You've got to be kidding. That guy just saw the flick of an old guy's right foot in the seat in front and turned him into the theme of 'The Devil in Downtown', a forthcoming clerihew. He claims he once spent a week in an abandoned cottage in Spain to feel the regular coldness of the hearth. Talk about Byron! This guy is poisonously brilliant. With luck, and good career management, he'll die tragically young.

So that's all there is to research in creative writing and obviously, should you now be wondering: you'd be plum crazy to go to university or college to undertake it – that would be a big waste of time.

In fact, you might be a whole lot better off not to have any formal education at all, because most of what can be learnt about Creative Writing comes about through travelling to places, reading a whole heap, drawing on your increasingly less personal life, watching, that kind of stuff.

That's research in creative writing. Everything else is, fairly much, junk.

B.

I asked, at the outset, if you would bear with me. But you've done that too long already, so I apologize.

Let's now consider, employing both argument and a shift in writing tone and viewpoint, another option. It is one of the creative writer's key tools – tonal address – the sense of an engagement between writer and reader, the day-to-day but still frequently wonderful complexions of language, syntax, word placement.

Here evolves an alternate strategy, and an alternate argument.

If creative writing occupies a space as a site of knowledge – and it is surely impossible to suggest that some form of knowledge is *not* acquired and accessed through creative writing – then it stands to reason that academe can investigate the nature, approach and dimensions of this site of knowledge, and contribute to the application and understanding of it. It certainly does so with many other sites of knowledge. If this is the case, how might it do so with creative writing?

There is little argument against the idea that the primary mechanism of engagement with the world employed by the creative writer is a piece of creative writing. Whether short story, screenplay, poem, novel, new media text, or otherwise, the creative writer investigates some aspect of the world through their creative practice. Depending on the nature of the end result – and, indeed, even in today's critically liberal higher education, this is true – depending on the nature of the end result, someone in academe will potentially analyse the final creative work and construct critical argument concerning it. And yet, to suggest this type of analysis is the only critical process at work would be naïve at best.

The creative writer engages in, and constructs alongside their creative practice, an active critical understanding of a specific kind. This critical understanding is in part based on a development of a craft, a set of skills that are practical, applied, pragmatic; the creative writer learns what works, and aims to employ this learning. But this is far from the end of things. The creative writer's critical understanding is also based on a sense of genre, form and convention. The novelist has some sense of the nature of the novel; the screenwriter has some sense of the nature of the film; the poet has some sense of the nature, or natures, of poetry. It is impossible to say that the better that understanding the better the writer will be; the process and the relationship is more complex than that, but there is a connection. This connection is not unlike the connection that the 'post-creation' literary, film, theatre critic has to the creative text; however, it has a different scope because it is used in an applied way to assist the writer in the construction of further new creative work, sometimes well beyond the work at hand, as well as assisting the writer in comparing and contrasting their work with that of other writers, post the act of writing.

The creative writer researches their sense of critical understanding, 'in process', whether prior, during or after the production of a single work, and most directly in relation to immediate or future work, planned, or as yet unplanned. To put it another way, the creative writer is engaged in critical understanding in the same way as a creature in the animal kingdom is engaged in observing, learning, applying, fundamentally in order to ensure their survival. This can be called *responsive critical understanding*, and it is both the purpose and the product of creative writing research.

The same kind of understanding ensures that the creative writer seeks to draw on as wide a range of knowledge as possible, or as applicable. That is, unlike the literary critic, who will draw largely on their knowledge of literary texts, critical methods, theoretical positions and current thinking among their critical peers, the creative writer (let's say a novelist, as one example in this case) is not restricted to the site of knowledge defined as 'literary criticism'. Even taking into account the liberalization of critical apparatus – which the latter twentieth century saw on the back of post-structural discourses and new multidimensional senses of text, authorship and readership – even taking this into account, the literary critic does not draw on the vast sites of knowledge that the creative writer draws upon. It simply is neither a natural need for the literary critic, nor is it a requirement of their professional role.

So what is creative writing research?

It can, indeed, be experiential, the result of drawing down on personal experience, the personally historical, the biographical, the more or less ordinary or adventurous undertakings of the writer in the world. It is also about the emotive, the dispositional and the psychological. Indeed, the personal dimension in creative writing research does not stop, as it most often does in many other subjects of research, at the social or physical environment, at structures and holistic meaning; creative writing research deals with human agency, human intention, behaviour, reasons and meanings, as well as more or less discernible holistic facts of the world.

Creative writing research also often involves books or some other evidence of a writer's practice, but also books in relation to the foundations of knowledge in a vast range of fields, fields that might at any point be of use to the creative writer. It also involves formal, structural and stylistic research into the tools at hand, the mechanism, the craft of creative writing. Some of this might be undertaken via 'research-through-practice'; that is, the act of creating. Other elements of this might be discovered through critical research, after writing, by the writer, in relation to their own work, or in relation to the work of other writers.

Creative writing research combines the individual, the holistic, the project-specific and more general, the process-based and the product-based. It is distinctive in nature, being based largely in the realm of words and relating to the creative use of those words, and, though the creative works and critical responses that are produced spread over a vast range, it maintains a sense of its distinctiveness from other fields, other arts, other sites of knowledge.

2. KEY POINTS

A creative writer's responsive critical understanding is *always* the result of some kind of investigation; whether this is defined as research by one creative writer or another mostly relates to creative writers not being encouraged to think of their range of investigations as 'research', and certainly not always making these investigations public.

Each creative writer's response to the world is a combination of personal and social circumstances. To an extent, the degree of responsive understanding is determined by how far the creative writer has investigated these circumstances. For the creative writer, as with other people, the degree of their understanding is impacted upon by controlled and fortuitous occurrences, by intended consequences and by unintended consequences. Likewise, the range of responsive understanding of any one creative writer is often heavily determined by what is necessary to produce a given piece of creative writing – though this range of understanding is not necessarily a defining factor in the quality of the creative work produced.

A creative writer commences a piece of writing, quite naturally engaged in a combination of personal and social circumstances. This is a starting point in a discussion of creative writing research; but it is far from an end point. Creative writers are impacted upon by specific elements of the activity in which they are engaged, and these too can be the subject of research-through-practice and of research.

To determine key points of creative writing research, two investigative examples suffice: the aesthetic (or artistic nature of the act that is creative writing) linked to the formal or constructivist nature of their work, and the cultural (or humanly interactive nature of what creative writers do, most often involving communication with others).

A. The art of creative writing

Fine Art, Music and Dance all have a concern for the tools of their art practice and the way in which these are used to produce a final result. While a long discussion of whether a creative writer uses a pencil, a computer, or piece of charcoal and a length of bark might be beyond most creative writers' research interests, it's almost certain that all writers have a concern with words, their meaning, their arrangement, and their impact on their audience. This might be considered under the aesthetics of creative writing or under the constructivist nature of it; either way, the writer seeks additional knowledge of the nature of words, and of their use. The most vexed question here, perhaps, is where to draw the line between writing that is purely communicative and writing that is creative. Is there, in fact, any line at all? If there is, how is it determined? If it is determined, who determines it, and why?

Examine two creative writers who might be considered to have produced modern classics, Ernest Hemingway and Vladimir Nabokov: one was critically touted for his use of spare, journalistic prose and the other for his use of the lyrical and self-conscious. Take the case of contemporary screenwriters Nora Ephron and Sophia Coppola. In both cases, simply looking at the basics of a writer's style does not legitimate the label 'creative writing'. Nor does creative writing length – consider the haiku versus the epic and, while the novel might distinguish itself from the novella according to length, this is only one part of the formal differences. Nor does packaging or presentation distinguish: simply saying on a book's cover that something is a 'literary classic' does not make it so, as publishers have long discovered. Nor does genre: various plays, films, works of feature journalism and multimedia pieces have made their mark on the writing arts as key pieces of creative writing, without necessarily having the self-conscious desire to consider themselves as creative writing 'types'.

Here, then, is one area of creative writing research that is commonly, if not constantly, undertaken. The creative writer, whether for pragmatic applied reasons or even simply for personal interest, researches the aesthetics, the form, the type and style of creative writing. There is a balance maintained between application and understanding, between creator and critic; it is a firmly research-oriented, sometimes in process and sometimes of product, and the key for creative writers and to creative writing.

B. The cultures of creative writing

Generically labelled 'cultural', a second example of creative writing research is connected with such things as geographic location, ethnic background, gender, age or sexual orientation. In other words, the creative writer might – and frequently does – closely consider the nature of their world. So cultural research, in that sense, is about the grounding of the interaction between individual and holistic interpretations of what is around us; simply, the individual writer and her or his environment.

One criticism here might be that *all* human beings do this; it is not conscious, or distinctive to the creative writer and, therefore, it is not really, specifically 'research'. The counter argument is that while it is a common human practice to assess and be informed about the nature of their world, it is not *common* human practice to make from that information a piece of creative work that models this information. That is, a work of creative writing often functions both as a research-through-practice exploration for the writer, a mode of personal investigation, and as the modelling for details about the world that have been discovered prior to, or during, the process of writing creatively, and offered up to the reader or audience.

Such models as creative writers produce have heuristic purposes. That is, they serve as guides for an investigation or towards answers to questions. Thus, in part, the reason for the passionate interest of many readers in works of creative writing. It is not only that these readers 'enjoy a good story' or 'are moved by a piece of poetry' or 'really identified with the characters' in a film or a play; it is also that the creative writer has provided something of a guide to the investigation of a issue, a way of considering a problem, or simply some idea of how to move from what is already known to what is currently unknown.

As models are the basis on which theories are built, tested, reconsidered, and rebuilt, the heuristic nature of creative writing works to construct for the reader, and for the writer, a hypothesis. 'What if?' is the question that drives the process of creative writing, and the reception of its results.

'What if this was my life?' 'What if my daily routine took this turn?' 'What if this picture was in front of me?' 'What if this disaster had befallen me?' 'What if I had this opportunity?' The list is infinite. The creative writer inserts themselves into the interpretative position; empathetically, providing a way for the reader to follow through a speculation, effectively alongside the writer themselves. This makes works of creative writing source models; they provide experimental opportunities and analogies and might even determine how certain, more or less universal, laws might or might not look. For example, is it a law that if someone is evil they will eventually get their just desserts? Is it a law that if confronted by human disaster the person of character will find strength in themselves, no matter how weak they might previously have seemed? Is it a law that there is a world that does exist and can be accessed by physical means; but that there is also a world of thought, memory and imagination that might not be visible but makes itself known in the physical world in a number of discernible ways?

C. Responsive critical understanding

Modelling undertaken, and investigated, by creative writers is a form of research that is both multivalent and yet relatively accessible. It is also responsive to the needs of the creative writer and, generally, responds to the world around them. It combines empirical investigation with theoretical examination. It moves both towards solutions and, in reverse, towards observations, concepts, and a range of influences that are common to humankind, and thus often widely recognizable. But, even though the presentation of what could be called both the research results and, simultaneously, the research experiment can often be understood by the non-specialist, this does not mean that the mode of research in creative writing is non-specific.

A creative writer's responsive critical understanding is frequently applied knowledge that can be outlined either separately to the creative work of a writer, or incorporated into the modes and methods of creative practice. Equally, it can be knowledge of a kind not dissimilar to that in a great many fields but *focused in relation to a particular creative writing project*, or group of projects. In other words, creative writing research that is not based in the writing arts but in fields that inform the creative writer in other ways is not the same as research in those particular informing fields; and yet it draws on those fields and it might even utilize the epistemological and ontological positions adopted by those fields as a way of entering their sites of knowledge. Here, the history of the study of creative writing at university or college is important.

From the earliest days of Plato's Academy to the modern university, subjects studied at institutions of higher learning have grown increasingly in their formal dimensions. Particularly in the twentieth century, and particularly in what might come under the heading of 'developed countries', this has occurred as a result of new ideas about educational practice, pedagogic (referring to that concerned with children) and andragogic (referring to that concerned with adults). Equally, it has been driven by the changing nature of the economic, political and social state of higher education. Issues have included, at various points, challenges to real or perceived elitism in universities, questions relating to vocational versus non-vocational education, notions of lifelong learning and the role of universities in developing an educated populace and, more expansively, issues of the relationship between higher education and the State.

While in some ways, arts practice seems at odds with formalization of process and of outcome, it has not been hermetically sealed from such changes in educational ideas that have occurred and, without doubt, there have been both positive and negative aspects to this. It is unusual today to see any higher learning in universities and colleges not tied to systems of validation, approval, course documentation, establishment and assessment of modes of teaching, extensively stated styles and types of student assessment, statistically recorded outcomes, approved and highly documented results and much comparative analysis, which might compare incoming and outgoing students in one institution with that in a range of others, or might look to consider the nature of a particular field of study across a national or even international range.

In all this, creative writing research has been developing substantially in universities and colleges. At postgraduate level, Master of Arts (MA), Master of Fine Arts (MFA) and doctoral degree work – whether Doctor of Philosophy (e.g. PhD, DPhil), Doctor of Creative Arts (DCA), Doctor of Arts or Doctor of Fine Arts (DA, DFA) – has increased both in number of programmes and, as logic might dictate, number of candidates. Doctoral study, in particular, which tends to locate itself in research, first and foremost, and to be the final degree in any given field of university study, has had strong growth in the United Kingdom and Australasia, and in the US, despite the stated preference of the Association of Writers and Writing Programs (AWP), the primary organization concerned with creative writing in higher education in North America, for the MFA.

Even ignoring the changes in higher learning practice that have occurred, it would be disingenuous for anyone to argue that teaching and learning creative writing merely involves locating a few creative writers on campus and having them involved in something broadly equivalent to osmosis. Simply, creative writers are involved in a higher learning that involves research activity, whether it is research-through-practice or research before or after practice. As a research activity creative writing research is distinctive, discernible and for those of us who value the writing arts, significant.

3. NOTABLE READINGS

It seems, at first glance, that very little has been written about creative writing research. Certainly, where things have been written that are relevant they have not always declared themselves as creative writing research – or, at least, not called themselves this openly – or they have tended to be caught up in discussions around other subjects, such as English Literature, where quite a number of creative writers and Creative Writing researchers have been based.

The following is a combination of books, articles and other items that are either general, or current, to my own creative writing research. As creative writing research involves an amalgam, an intersection, an accumulation – any of these words and their synonyms might fit its modes, depending on the circumstances – the following list is merely indicative.

I've gone for a kind of personal 'Top Eight', but I'd probably shift one or two pieces in, or out, if composing the list next month, or next week, or even tomorrow. The first few I will explain in detail; the others just with a note or two.

Whereas literary research, to take one example, might utilize and even aim to produce widely applicable models and theories, creative writing research most often does so as a secondary consequence of a practice or of a consideration of practice or its end product, driven by a writer's curiosity and aiming to inform the writer. Creative writing research, therefore, is very project- and person-specific; its accumulative effect is a better understanding of creative writing, but its intention is most often driven by personal need and where holistic discoveries are made, beyond the formal research undertaken in Higher Education, they often do not get recorded at all.

It has therefore been, undoubtedly, the growth in research at graduate level that has assisted most in raising the level of open discussion about creative writing, its modes, its results, its types and styles and intentions, its past, present and future. I say 'assisted' – even though I suspect a few individuals might question if this growth in open discussion is not connected with the formalization of Higher Education mentioned earlier and, in that sense, represents a kind of 'institutionalization' of creative writing – I say 'assisted' because to have something that is capable of being talked about openly, shared between those who practise and consider it, and given the benefit of human exchange, and then have it considered restricted from this kind of exchange because it is thought, somehow, to be the result of a process that is unapproachable or unfathomable or shouldn't be over-scrutinized, is not merely self-defeating but seems disreputable. If we're capable of exchanging such knowledge, what argument can there legitimately be against it?

1. Ian Watt, *The Rise of the Novel* (Berkeley, CA: University of California), 1957

In one way, this book has little reason for being here; in another way, it feels like it is a primary text. Watt's book appeared on a university reading list in my first year of university, and it has little reason for being here because, embarrassingly, I didn't read it in its entirety. It was over three hundred pages long and the university lecturers I had seemed happy enough to quote me chunks small enough for a time-cutting student to consume without venturing into the entire text itself. I had *Little Dorrit* to read, after all, and *Paradise Lost*, among other gargantuan efforts, and the surf and my surfboard beckoned in between times! If these well-informed lecturers were going to give me a précis of Watt's book then who was any fresher to refuse it?

And yet, this book seems far more important than that, because prior to reading Watt's title on the Introduction to English Literature reading list, I hadn't thought about the idea of the novel being a form that had 'risen'. I assumed – as the lecturers obviously realized would be the case for most of us – that the novel had always existed as the form, and that studying it was merely a matter of knowing on what part of the timeline any particular work appeared. Reading and writing at school had been a pretty historicist affair, come to think of it; and we followed it through with the assumption that novels, plays, poems all existed as a matter of course – much like the weather or the teacher out front who'd ask one of us or another to read a piece of them out loud. Watt's was a book that changed this sense of rigidity considerably: if the novel *began* somewhere then it stood to reason that other forms had existed before it, and other forms might well exist after it. Not only that, if the novel was a form born from a certain cultural and social condition, as well as a historical one, then a reader and, as it occurred to me later, a writer would need to know a bit about where they were.

At the opening of Chapter One of his book Watt says: 'There are still no wholly satisfactory answers to many of the general questions which anyone interested in the early eighteenth-century novelists and their works is likely to ask ...' (p. 9). I was pleased about this. The novel, even three hundred years later, was apparently still mysterious, still an Everest to write and to decipher. There was, then, good reason to read or (if anyone I knew could *ever* do such a thing) write one. It was still an adventure. I probably wrote my first novel partially because of what I discovered in the chunks of Watt's book I was fed as a fresher; it made me aware of creative writing history, the role of the writer in the writing arts, and the importance of the whole enterprise to people in general.

2. Vladimir Nabokov, *Lolita* (London: Weidenfeld), 1959

What *really* was my first reaction to this book? I try to pin it down and the thought bounces around. Nabokov's narrator, Humbert Humbert, writes: 'My sin, my soul. Lo-lee-ta: the tip of the tongue taking a trip of three steps down the palate to tap, at three on the teeth. Lo. Lee. Ta' (p. 11).

I'm a little frightened to admit it, but I feel about Nabokov's novel much the same as Humbert Humbert does about his Lolita. I knew about Nabokov's book before I bought a copy. As with most people who *hear* about *Lolita* before they read it, the knowledge I had was mostly along the lines that it was not pornography but, rather, a literary classic. And yet, also, that its dubious subject matter – involving a girl of twelve, or fourteen, or something (rumour bred all variety of interpretations before I actually got hold of the book), and some kind of encounter with a middle-aged man – was reason enough for those who were 'not lovers of the writing arts' to confuse Nabokov's intentions and think he was advocating paedophilia.

So *Lolita* revealed two initial things: firstly, that it was possible for a great work of literature to draw criticism that was not only misinformed about its subject matter but about the art of creative writing itself; secondly, that the writer and the finished object in creative writing (in this case, Nabokov and his finished book, *Lolita*) were inseparable. Whatever might at any point be said about the independence of the final text from the creative writer felt, even in commonsense terms, to be wrong-headed. This initial feeling matched research I'd undertaken previously on the nature of human history, the different ways explanation of the past might be construed, and the textured aspects of historiography that sought to better explain how people and their world evolved. You obviously couldn't remove the agential input of the creative writer from the final product and think you were reaching a valid explanation of a book, a story, a poem, or similar. Because that was the case, surely you equally couldn't avoid a discussion of the process of producing a work of creative writing and think you were getting as close as possible to understanding it?

Beyond these initial feelings, *Lolita* and Nabokov also revealed that the language of prose could be as lyrical and as evocative as the language of poetry. It made me aware, too, that I was someone who liked the voice of narrators to be idiosyncratic, a little self-possessed, a little self-serving. I liked the writer and narrator to fly a kind of pirate flag in the world of prose, sail on through it, giving me a wild swashbuckling ride. It was a personal choice, my taste, but *Lolita* let me find that, and that was its importance.

Following *Lolita*, and no doubt partly because of it, I discovered the short stories of Donald Barthelme, the short novels of Richard Brautigan, Paul Theroux's *Picture Palace*. Just for starters. In addition, I suddenly felt I understood better the work of such writers as Gabriel Garcia Marquez, Manuel Puig, Salman Rushdie and Italo Calvino. From there, comparing and contrasting, the work of other writers (e.g. Toni Morrison, Virginia Woolf, J. M. Coetzee) began to be more clear to me, not only as a reader but as a creative writer. All these revealed something about my own creative writing, how I viewed my work and, ultimately, how I set about undertaking it. It was *Lolita* and Nabokov that provided that key breakthrough; the rest was about application of this new knowledge.

3. *New Writing: The International Journal for the Practice and Theory of Creative Writing* (MLM, 2004–onwards)

It is, in one sense, completely unfair to mention this journal. However, even though I'm speaking as this journal's Editor-in-Chief, I'm still going to ask the reader to believe I'm doing so as honestly as humanly possible.

New Writing was launched to be a platform for research in creative writing. Work submitted to the journal is, and has been, first rate, and reflects the growth and development of research discussions world wide, at least formally over the past half-century, and informally for much longer. Much of the work in *New Writing* has evolved from direct contact between creative writers and universities and colleges; some comes from Masters and Doctoral students and/or their supervisors – though being part of academe, or on a creative writing programme, is very far indeed from a prerequisite for submitting work. The journal accepts both critical and creative work in creative writing.

Some contributors, to date, have been members of writers' organizations such as the Association of Writers and Writing Programs (AWP) in the US, the National Association of Writers in Education (NAWE) in the UK, and the Australian Association of Writing Programs (AAWP) in Australia. Some have not been, or perhaps would not even want to be, members of any organization. Each of these organizations has a magazine or journal of its own. *New Writing* aims to be independent in that respect. It also aims to publish so that libraries world wide, as well as individuals, can subscribe, and to provide a platform for the meeting of all involved in creative writing research-through-practice or research.

Editing *New Writing* provides wonderful insights into so much that people are doing in creative writing that it's next to impossible to nail down one element that's livelier than another. Everything that finds its way 'across the desk' is revealing, some of it is fascinating, and the existence of such liveliness is well worth celebrating.

4. E. Le Roy Ladurie, *Montaillou* (London: Penguin), 1980

Described on its cover as 'the world-famous portrait of life in a medieval village' this is an example of historiography at its best. Ladurie reveals how discovering even seemingly mundane, 'clerical' pieces of information can help weave a fascinating story. Thus, not only a brilliant piece of historiography but, also, a great example of the ways in which writing about human activity involves a well-developed sense of the multilayered nature of experience.

5. A. Giddens, *The Constitution of Society: Outline of a Theory of Structuration* (London: Polity), 1986

Structurationism, as Giddens labels it (though others, not labelling it as such, use similar methodologies), comes largely from work by theorists in Social History and Sociology. What strikes me as useful in the theory is the ideas about synthesis that drive it. Those working the structurationist vein see the influences of individuals, social structures and historical cycles as highly interactive. They recognize such things as dispositions and human nature, while also incorporating ideas about individual and social action, social institutions and social structures. The theory makes much of how an interaction of all these things shapes the world, and this seems both a valid and a useful way of investigating it.

6. Garrison Keillor (ed.), *The Best American Short Stories* (Boston, MA: Houghton Mifflin), 1998.

This is Keillor's turn as Editor of this annual volume; but, really, any annual volume of this collection will suffice. It provides a snapshot of the contemporary American short story. Some are fabulous; others average. But each annual volume investigates the short story form in some way or another. To my mind: inspiring, as well as essential research for anyone writing short stories.

7. M. Woodmansee and P. Jaszi, *The Construction of Authorship: Textual Appropriation in Law and Literature* (Durham, NC: Duke University Press), 1994

What made this immediately different for me was that it was a book about authorship largely from a legal point of view. Because I had not encountered one before, this one opened up many possibilities. Most interestingly, the book provides an insight into what are essentially pragmatic and historical reasons why our ideas about authorship have changed over time. In creative writing terms it reveals, both directly and indirectly, why it is spurious to think of the creative writer in a fixed way; the writer, and creative writing, needs grounding in context.

8. H. Bergson, *Matter and Memory*, trans. N. M. Paul and W. S. Palmer (New York: Zone Books), 1991, first published in English in 1911; *Creative Evolution*, trans. Arthur Mitchell (New York: Dover), 1998, first published in English in 1911; and *Time and Free Will: An Essay on the Immediate Data of Consciousness* (New York: Macmillan), 1919, first published in English in 1910

I'm cheating here, because this really is three entries rather than one. But the fact is, I can't remember which of Bergson's books I read first; nor can I separate them in importance. Similarly, this is not as extensive a list of Bergson's works as I'd like to include. Bergson's ideas, such as those concerned with 'Intuition', time and duration (*durée*), consciousness, intelligence versus the intellect, and creative life all have useful connections to creative writing

4. SPECULATIONS

In a chapter on Creative Writing research, and based on my earlier comment that much creative writing research is person- and project-specific, exercises not connected with specific topics relevant to the individual reader's particular work would be out of place. The following, therefore, are seen as indicative research proposals rather than definitive exercises. But they aim to stimulate some thoughts.

Proposal One

'Human action is a combination of human nature and individual dispositions, individual or group acts, and the structures, institutions and cycles of cultures and societies.' Can a creative writer investigate this? If so, how? How is a final piece of creative writing a combination of these factors – or is it?

Proposal Two

'When subject and form meet well a piece of creative writing evolves relatively naturally, without self-conscious need to insist on shape and style. When they do not meet well each element must be (somehow) "gotten" into place, and the results, while not always noticeably different to readers or audience, *feel* telltale to the writer?' If this is true, what's the reason for this, and how does it relate to interaction between subject and form, writer and finished work? If it is not true, what might be a truer statement?

Proposal Three

'No two contemporary creative writers approach a topic in the same way.' If this statement is true, how might a comparison of two contemporary writers reveal something about the nature of the act of creative writing? If it is not true, what might be a truer statement?

Notes

Chapter 1: Short Fiction

1. In 1922, the University of Iowa began to accept creative works, including literary works, as theses for advanced degrees; in 1936, Iowa established the first formal MFA degree programme in creative writing (www.uiowa.edu/~iww/about.htm). By the 1970s, MFA programmes, as well as MA programmes for which it was possible to submit creative theses, were legion in the country. By the late 1970s, two PhD programmes in creative writing – at the University of Utah and at the University of Houston – had arisen; there are now over a dozen such programmes in the US. Though I'm interested to note how quickly the creative PhD has spread in Australia and the UK just in the last few years, I'm equally interested to learn that, at least in the UK, graduate student research in creative writing tends to focus not on the creative work *per se*, but rather on creative writing pedagogy – the idea presumably being that the proper study of writers is the teaching of writing. We in the US, on the other hand, have scarcely been asked to consider pedagogy at all, which is doubtless one reason why we tend to wring our hands helplessly over our qualms about the workshop.

2. Because Mr Hickey presents this flattening specifically as a masculinization of art, I have used the male rather than the female pronoun to refer to the painter here.

Chapter 4: Writing for Children and Young Adults

1. When I use the phrase 'children's literature' or 'writing for young people', I mean to include writing for young adults.

2. Australia and the US recently signed a free trade agreement. During negotiations debates raged over 'intellectual property' rights. For instance, in 2004, 'Out of every four dollars of copyrightable material three dollars goes out of Australia and mainly to the US' (McPhee, 2004: 4).

3. Young adult and recently children's novelist Sonya Hartnett, whose adult novel *Of a Boy* opened doors to her in the UK, has written an incisive and depressing article comparing the treatment by reviewers, critics and festival organizers of children's writers in Australia and the UK in *The Bulletin* (Hartnett, 2004).

4. Information about these Children's Choice Awards can be accessed on various websites. In the UK, 'the only major children's book prize . . . decided by the reader' is the Red House Children's Book Award (www.redhousechildrensbookaard.co.uk/about.htm). The Nestlé Children's Book Prize (www.booktrusted.co.uk/nestle/factsheet.html) allows adult judges to select a shortlist and children then choose, but

the young judges have to win a competition run through schools to have the chance to vote at all. In the US the Children's Book Council (www.cbcbooks.org/readinglists/childrenschoices) explains its joint project with the International Reading Association on their website (also see www.reading.org/resources/tools/choices.html). In Australia, each state plus the Australian Capital Territory have their own children's choice awards with appropriate acronyms: BILBY, COOL, CYBER, KANGA, KOALA, KROC, WAYRBA, YABBA (www.eddept.wa.edu.au/cmis/eval/fiction/awards/aw1.htm). There is also a national award. See 'References and Some Additional Sources' for a list of selected websites.

5. Donelson and Pace Nilsen examine the various uses of the term and settle on their own definition for the purposes of their study: '... readers between the approximate ages of 12 and 20' (1997: 6).

6. 'When the paper is folded into a certain configuration they print 8 pages on one side ... and 8 on the other. This folds into what is called a 16-page signature. Picture books usually comprise two 16-page signatures stitched together and attached to a three-piece cardboard case with a pair of endpapers. ... It has all got to do with folding, casing and printing machines.' My sincere thanks to publisher and editor Sue Williams (co-founder of Omnibus and Working Title Presses) for this information (30 May 2005).

Chapter 6: Playwriting

1. For a social history of Creative Writing in the academy, see M. Wandor, *The Author is not Dead, Merely Somewhere Else: Creative Writing after Theory* (2006).

2. See 'The Royal Smut-Hound' by Kenneth Tynan, in M. Wandor, *Post-war British Drama: Looking Back in Gender* (2001), pp. 98–111.

3. See M. Wandor, *Carry On, Understudies* (1986); P. Ansorge, *Disrupting the Spectacle* (1975); N. Khan, *The Arts Britain Ignores* (1976); S. Craig, *Dreams and Deconstructions* (1980).

4. T. Eagleton, *Literary Theory* (1983, 1996); V. Cunningham, *Reading After Theory* (2002).

5. See S. Shepherd, and M. Wallis, *Studying Plays* (1998), p. 1.

6. K. Elam, *The Semiotics of Theatre and Drama* (1997). Originally published in 1980.

7. See M. Wandor, 'Value Judgements: you gotta love 'em', *New Writing: The International Journal for the Practice and Theory of Creative Writing* (forthcoming).

Chapter 7: Scriptwriting for Radio

1. In this chapter I deal almost exclusively with radio drama, and teaching, in the UK. For possibilities in the US, and some advice about scriptwriting, see Tony Palermo, (www.ruyasonic.com), and for a world perspective, see Tim Crook, 'International Radio Drama – Social, Economic and Literary Contexts' (www.irdp.co.uk).

2. Undergraduate student in a critical commentary. For a range of student comments about studying creative writing, see Steve May, 'Teaching Creative Writing at

Undergraduate Level: Why, how and does it work?' (www.english.ltsn.ac.uk/explore/projects/archive/creative/creative3.php).

3. Extracts from the Radio 4 *Commissioning Guidelines 1998/9* (BBC, 1998), Refs 40013/T/1130/WD and 40019/U/1415/WD.

4. In my first 15 years as a radio writer I sold approximately 30 plays, all of them based on my own ideas. Of my last seven projects six have been based on ideas supplied by a producer, only one has been my own original idea. Lance Dann, a PhD student at Bath Spa University, is currently undertaking research into changes in the commissioning process for radio drama in the UK (sponsored by the Society of Authors), and how those changes have affected output. Certain trends emerge already: new writers tend now to be headhunted by producer/directors, from theatre or non-script forms. The unsolicited manuscript has a significantly smaller chance of getting bought than it did in the mid-1980s.

5. A sad fact confirmed by the BBC's own Writersroom co-ordinator on a recent visit to our institution.

6. Only in the mid-1990s standard BBC recording practice used reel-to-reel tape, which was edited by hand and razor. Nowadays digital editing is the norm, though the matter is complicated by different parts of the BBC using different equipment.

7. See Tim Crook, 'International Radio Drama'.

8. For example Shaun MacLoughlin, *Writing for Radio* (2004), and the more venerable but still useful William Ash, *The Way to Write Radio Plays* (1985).

9. See Peter Lewis, *Radio Drama* (1981). Tim Crook, *Radio Drama: Theory and Practice* (1999), and Vincent McInerny, *Writing for Radio* (2001), combine the practical and the theoretical.

10. An exception is the work of Lee Hall, writer of the feature film *Billy Elliott*. See Lee Hall, *Plays* (2002).

11. You can probably get hold of Orson Welles's *War of the Worlds* (I recently got it as a free gift from a petrol station) and several versions of Dylan Thomas's *Under Milk Wood*. Otherwise (as of March 2005) the BBC Radio Collection boasted but ten dramas: works by Shakespeare and Noel Coward, and The Mysteries.

12. It's significant that the bestsellers in the BBC Audio Collection are 'classic' comedy shows from the 1950s and 1960s, for example *Round the Horn*, or *Beyond our Ken*, and as of May 2005 Douglas Adams's *Hitchhiker's Guide to the Galaxy*.

13. *Commissioning Guidelines*, Ref. 40019/U/1415/WD.

14. Steve May, 'Teaching Creative Writing'.

15. Arthur Conan Doyle, 'The Adventure of the Lion's Mane', in *The Casebook of Sherlock Holmes* (1986), and given a somewhat postmodern treatment by Bert Coules for BBC Radio 4 in 1995 (www.bertcoules.co.uk/casebook.htm).

16. One solution concocted by a group of undergraduates went thus: the victim's disenchanted wife had befriended a marine biologist, who then supplied her with the creature, which she introduced into her husband's bath, later disposing of his body in the sea.

17. For more on scenes in radio plays see, 'A note on presentation and drafting' below.

18. Of course, *Waiting for Godot* breaks this rule, but only works insofar as Beckett is thoroughly immersed in and playing with the rule.

19. *The Governor*, dir. Richard Wortley, BBC Radio 3 (1989).
20. The opening of *A Selection of Ordinary Household Sounds*, BBC Radio 4 (1993).
21. For Script Smart, a formatting tool approved by the BBC, visit www.bbc.co.uk/writersroom/scriptsmart/index.shtml
22. 'Writing Drama For BBC Radio and Television: Guidelines for Unsolicited Work', BBC pamphlet, May 2001, pp. 15 and 18. The most recent handouts have achieved an uneasy truce on this matter.

Chapter 11: Workshopping

1. This is not to say that sharing examples of published literary work is not an important element of teaching. Most of the time, however, reading can be assigned outside of class.
2. Obviously great texts are produced throughout the Western and non-Western world; this reference to the English-speaking world pertains to the fact that the writing workshop in higher education is relatively unique to this world.
3. For a complete survey of the condition of teacher training in graduate programmes in the US, see Dr Kelly Ritter's landmark article in *College English*, November 2001.

References and Some Additional Sources

Addonizio, K. and Laux, D., *The Poet's Companion: A Guide to the Pleasures of Writing Poetry* (New York: W. W. Norton), 1997.

Ahlberg, A. and Ahlberg, J., *It Was a Dark and Stormy Night* (Harmondsworth: Puffin), 1994.

Altbach, P. G. and Hoshino, E. S. (eds), *International Book Publishing: An Encyclopedia* (Hamden, CT: Garland), 1995.

Alvermann, D. E., *Adolescents and Literacies in a Digital World* (New York: Peter Lang), 2002.

Ansorge, P., *Disrupting the Spectacle* (London: Pitman), 1975.

Ash, W., *The Way to Write Radio Plays* (London: Elm Tree Books), 1985.

Auden, W. H., *The Dyer's Hand* (reissue edn) (New York: Vintage), 1990.

Baker, J., *Window* (London: Julia MacRae Books), 1991.

Barnett, A. and Turchi, P. (eds), *The Story Behind the Story* (New York: W. W. Norton), 2004.

Bartholomae, D. and Petrosky, A., *Ways of Reading: An Anthology for Writers* (7th edn) (Bedford: St Martin's Press), 2005.

Bassnett, S. and Grundy, P., *Language through Literature: Creative Language Teaching* (London: Longman), 1993.

Behn, R. and Twichell, C. (eds), *The Practice of Poetry: Writing Exercises from Poets Who Teach* (New York: HarperCollins), 1992.

Beiguelman, G., 'Egoscope' (www.desvirtual.com/egoscopio/english/about_more.htm).

Bell, M. S., *Narrative Design: Working with Imagination, Craft, and Form* (New York: W. W. Norton), 1997.

Bennett, A. and Royle, N., 'Creative Writing', in *An Introduction to Literature, Criticism and Theory* (3rd edn) (London: Longman), 2004, pp. 85–92.

Bergson, H., *Time and Free Will: An Essay on the Immediate Data of Consciousness* [first published in English 1910] (New York: Macmillan), 1919.

Bergson, H., *Matter and Memory* [first published in English 1911], trans. N. M. Paul and W. S. Palmer (New York: Zone Books), 1991.

Bergson, H., *Creative Evolution* [first published in English 1911], trans. A. Mitchell (New York: Dover), 1998.

Bernheimer, C. and Kahane, C. (eds), *In Dora's Case: Freud, Hysteria, Feminism* (London: Virago), 1985.

Bilton, A., *An Introduction to Contemporary American Fiction* (Edinburgh: Edinburgh University Press), 2002.

Birkerts, S., 'The Poet in an Age of Distractions', in *The Electric Life: Essays on Modern Poetry* (New York: William Morrow), 1989a, pp. 29–40.

Birkerts, S., *The Electric Life: Essays on Modern Poetry* (New York: William Morrow), 1989b.

Bishop, W., 'On Learning to Like Teaching Creative Writing', in W. Bishop and H. Ostrom (eds), *Colors of a Different Horse: Rethinking Creative Writing, Theory and Pedagogy* (Urbana, IL: National Council of Teachers of English), 1994.

Bishop, W., *Released Into Language: Options for Teaching Creative Writing* (2nd edn) (Portland, ME: Calendar Island Publishers), 1998.

Bishop, W., *On Writing: A Process Reader* (New York: McGraw-Hill), 2003a.

Bishop, W., *The Subject Is Writing: Essays by Teachers and Students* (Portsmouth, NH: Boynton/Cook), 2003b.

Bishop, W. and Ostrom, H. (eds), *Colors of a Different Horse: Rethinking Creative Writing and Pedagogy* (Urbana, IL: National Council of Teachers), 1994.

Bishop, W. and Starkey, D. (eds), *In Praise of Pedagogy: Poetry, Flash Fiction, and Essays on Composing* (Portsmouth, NH: Boynton/Cook), 2000.

Blacklock, D., 'Reading SOLO', *Practically Primary*, Vol. 2, No. 2 (June 1997), 24–6.

Bly, C., *The Passionate, Accurate Story: Making Your Heart's Truth into Literature* (Minneapolis, MN: Milkweed), 1990.

Boden, M., *Dimensions of Creativity* (Cambridge, MA: The MIT Press), 1994.

Boden, M., *The Creative Mind: Myths and Mechanisms* (2nd edn) (London: Routledge), 2004.

Boisseau, M. and Wallace, R., *Writing Poems* (6th edn) (New York: Longman), 2004.

Bolter, J. and Grusin, R., *Remediation: Understanding New Media* (Cambridge, MA: The MIT Press), 2000.

Bradbury, M., *The Modern British Novel* (London: Penguin), 1994.

Bradford, C., *Reading Race: Aboriginality in Australian Children's Literature* (Melbourne: Melbourne University Press), 2001.

Brian, J., *What's in the River?*, illus. J. Dawson (Norwood, SA: Omnibus Books), 2001.

Brooke-Rose, C., *Stories, Theories and Things* (Cambridge: Cambridge University Press), 1991.

Brotchie, A. (complier) and Gooding, M. (ed.), *The Book of Surrealist Games* (Berkeley, CA: Shambhala Publications), 1995.

Browne, A., *Zoo* (London: Red Fox), 1992.

Bruccoli, M., *Some Sort of Epic Grandeur* (2nd revised edn) (Columbia, SC: University of South Carolina Press), 2002.

Burke, K., *Language as Symbolic Action* (Berkeley, CA: University of California Press), 1966.

Burke, P., *The Art of Conversation* (Ithaca, NY: Cornell University Press), 1993.

Burton, D., 'Through A Glass Darkly – Through Dark Glasses: Sylvia Plath's *The Bell Jar*', in R. Carter (ed.), *Language and Literature: A Reader in Stylistics* (London: Allen and Unwin), 1982, pp. 195–216.

Calvino, I., *The Literature Machine* (London: Secker and Warburg), 1986.

Camoin, F., 'The Workshop and Its Discontents', in W. Bishop and H. Ostrom (eds), *Colors of a Different Horse: Rethinking Creative Writing, Theory and Pedagogy* (Urbana, IL: National Council of Teachers of English), 1994, pp. 3–7.

Capote, T., *In Cold Blood* (London: Hamish Hamilton), 1966.

Carter, R. (ed.), *Language and Literature: A Reader in Stylistics* (London: Allen and Unwin), 1982.

Cartmell, D. and Whelehan, I. (eds), *Adaptations: From Text to Screen, Screen to Text* (London: Routledge), 1999.

Caves, R. E., *Creative Industries: Contracts between Art and Commerce* (Cambridge, MA: Harvard University Press), 2000.

Chambers, A., 'The Reader in the Book', in P. Hunt (ed.), *Children's Literature: The Development of Criticism* (London: Routledge), 1990, pp. 91–114.

Children's Choice Award Websites:
www.booksellers.co.nz/childs.htm (New Zealand)
www.booktrusted.co.uk/nestle/factsheet.html (UK)
www.cbcbooks.org/readinglists/childrenschoices (US)
www.eddept.wa.edu.au/cmis/eval/fiction/awards/aw1.htm (Australia)
www.pnla.org/yrca (Canada)
www.reading.org/resources/tools/choices.html (US)
www.redhousechildrensbookaard.co.uk/about.htm (UK)

Coetzee, J. M., *Foe* (London: Secker & Warburg), 1986.

Coleridge, S. T., 'Kubla Khan', in *Selected Poetry and Prose of Coleridge*, ed. D. Stauffer (New York: The Modern Library), 1951, pp. 44–5.

Conan Doyle, A., 'The Adventure of the Lion's Mane', in *The Casebook of Sherlock Holmes* (London and Glasgow: Collins), 1986.

Conroy, F., *Stop-Time* (New York: Viking), 1967.

Cook, J., 'Creative Writing as a Research Method', in G. Griffin (ed.), *Research Methods for English Studies* (Edinburgh: Edinburgh University Press), 2005, pp. 195–212.

Craig, S., *Dreams and Deconstructions* (Ambergate: Amber Lane Press), 1980.

Crook, T., *Radio Drama: Theory and Practice* (London and New York: Routledge), 1999.

Csikszentmihalyi, M., *Creativity: Flow and the Psychology of Discovery and Invention* (New York: Harper Perennial), 1997.

Cunningham, V., *Reading After Theory* (Oxford: Blackwell), 2002.

Currie, M. (ed.), *Metafiction: A Critical Reader* (New York: Longman), 1995.

Currie, M., 'Criticism and Creativity: Poststructuralist Theories', in J. Wolfreys (ed.), *Introducing Literary Theory* (Edinburgh: Edinburgh University Press), 2001, pp. 152–68.

Dawson, P., *Creative Writing and the New Humanities* (London: Routledge), 2004.

Day, D., *Malcolm Lowry: A Biography* (New York: Oxford University Press), 1973.

Delbanco, A., *Speaking of Writing: Selected Hopwood Lectures* (Ann Arbor, MI: University of Michigan Press), 1990.

Didion, J., *Slouching Towards Bethlehem* (New York: Farrar, Straus & Giroux), 1968.

Dillard, A., *Pilgrim at Tinker Creek* (New York: Harper's Magazine Press), 1974.

Disher, G., 'Arrested Development', *Viewpoint*, Vol. 5, No. 4 (Summer 1997), 3–5.

Domina, L., 'The Body of My Work is Not Just a Metaphor', in W. Bishop and H. Ostrom (eds), *Colors of a Different Horse: Rethinking Creative Writing, Theory and Pedagogy* (Urbana, IL: National Council of Teachers of English), 1994, pp. 27–34.

Donelson, K. L. and Pace Nilsen, A., *Literature for Today's Young Adults* (5th edn) (New York: Longman), 1997.

Doonan, J., *Looking at Pictures in Picture Books* (Stroud: The Thimble Press), 1993.

Duke, K., *Aunt Isabel Tells a Good One* (New York: Puffin Books), 1992.

Eagleton, T., *Literary Theory: An Introduction* (Oxford: Blackwell), 1983.

Eagleton, T., *Literary Theory: An Introduction* (2nd edn) (Oxford: Blackwell), 1996.

Eco, U., *Six Walks in Fictional Woods* (London: Harvard University Press), 1994.

Egri, L., *The Art of Dramatic Writing* (New York: Simon and Schuster), 1960.

Egri, L., *The Art of Creative Writing* (Secaucus, NJ: Citadel Press), 1993.

Elam, K., *The Semiotics of Theatre and Drama* (London: Routledge), 1997.

Engel, J., *Oscar-winning Screenwriters on Screenwriting* (New York: Hyperion Books), 2002.

Evans, C., *English People: The Experience of Teaching and Learning English in British Universities* (Buckingham: Open University Press), 1993.

Fenza, D. W., 'Creative Writing and Its Discontents', *The Writer's Chronicle* (March/April 2000) (www.awpwriter.org/magazine/writers/fenza01.htm) (also available from the NAWE Archive: www.nawe.co.uk).

Field, S., *The Definitive Guide to Screenwriting* (London: Ebury Press), 2003.

Florida, R., *The Rise of the Creative Class* (New York: Basic Books), 2002.

Forché, C. and Gerard, P. (eds), *Writing Creative Nonfiction: Instruction and Insights from the Teachers of the Associated Writing Programs* (Cincinnati, OH: Story Press), 2001.

Ford, R., 'Goofing Off While the Muse Recharges', in *Writers on Writing: Collected Essays from the New York Times*, intro. J. Darnton (New York: Holt), 2001, pp. 65–70.

Forster, E. M., *Aspects of the Novel* (San Diego, CA: Harvest/HBJ), 1956.

Foster, H., *The Return of the Real: Critical Models in Art and Theory since 1960* (Cambridge, MA: The MIT Press), 1996.

Foucault, M., 'What is an Author?', trans. D. F. Bouchard and S. Simon, in D. F. Bouchard (ed.), *Language, Counter-Memory, Practice* (Ithaca, NY: Cornell University Press), 1977, pp. 124–7.

Fox, M., *Possum Magic*, illus. J. Vivas (Adelaide: Omnibus Books), 1983.

Fox, M., *Mem's the Word* (Ringwood: Penguin Books), 1990.

Fox, M., *Reading Magic: Why Reading Aloud to Our Children Will Change Their Lives Forever* (San Diego, CA: Harcourt), 2001; also published as *Reading Magic: How Your Child Can Learn to Read Before School and Other Read-aloud Miracles* (Sydney: Pan Macmillan), 2001.

Francis, L. and Bruchac, J. (eds), *Reclaiming the Vision: Past, Present, and Future Native Voices for the Eighth Generation* (New York: Greenfield Press), 1996.

Frensham, R. G., *Teach Yourself Screenwriting* (London: Teach Yourself Books), 1996.

Freud, S., *Case Histories I: 'Dora' and 'Little Hans'* [1905], ed. and trans. A. Richards (London: Penguin), 1977.

Froug, W., *The New Screenwriter Looks at the New Screenwriter* (Hollywood, CA: Silman-James Press), 1992.

Fussell, P., *Poetic Meter and Poetic Form* (New York: McGraw-Hill Education), 1979.

Garber, E. and Ramjerdi, J., 'Reflections on the Teaching of Creative Writing: A Correspondence', in W. Bishop and H. Ostrom (eds), *Colors of a Different Horse: Rethinking Creative Writing, Theory and Pedagogy* (Urbana, IL: National Council of Teachers of English), 1994, pp. 8–26.

Gardner, J., *On Moral Fiction* (New York: Basic Books), 1978.

Garrett, J., 'To the Reader', Editorial, *Bookbird: Special Double Issue: 'Bad' Books, 'Good' Reading?*, Vol. 33, No. 3/4, (Fall–Winter 1995–96), 2–4.

Gibbons, R. (ed.), *The Poet's Work* (Chicago, IL: University of Chicago Press), 1989.

Giddens, A., *The Constitution of Society: Outline of a Theory of Structuration* (London: Polity), 1986.

Gide, A., *Journals 1889–1949*, trans. and ed. J. O'Brien (New York: Penguin), 1984.

Goldsmith, K., 'Uncreativity as a Creative Practice', *Drunken Boat 5* (Winter 2002–03) (http://drunkenboat.com/db5/goldsmith/uncreativity.html).

Goodman, S. and O'Halloran, K. (eds), *The Art of English: Literary Creativity* (Milton Keynes: Open University Press), forthcoming.

Gordimer, N., 'Nadine Gordimer with Hermione Lee', in S. Nasta (ed.), *Writing Across Worlds: Contemporary Writers Talk* (London: Routledge), 2004.

Graham, B., *Greetings from Sandy Beach* (Melbourne: Lothian Books), 1990.

Guest, B., *Forces of Imagination: Writing on Writing* (Berkeley, CA: Kelsey Street), 2002.

Gulino, P. J., *Screenwriting: The Sequence Approach* (New York and London: Continuum), 2004.

Gutkind, L., 'What's in this Name – And What's Not?', *Creative Nonfiction*, No. 1 (December 1993) (available at www.creativenonfiction.org/thejournal/articles/issue01/01editor.htm).

Gutkind, L., 'Style and Substance', *Creative Nonfiction*, No. 10 (October 1998) (available at www.creativenonfiction.org/thejournal/articles/issue10/10editor.htm).

Haake, K., *No Reason on Earth* (Seattle, WA: Dragon Gate Press), 1986.

Haake, K., *The Height and Depth of Everything* (Reno, NV: University of Nevada Press), 2001.

Haake, K., Ostrom, H. and Bishop, W., *Metro: Journeys in Writing Creatively* (New York: Addison Wesley), 2001.

Hall, L., *Plays* (London: Methuen), 2002.

Harper, G., 'Creative Writing in Higher Education: Introducing Gramography', *Writing in Education*, No. 12 (Summer 1997) (available from the NAWE Archive: www.nawe.co.uk).

Hartnett, S., 'Closed Book', View (Arts and Entertainment), *The Bulletin*, 4 May 2004, 60–2.

Hayles, N. K., *Writing Machines* (Chicago, IL: University of Chicago Press), 2003.

Hayles, N. K., 'The Time of Digital Poetry: From Object to Event', in A. Morris and T. Swiss (eds), *New Media Poetics: Contexts/Technotexts/Themes* (Cambridge, MA: The MIT Press), forthcoming.

Heaney, S., 'Feeling into Words', lecture given at the Royal Society of Literature, 17 October 1974 (reprinted in R. Gibbons (ed.), *The Poet's Work* (Chicago, IL: University of Chicago Press), 1989, pp. 263–82).

Heaney, S., *Place of Writing* (Grand Rapids, MI: Baker Book House), 1989.

Heiss, A. M., *Dhuuluu-Yala (To Talk Straight) – Publishing Indigenous Literature* (Canberra: Aboriginal Studies Press), 2003.

Henry, B. and Zawacki, A. (eds), *The Verse Book of Interviews: 27 Poets on Language, Craft & Culture* (Amherst, MA: Verse Press), 2005.

Herrington, A. and Curtis, M., *Persons in Progress: Four Stories of Writing and Personal Development in College* (Urbana, IL. National Council of Teachers of English), 2000.

Hickey, D., *The Invisible Dragon: Four Essays on Beauty* (Los Angeles, CA: Art Issues Press), 1993.

Holland, S. (ed.), *Creative Writing: A Good Practice Guide* (London: English Subject Centre), 2003.

Hollander, J., *Making Your Own Days: Rhyme's Reason: A Guide to English Verse* (3rd edn) (New Haven, CT: Yale University Press), 2001.

Hollindale, P., 'Ideology and the Children's Book', *Signal*, No. 55 (January 1988), 3–22.

Howard, D., *How to Build a Great Screenplay* (New York: St Martin's Press), 2004.

Howard, D. and Mabley, E., *The Tools of Screenwriting* (New York: St Martin's Griffin Press), 1993.

Hugo, R., *The Triggering Town: Lectures and Essays on Poetry and Writing* (New York: W. W. Norton), 1992.

Hunt, P. (ed.), *Children's Literature: The Development of Criticism* (London: Routledge), 1990.

Hunt, P., *Criticism, Theory, and Children's Literature* (Oxford: Blackwell), 1991.

Hunt, P., *An Introduction to Children's Literature* (Oxford: Oxford University Press), 1994.

Hunt, P., 'The Complete History of 20th and 21st Century Children's Literature in 35 Minutes', in S. Van der Hoeven (ed.), *Time Will Tell: Children's Literature into the 21st Century: Proceedings from the Fourth National Conference of the Children's Book Council of Australia* (Adelaide: CBC), 1998, 30–5.

Hunter, J. P., *Before Novels: The Cultural Contexts of Eighteenth-century English Fiction* (New York: Norton), 1990.

Hutchins, P., *The Very Worst Monster* (London: The Bodley Head), 1985.

Illich, I., 'The Alternative to Schooling' [1965], in J. Bowen and P. R. Hobson, *Theories of Education: Studies of Significant Innovation in Western Educational Thought* (Brisbane: Wiley), 1974.

Illich, I., 'Text and University: on the idea and history of a unique institution', trans. L. Hoinacki (www.pudel.uni-bremen.de/pdf/TEXTANTL.pdf), 1991.

Illich, I., *In the Vineyard of the Text: A Commentary on Hugh's 'Didascalicon'* (Chicago, IL: University of Chicago Press), 1993.

Ito, M., 'Technologies of Childhood Imagination: Yugioh, Media Mixes, and Everyday Cultural Production' (available at www.itofisher.com/mito/archives/000074.html), 2005.

James, H., *The Complete Notebooks of Henry James*, ed. L. Edel and L. H. Powers (Oxford: Oxford University Press), 1987.

Jennings, P., *Unreal!* (Ringwood: Puffin), 1985, and numerous collections of stories since (www.pauljennings.com.au).

Jennings, P., 'We need to share our stories in order to work out who we are …', in M. Ricketson, *Paul Jennings: 'The Boy in the Story is Always Me'* (Ringwood: Viking), 2000, 294–300 (Afterword).

Jennings, P., *The Reading Bug … and how you can help your child to catch it* (Camberwell: Penguin), 2003.

Jewitt, C. and Kress, G. (eds), *Multimodal Literacy: New Literacies and Digital Epistemologies* (Vol. 4) (New York: Peter Lang), 2003, pp. 1–18.

Johnson, T. (ed.), *Emily Dickinson: The Complete Poems* (London: Faber & Faber), 1970.

Keillor, G. (ed.), *The Best American Short Stories* (Boston, MA: Houghton Mifflin), 1998.

Kellner, D., 'New Media and New Literacies: Reconstructing Education for the New Millennium', in L. A. Lievrouw and S. Livingstone (eds), *Handbook of New Media: Social Shaping and Consequences of ICTs* (Thousand Oaks, CA: Sage Publications), 2002, pp. 90–104.

Khan, N., *The Arts Britain Ignores* (London: Arts Council Press of Great Britain), 1976.

'Kindy girl, 5, in handcuffs', *Sunday Mail* (Adelaide), 24 April 2005 (Dow Jones Reuters: http://global.factiva.com/en/arch/print_results.asp).

Kingston, M. H., *The Woman Warrior* (New York: Random House), 1976.

Kinzie, M., *A Poet's Guide to Poetry* (Chicago, IL: University of Chicago Press), 1999.

Kirk, J., 'What's a Good Book?', in *At Least They're Reading: Proceedings of the First National Conference of the Children's Book Council of Australia* (Melbourne: D. W. Thorpe, 1992, p. 149.

Komunyakaa, Y., *Blue Notes: Essays, Interviews, and Commentaries* (Ann Arbor, MI: University of Michigan Press), 2000.

Kooser, T., *The Poetry Home Repair Manual: Practical Advice for Beginning Poets* (Lincoln, NE: University of Nebraska Press), 2005.

Kress, G., *Literacy in the New Media Age* (New York: Routledge), 2003.

Kress, G., Jewett, C. and Tsatsarelis, C., 'Knowledge, Identity, Pedagogy: Pedagogic Discourse and the Representational Environment of Education in Late Modernity', *Linguistics and Education*, Vol. 11, No. 1 (March 2000), 7–30.

Kroll, J., 'The Imaginative Leap' (Margaret Mahy interviewed by Jeri Kroll), *Lowdown: Youth Performing Arts in Australia*, Vol. 9, No. 3 (May 1987), 63–5.

Kroll, J., 'Imagination and Marketability: What Do Writers Do for a Living?', *TEXT*, Vol. 2, No. 1 (April 1998), 1–9 (available at www.griffith.edu.au/school/art/text/april98/kroll.htm).

Kroll, J., *Fit for a Prince*, illus. D. Hatcher (Norwood, SA: Omnibus Books), 2001.

Kroll, J., 'The Resurrected Author: Creative Writers in 21st-century Higher Education', *New Writing: The International Journal for the Practice and Theory of Creative Writing*, Vol. 1, No. 2 (2004), 89–102.

Kroll, J. and Evans, S., 'How to Write a "How to Write" Book: The Writer as Entrepreneur', *TEXT*, Vol. 9, No. 1 (April 2005), 1–26 (available at http://www.griffith.edu.au/school/art/text/april05/krollevans.htm).

Kupfer, F., *Before and After Zachariah: A Family Story About a Different Kind of Courage* (Chicago, IL: Academy of Chicago Publications), 1988.

Kupfer, F., 'Everything But the Truth', originally published in *The Women's Review of Books*, Vol. 8, No. 10 (July 1996), 1; reprinted in R. L. Root, Jr, and M. Steinberg (eds), *The Fourth Genre: Contemporary Writers of/on Creative Nonfiction* (3rd edn) (New York: Longman), 2004, pp. 291–3.

Lammon, M., 'An Interview with David McKain and Margaret Gibson', *AWP Chronicle*, Vol. 23, No. 5 (March/April 1991), 1–7.

Landow, G. P., *Hypertext 2.0: The Convergence of Contemporary Critical Theory and Technology* (Baltimore, MD: The Johns Hopkins University Press), 1997.

Lankshear, C. and Knobel, M., *New Literacies: Changing Knowledge and Classroom Learning* (Philadelphia, PA: Open University Press), 2003.

Lankshear, C. and Knobel, M., '"New" Literacies: Research and Social Practice'. Opening plenary address presented at the Annual Meeting of the National Reading Conference, San Antonio, TX (available at: www.geocities.com/Athens/Academy/1160/nrc.html), 2004.

Leander, K. M. and McKim, K., 'Tracing the Everyday "Sitings" of Adolescents on the Internet: A Strategic Adaptation of Ethnography across Online and Offline Spaces', *Education, Communication, & Information*, Vol. 3, No. 2 (2003), 211–40.

Le Roy Ladurie, E., *Motaillou* (London: Penguin), 1980.

Levine, A., 'From Outside Over There: Publishing Books That Began Elsewhere', in B. Alderman and S. Page (eds), *The Third Millennium: Read On!: Proceedings of the Fifth National Conference of the Children's Book Council of Australia* (Canberra: CBC), 2000, 17–27.

Lewis, C. and Fabos, B., 'Instant Messaging, Literacies, and Social Identities', *Reading Research Quarterly*, Vol. 40, No. 4 (2005), 470–501.

Lewis, P., *Radio Drama* (London: Longman), 1981.

Lewis, V. V. and Mayes, W. M., *Valerie and Walter's Best Books for Children: A Lively, Opinionated Guide* (2nd edn) (New York: Quill), 2004.

Light, G., 'Conceiving Creative Writing in Higher Education', *The Creative Writing in Higher Education Journal*, Vol. 1 (2000) (available at www.nawe.co.uk/forum.html).

Light, G., 'How Students Understand and Learn Creative Writing in Higher Education' (available from the NAWE Archive: www.nawe.co.uk).

Livingstone, S., *Young People and New Media* (London: Sage), 2002.

Lodge, D. and Wood, N. (eds), *Modern Criticism and Theory: A Reader* (3rd edn) (London: Longman), 2006.

Lukens, R. J., *A Critical Handbook of Children's Literature* (6th edn) (New York: Longman), 1999.

Lurie, M., *Madness* (Sydney: Collins/Angus and Robertson), 1991.

McInerny, V., *Writing for Radio* (Manchester: Manchester University Press), 2001.

McKee, R., *Story, Substance, Structure, Style and the Principles of Screenwriting* (London: Methuen), 1999.

MacLoughlin, S., *Writing for Radio* (Bristol: Soundplay Books), 2004.

McPhee, H., 'Writers in the Global Australian Village', The Australian Society of Authors Colin Simpson Lecture, 2004, 1–17 (available at www.asauthors.org/cgi-bin/asa/information.cgi/ Show?_id=info1150&sort=DEFAULT&search=colin%20simpson%20lecture).

McPhee, J., *The Pine Barrens* (New York: Farrar, Straus & Giroux), 1968.

McRae, J., *Literature with a small 'l'* (London: Macmillan), 1991.

Mahy, M., *The Man Whose Mother was a Pirate*, illus. B. Froud (London: Dent & Sons), 1972.

Mahy, M., *The Man Whose Mother was a Pirate*, illus. M. Chamberlain (Melbourne: Dent & Sons), 1985.

Mailer, N., *Executioner's Song* (Boston, MA: Little, Brown), 1979.

Marr, D., *Patrick White: A Life* (New York: Knopf), 1992.

Marsden, J., The Australian Society of Authors Colin Simpson Lecture, 2005 (available at www.asauthors.org/papers/2005/colin_simpson_2005.pdf).

Marshall, B. K., *Teaching the Postmodern: Fiction and Theory* (London and New York: Routledge), 1992.

Maybin, J. and Swann, J. (eds), *The Art of English: Everyday Creativity* (Milton Keynes: Open University Press), forthcoming.

Mayers, T., *(Re)Writing Craft: Composition, Creative Writing and the Future of English Studies* (Pittsburgh, PA: University of Pittsburgh Press), 2005.

Memmott, T., *[N]+Semble* (available at http://memmott.org/talan/rtp27/), 2005.

Menand, L., 'How to Frighten Small Children: The Complicated Pleasure of Kids', Books, *The New Yorker*, 6 October 1997, 112, 114–19.

Merchant, G., 'Teenagers in Cyberspace: An Investigation of Language Use and Language Change in Internet Chatrooms', *Journal of Research in Reading*, Vol. 24, No. 3 (2001), 293–306.

Miller, B. and Paola, S., *Tell It Slant: Writing and Shaping Creative Nonfiction* (Boston, MA: McGraw-Hill), 2003.

Milne, A. A., 'Children's books ... are books chosen for us by others', in P. Hunt (ed.), *An Introduction to Children's Literature* (Oxford: Oxford University Press), 1994.

Montfort, N., *Twisty Little Passages: An Approach to Interactive Fiction* (Cambridge, MA: The MIT Press), 2003.

Morris, A., 'New Media Poetics: As We May Think/How to Write', in A. Morris and T. Swiss (eds), *New Media Poetics: Contexts/Technotexts/Themes* (Cambridge, MA: The MIT Press), forthcoming.

Motte, W. F. (trans. and ed.), *Oulipo: A Primer of Potential Literature* (Normal, IL: Dalkey Archive), 1998.

Moxley, J., *Creative Writing in America* (Urbana, IL: National Council of Teachers), 1989.

Murray, D., *A Writer Teaches Writing* (2nd edn) (Stamford, CT: Heinle), 2003.

Myers, D. G., *The Elephants Teach* (Englewood Cliffs, NJ: Prentice Hall), 1995.

Myers, J., *The Portable Poetry Workshop* (Boston, MA: Wadsworth), 2005.

Nabokov, V., *Lolita* (London: Weidenfeld), 1959.

Nash, W., *An Uncommon Tongue: The Uses and Resources of English* (London: Routledge), 1992.

New Writing: The International Journal for the Practice and Theory of Creative Writing (MLM, 2004–ongoing).

Nims, J. F. and Mason, D., *Western Wind: An Introduction to Poetry* (4th edn) (New York: McGraw-Hill), 1999.

Nodelman, P., *Words About Pictures: The Narrative Art of Children's Picture Books* (Athens, GA: University of Georgia Press), 1988.

Oliver, M., *A Poetry Handbook* (San Diego, CA: Harcourt Brace), 1995.

Orr, G. and Voigt, E. B. (eds), *Poets Teaching Poets: Self and the World* (Ann Arbor, MI: University of Michigan Press), 1996.

Ostriker, A. *Writing Like a Woman* (Ann Arbor, MI: University of Michigan Press), 1983.

Ostrom, H., 'Of Radishes and Shadows, Theory and Pedagogy', in W. Bishop and H. Ostrom (eds), *Colors of a Different Horse: Rethinking Creative Writing, Theory and Pedagogy* (Urbana, IL: National Council of Teachers of English), 1994, pp. xi–xxiii.

O'Toole, S., *Transforming Texts* (London: Routledge), 2003.

Paterson, K., 'Heart in Hiding', in W. Zinsser (ed.), *Worlds of Childhood: The Art and Craft of Writing for Children* (Boston, MA: Mariner Books), 1998, pp. 139–71.

Peters, R.S., 'Education as Initiation', in J. Bowen and P. R. Hobson, *Theories of Education: Studies of Significant Innovation in Western Educational Thought* (Brisbane: Wiley), 1974.

Pinksy, R., *The Sounds of Poetry: A Brief Guide* (New York: Farrar, Straus and Giroux), 1999.

Poch, J., 'Clichés in Contemporary Poetry', *The Writer's Chronicle*, Vol. 37, No. 6 (2005), 58–9.

Pope, R., *Textual Intervention: Critical and Creative Strategies for Literary Studies* (London: Routledge), 1995.

Pope, R., *The English Studies Book* (London and New York: Routledge), 1998.

Pope, R., *The English Studies Book: Language, Literature, Culture* (2nd edn) (London and New York: Routledge), 2002.

Pope, R., 'Rewriting Texts, Reconstructing the Subject', in T. Agathocleous and A. Dean (eds), *Teaching Literature: A Companion* (New York: Palgrave), 2003, pp. 105–24.

Pope, R., *Creativity: Theory, History, Practice* (Oxford and New York: Routledge), 2005.

Provoost, A., ' "So Here's the Bad News": The Child as Antagonist', trans. J. Nieuwenhuizen, in *Reading Minds* (Amsterdam: Majo de Saedeleer: Stichting Lezen), 2004, pp. 9–41.

Rhys, J., *Wide Sargasso Sea* (Harmondsworth: Penguin), 1972.

Rice, P. and Waugh, P. (eds), *Modern Literary Theory: A Reader* (4th edn) (London and New York: Arnold), 2001.

Ricketson, M., *Paul Jennings: 'The Boy in the Story is Always Me'* (Ringwood: Viking), 2000.

Ritter, K., 'Professional Writers/Writing Professionals: Revamping Teacher Training in Creative Writing Ph.D. Programs', *College Writing*, Vol. 64, No. 2 (November 2001).

Roorbach, B., *Contemporary Creative Non-Fiction: The Art of Truth* (New York: Oxford University Press), 2001.

Root, Jr, R. L. and Steinberg, M. (eds), *The Fourth Genre: Contemporary Writers of/on Creative Nonfiction* (3rd edn) (New York: Longman), 2004.

Rothenberg, J., *Writing Through: Translations and Variations* (Middletown, CT: Wesleyan University Press), 2004.

Rubenstein, R., 'Gathered, Not Made: A Brief History of Appropriative Writing', *The American Poetry Review* (March/April 1999) (also available at www.ubu.com/papers/rubenstein.html).

Rushdie, S., *Midnight's Children* (New York: Penguin), 1995.

Sapnar, M., ' "The Letters Themselves": An Interview with Ana Maria Uribe', *The Iowa Review Web* (www.uiowa.edu/~iareview/tirweb/feature/uribe/uribe.html), 2002.

Saxby, M., 'The Gift of Wings: The Value of Literature to Children', in M. Saxby and G. Winch (eds), *Give Them Wings: The Experience of Children's Literature* (2nd edn) (South Melbourne: Macmillan), 1991, pp. 3–18.

Saxby, M., *The Proof of the Puddin': Australian Children's Literature 1970–1990*, (Sydney: Ashton Scholastic), 1993.

Saxby, M., 'On the Side of the Angels', The Inaugural Courtney Oldmeadow Memorial Lecture, 1982, ed. J. Prentice (Melbourne: Dromkeen Society Publication), 2002, pp. 1–6.

Scholes, R., *The Rise and Fall of English: Reconstructing English as a Discipline* (New Haven, CT and London: Yale University Press), 1998.

Scholes, R., Comley, N. and Ulmer, G., *Text Book: Writing through Literature* (3rd edn) (New York: St Martin's Press), 2002.

Scott-Mitchell, C., 'Further Flight: The Picture Book', in M. Saxby and G. Winch (eds), *Give Them*

Wings: The Experience of Children's Literature (2nd edn) (South Melbourne: Macmillan), 1991, pp. 75–90.

Seger, L., *Advanced Screenwriting* (Los Angeles, CA: Silman-James Press), 2003.

Sendak, M., *Where the Wild Things Are* (New York: Harper and Row), 1963.

Sendak, M., 'Visitors from my Boyhood', in W. Zinsser (ed.), *Worlds of Childhood: The Art and Craft of Writing for Children* (Boston, MA: Mariner Books) 1998, pp. 17–37.

Shapard, R. (ed.), *Sudden Fictions* (Salt Lake City, UT: Gibbs M. Smith), 1987.

Shapard, R. with Thomas, J. (eds), *Sudden Fiction International* (New York: W. W. Norton), 1989.

Sharples, M., *How We Write* (London: Routledge), 1999.

Sheahan-Bright, R., 'It's a Supermarket: Children's Publishing and the Mass Market', *Magpies*, Vol. 14, No. 2 (May 1999), 10–13.

Shelnutt, E., 'Notes from a Cell: Writing Programs in Isolation', *AWP Chronicle* (February 1990), 1ff.

Shepherd, S. and Wallis, M., *Studying Plays* (London: Arnold), 1998.

Shields, C., 'Opting for Invention over the Injury of Invasion', in *Writers on Writing: Collected Essays from the* New York Times, intro. J. Darnton (New York: Holt), 2001, pp. 211–16.

Smiley, J., in *AWP Chronicle*, Vol. 26, No. 5 (Fairfax: AWP), 1994, 1.

Spiro, J., *Creative Poetry Writing* (Oxford and Toronto: Oxford University Press), 2004.

Spiro, J., *Creative Story Telling* (Oxford and Toronto: Oxford University Press), forthcoming.

Spurling, H., *Paul Scott: A Life* (London: Hutchinson), 1990.

Stafford, W., *Writing the Australian Crawl* (Ann Arbor, MI: University of Michigan Press), 1978.

Stam, R., *Literature through Film: Realism, Magic, and the Art of Adaptation* (Oxford: Blackwell), 2005.

Starkey, D., *Teaching Writing Creatively* (Portsmouth, NH: Heinemann), 1998.

Starkey, D. (ed.), *Genre By Example* (Portsmouth, NH: Heinemann), 2001.

Stegner, W., *On The Teaching of Creative Writing* (Hanover, NH: University of New England Press), 1988.

Stephens, J., *Language and Ideology in Children's Fiction* (London: Longman), 1992.

Sternglass, M. S., *Time to Know Them: A Longitudinal Study of Writing and Learning at the College Level* (Mahwah, NJ: Lawrence Erlbaum), 1997.

Stoppard, T., *Rosencrantz and Guildenstern Are Dead* (London: Faber & Faber), 1967.

Strickland, S., 'Poetry in the Electronic Environment', *electronic book review* (www.electronic bookreview.com/v3/servlet/ebr?command=view_essay&essay_id=stricklandtwoele), 1997.

Strickland, S. with Lawson, C., *V: Vniverse* (available at www.vniverse.com), 2002.

Susina, J., 'Editor's Note: Kiddie Lit(e): The Dumbing Down of Children's Literature', *The Lion and the Unicorn*, Vol. 17, No. 1 (June 1993), v–ix.

Swenson, M., *Made with Words* (Ann Arbor, MI: University of Michigan Press), 1998.

Swiss, T. and Nakamura, M., *Hey Now* (available at http://bailiwick.lib.uiowa.edu/swiss/web/heynow.html), 2002.

Talese, G., *Thy Neighbor's Wife* (New York: Doubleday), 1980.

Thiele, C., 'Writing for Children: A Personal View', The Second Courtney Oldmeadow Memorial Lecture, 1983, ed. J. Prentice (Melbourne: Dromkeen Society Publication), 2002, pp. 1–5.

Thomas, A., 'Digital Literacies of the Cybergirl', *E-Learning*, Vol. 1, No. 3 (2004), 358–82.

Todd, M. L. and Higginson, T. W. (eds), *Emily Dickinson: Poems* [1890] (Series 1 & 2, 1990–91) (New Jersey: Avenel), 1990.

Trelease, J., *The Read-Aloud Handbook* (New York: Penguin), 1982.

Turner, A. (ed.), *Poets Teaching the Creative Process* (New York: Longman), 1980.

Tynan, K., 'The Royal Smut-Hound', in M. Wandor, *Post-war British Drama: Looking Back in Gender* (London: Routledge), 2001, pp. 98–111.

Ventura, M., 'The Talent of the Room', *LA Weekly*, 21–27 May 1993 (also available at www.kelleyeskridge.com/Links/TalentOfTheRoom.htm).

Wagner, J., *John Brown, Rose and the Midnight Cat*, illus. R. Brooks (Ringwood: Penguin), 1977.

Walcott, D., *Omeros* (London: Faber & Faber), 1990.

Wandor, M., *Carry On, Understudies* (London: Routledge), 1986.

Wandor, M., 'A Creative Writing Manifesto', in S. Holland (ed.), *Creative Writing: A Good Practice Guide* (London: English Subject Centre), 2003, pp. 13–14.

Wandor, M., 'Creative Writing and Pedagogy 1: Self Expression? Whose Self and What Expression', *New Writing: The International Journal for the Practice and Theory of Creative Writing*, Vol. 1, No. 2 (2004), 112–23.

Wandor, M., *The Author is not Dead, Merely Somewhere Else: Creative Writing after Theory* (Basingstoke: Palgrave Macmillan), 2006.

Wandor, M., 'Value Judgements: you gotta love 'em', *New Writing: The International Journal for the Practice and Theory of Creative Writing*, forthcoming.

Wardrip-Fruin, N. and Harrigan, P. (eds), *First Person: New Media as Story, Performance, and Game* (Cambridge, MA: The MIT Press), 2004.

Wardrip-Fruin, N. and Montfort, N. (eds), *The New Media Reader* (Cambridge, MA: The MIT Press), 2003.

Watt, I., *The Rise of the Novel* (Berkeley, CA: University of California), 1957.

Waugh, P., *Metafiction: The Theory and Practice of Self-conscious Fiction* (London: Methuen), 1984.

Wells, R., 'The Well-Tempered Children's Book', in W. Zinsser (ed.), *Worlds of Childhood: The Art and Craft of Writing for Children* (Boston, MA: Mariner Books) 1998, pp. 39–61.

Wild, M., *Fox*, illus. R. Brooks (St Leonards: Allen and Unwin), 2000.

Wilen, L. and Wilen, J., *How to Sell Your Screenplay* (New York: Square One Publishers), 2001.

Wolfe, T., *Electric Kool-Aid Acid Test* (New York: Bantam), 1967.

Wolfreys, J. (ed.), *Introducing Literary Theory* (Edinburgh: Edinburgh University Press), 2001.

Wolfreys, J. (ed.), *Introducing Criticism at the 21st Century* (Edinburgh: Edinburgh University Press), 2002.

Woodmansee, M. and Jaszi, P., *The Construction of Authorship: Textual Appropriation in Law and Literature* (Durham, NC: Duke University Press), 1994.

Woodruff, J., *A Piece of Work: Five Writers Discuss Their Revisions* (Iowa City, IA: University of Iowa Press), 1993.

Woolf, V., *A Change of Perspective: Collected Letters III, 1923–28*, ed. N. Nicolson (London: Hogarth), 1977.

Young-hae Chang Heavy Industries, *Dakota* (available at www.yhchang.com/DAKOTA.html), 2001.

Zipes, J., *Sticks and Stones: The Troublesome Success of Children's Literature from Slovenly Peter to Harry Potter* (New York: Routledge), 2002.

Index